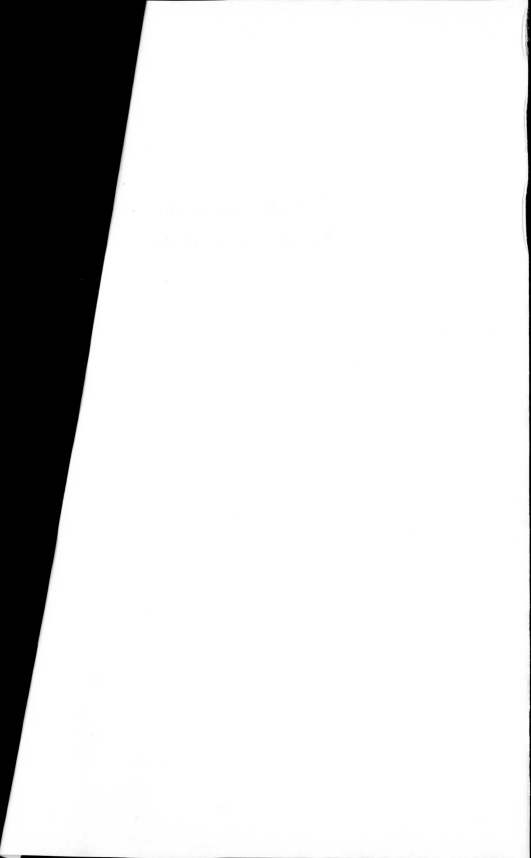

Huma

Immigr

HUMANIZING IMMIGRATION

HOW *to* TRANSFORM OUR RACIST *and* UNJUST SYSTEM

BILL ONG HING

BEACON PRESS • BOSTON

BEACON PRESS
Boston, Massachusetts
www.beacon.org

Beacon Press books
are published under the auspices of
the Unitarian Universalist Association of Congregations.

26 25 24 23   8 7 6 5 4 3 2 1

This book is printed on acid-free paper that meets the uncoated paper
ANSI/NISO specifications for permanence as revised in 1992.

Text design and composition by Kim Arney

Portions of chapter 6 were based on Bill Ong Hing,
"Systematic Failure: Mental Illness, Detention, and
Deportation," *UC Davis Journal of International Law &
Policy* 16, no. 2 (Aug. 27, 2010), https://jilp.law.ucdavis.edu.

*Library of Congress Cataloguing-in-Publication
Data is available for this title.*
Hardcover ISBN: 978-0-8070-0802-7
E-book ISBN: 978-0-8070-0803-4
Audiobook: 978-0-8070-1460-8

*For the children I met at the border
patrol detention facility in Clint, Texas,
in June 2019. Shame on our country for
your confinement under unconscionable
conditions. I pray every day that you
have recovered and that you are enjoying
the loving, safe life that you deserve.*

CONTENTS

PREFACE

M Y FIRST ENCOUNTER with a federal immigration agent occurred when I was a law student in 1973. I was working on
landlord-tenant cases at the Chinatown-North Beach office
of the San Francisco Neighborhood Legal Assistance Foundation
(SFNLAF) and wrapping up a successful rent reduction case on behalf of a Spanish-speaking client, Jorge Guzman. Because the attorney
working on the case couldn't speak Spanish and I have some fluency,
I worked on the case as a law clerk and as an interpreter. The housing
attorney asked me to hand a check over to Jorge at the final meeting
and explain the terms of the settlement. Jorge was ecstatic at our success in the battle with his landlord, but he told me that he was troubled
by something that happened at what was known at the time as the US
Immigration and Naturalization Service (INS) the day before. It seemed
that Jorge had gone to the INS building to ask how to file an immigration petition for his wife, who was in Mexico. Jorge was a lawful
permanent resident of the United States. He happened to run into an
immigration agent in the hallway, who asked to look at Jorge's "green
card." Jorge obliged, and the agent asked Jorge to accompany him to
his office. Jorge took a seat opposite the officer, who shocked Jorge by
shouting, "This card looks fake!" Jorge assured the agent that the card
was real. In front of Jorge, the agent took a pair of scissors and cut the
card in half to inspect it. The agent then said, "Actually, you're right.
It is real," and handed the pieces back to Jorge and told him to leave.

As Jorge showed me the pieces of the card, I sat in disbelief and
outrage. I asked Jorge if he remembered where the agent's office

was, and he told me he did. We walked the several blocks from the SFNLAF office, at 250 Columbus Avenue, to the Appraisers Building, at 630 Sansome Street, where the INS was located. Jorge told me that the agent's office was on the seventh floor, so we took the elevator up. Jorge recalled the exact door he had been led to the day before, and I knocked loudly. The door opened to a room with about eight desks, and an agent asked what we wanted. I asked Jorge if he saw the agent from the day before, and Jorge pointed to an agent across the room. I said, "We'd like to speak with the agent over there." The agent across the room greeted us with a stern "What do you want?" I said, "My client tells me that you took his green card yesterday and cut it in half with a pair of scissors, even though it's a real card. I really want you to do something about your mistake." The agent responded: "Yes, that happened. Don't worry about it. Just go down to Room 100 and tell them that Agent Smith sent you. They'll take care of you." I thought to myself, *Wow, vindication for Jorge!* As I explained to Jorge what happened, we happily rode the elevator back down to the first floor and looked for Room 100. It wasn't hard to find. It was a public information room that had a long line of about fifty people waiting to ask questions or pick up immigration forms. I admitted to Jorge that it wasn't such a victory after all. By the time we got to the front of the line, an hour later, the person on the other side of the counter handed us a form for a replacement card and told us to send it in with the appropriate filing fee. It eventually took over six months for Jorge to get a new card.

Agent Smith was the first, but certainly not the last, jerk working for the immigration service I would encounter over the course of my career. That first experience that Jorge opened my eyes to is emblematic of the institutionalized racism and othering in our immigration system that has led to the dehumanization of noncitizens that I have witnessed over the course of my career. The framework and policies that immigration officials work within seemingly gives them license to act cruelly, rudely, and even violently.

Working in that particular legal aid office as a law student was a blessing. The location stood at the border of the Chinese and Italian immigrant communities, with fascinating cultures and great food spots. Most importantly, from the perspective of an aspiring lawyer, the wide-ranging issues that clients brought to the legal aid office provided a great learning environment. Looking back, I can hardly believe that in the summer after my first year of law school, Ed Steinman—a veteran of the office who was starting his career as a law professor—asked me to assist him in representing Kinney Lau, a nine-year-old student, whose case was before the US Supreme Court. Kinney could not understand English but was placed in a classroom where everything was conducted in English. That sink-or-swim environment might work for some, but it wasn't working for Kinney. His case led to the landmark decision, *Lau v. Nichols* (1974), in which the Supreme Court ruled unanimously that the San Francisco Unified School District violated a provision of the Civil Rights Act of 1964 by not providing equal educational access to non-English-speaking students. *Lau* has become the basis for bilingual education and other innovative approaches that have been implemented across the country to allow immigrant children to participate in public education programs.

After graduating from law school, I jumped at the chance to work at SFNLAF and accepted the job offer to take over the immigration caseload. I mostly took on family immigration petitions and deportation defense cases for clients of Chinese and Mexican descent. Among the people I represented in dozens of deportation cases was the Cabral family. They had moved to San Jose, California, from Mexico in 1974, about the time I was graduating from law school. The father, Felipe, was a baker in a local *panaderia*, a Mexican pastry shop. Lucrecia, the mother, was a stay-at-home parent. The couple had four children—two daughters and two sons. The family entered without inspection by paying a smuggler to help them cross the border to, in Felipe's words, seek "a better life." But a couple years later, someone—a "friend," or enemy, or neighbor, or coworker—reported them to federal immigration agents, or *la migra*, as they are called in the Mexican community.

The arrests were violent. Agents came at four in the morning, surrounding the house and pounding on the front door. After several minutes, Sylvia, one of the daughters, answered the door and denied that anyone else was home. But the agents busted in, and eventually found the rest of the family hiding under the house. Everyone was arrested and dragged into federal detention. The date was May 20, 1976. Days later I met the Cabral family when I was doing my rounds as a legal services attorney assigned to interview immigrants who had been taken into custody by *la migra*. Many years later, another daughter, Maria Reyna, who was seventeen at the time of the raid, told me that "the incident was the most terrifying and traumatic experience of [her] life."

Unfortunately, there wasn't a whole lot that I could assert on behalf of the Cabral family, given the lack of rights provided under federal law to noncitizens without proper documents. In those days, however, it was easy enough to convince an immigration judge to allow Lucrecia and the children out of custody, pending the deportation hearing. Felipe was also released, after the family came up with $2,000 bail. So at least the family was out of custody as we prepared for the deportation hearing.

I visited the family in San Jose on a Sunday afternoon to prepare for the hearing. They showed me around their house and pointed out the trap door that family members had used to hide under the house. They were upset about the way that the agents had pushed their way into the house at 4 a.m. Sylvia said the agents had even looked through the kitchen cabinets. The family wanted me to develop a strategy that would allow them to complain at the hearing about the intrusive behavior. We decided that they would refuse to admit deportability at their hearing, thereby setting up a procedure that would allow us to object to the introduction of incriminating statements made at the time of arrest, on the grounds that members of the family were questioned during an illegal search and seizure by the agents. We knew that that wouldn't get too far under prevailing law at the time, but at least the family would be able to testify and complain about the conditions of the arrests. That was important to them.

The Cabral family took me in from the start. They were like families that I grew up knowing, loving, and respecting in my hometown of Superior, Arizona, a small copper-mining community in central Arizona that is predominantly Mexican American. The Cabrals, like the hundreds of other families I knew in Superior, were kind, warmhearted, friendly, hardworking, and decent. The children were fun-loving; the parents unwaveringly committed to their children, neighborhood, and church. They were in the United States to share a part of the American dream, not unlike the Gold Mountain image of America that Chinese migrants I knew had as well. (When word of the discovery of gold in California in 1849 spread across the ocean throughout Chinese provinces, thousands of Chinese migrants moved to the land that some, like my parents, came to call *gam saan*, or "gold mountain.")

Although the immigration judge was not sympathetic and ruled against the Cabrals, the family was passionate about their plight—so much so that, over the next decade, I made special motions and filed administrative and judicial appeals (including one to the US Supreme Court) on their behalf, and I tried to get Congress interested in their case. Fortunately, in 1986, Congress enacted the Immigration Reform Control Act, which granted legalization to individuals without documentation who were in the United States for at least five years, and the Cabral family was able to obtain legal status. Felipe passed away many years later, but I'm still in touch with the rest of this great *familia*. Maria Reyna, who now has her own family and works full time for an automobile company, volunteers on evenings and weekends for an immigrant rights organization in Redwood City, California. This is her way of helping others who are now facing what her own family endured.

The violence exhibited against the Cabrals, the rudeness toward Jorge, and the countless other demeaning experiences my clients have suffered through unnecessarily in search of a better life serve as the impetus for this book. It may sound like a cliché, but it really has been a privilege to work and fight with my clients arrested by immigration agents in the fields of the Salinas Valley; Iranian students rounded up by the Carter administration in 1979; Mexican migrants forced to look for work across the border because of US economic policies; those fleeing civil wars from Guatemala, El Salvador, and Nicaragua in the 1980s; Filipino war veterans seeking just recognition for their service to our country during World War II; Arabs and Muslims targeted by hate after 9/11; Cambodian refugees targeted for deportation; and more recent migrants from the Northern Triangle countries of Central America fleeing gang, cartel, and domestic violence. Certain clients, like Peter McMullen, the former member of the Provisional Irish Republican Army, and Leonid Kustura, who was deported on drug charges even though he had lived here since the age of three months, are hard to forget. It's also hard to forget some of the enforcement officials I've encountered, like Michael Smirnoff, an immigration agent who loved his nickname "Mr. Filipino" because he liked to target Filipinos for enforcement. There was the immigration detention guard, Mary Ann, who always chided me for speaking Spanish to my clients, because "you shouldn't help them because there's just too many of them coming." And the border patrol agent who stomped on my client's back after tackling my client during a farmworker raid. My good friend Mark Silverman was in the courtroom when I cross-examined that agent, and Mark had to restrain me because I got so upset at the agent's privileged and cavalier nature. Of course the actions and attitudes of these characters only fueled my drive to fight for immigrant rights, as did the fact that, around 2002, I learned the full extent of my parents' separate detentions in harsh conditions on Angel Island in San Francisco Bay in 1915 and 1926. In this book, I write about a few of my clients, including Luz Cardoza-Fonseca, Fethawit Tewelde, Juana Lopez-Telles, John Wong, Corazon Ayalde, and Antonio Sanchez, whose stories help to highlight potential or realized injustices and the craziness of our current immigration system. I also describe the experience that haunts me to this day: the inspection of the border patrol station at Clint, Texas, where many children and toddlers were separated from their caregivers at the border, left to fend for themselves.

violence. Certain clients, like Peter McMullen, the former member of the Provisional Irish Republican Army, and Leonid Kustura, who was deported on drug charges even though he had lived here since the age of three months, are hard to forget. It's also hard to forget some of the enforcement officials I've encountered, like Michael Smirnoff, an immigration agent who loved his nickname "Mr. Filipino" because he liked to target Filipinos for enforcement. There was the immigration detention guard, Mary Ann, who always chided me for speaking Spanish to my clients, because "you shouldn't help them because there's just too many of them coming." And the border patrol agent who stomped on my client's back after tackling my client during a farmworker raid. My good friend Mark Silverman was in the courtroom when I cross-examined that agent, and Mark had to restrain me because I got so upset at the agent's privileged and cavalier nature. Of course the actions and attitudes of these characters only fueled my drive to fight for immigrant rights, as did the fact that, around 2002, I learned the full extent of my parents' separate detentions in harsh conditions on Angel Island in San Francisco Bay in 1915 and 1926. In this book, I write about a few of my clients, including Luz Cardoza-Fonseca, Fethawit Tewelde, Juana Lopez-Telles, John Wong, Corazon Ayalde, and Antonio Sanchez, whose stories help to highlight potential or realized injustices and the craziness of our current immigration system. I also describe the experience that haunts me to this day: the inspection of the border patrol station at Clint, Texas, where many children and toddlers were separated from their caregivers at the border, left to fend for themselves.

I acknowledge that the country has the power to deny admission, to deport, and to criminalize noncitizens. However, that power should be implemented morally and ethically, with an understanding that we are dealing with real human beings. Furthermore, that power should be implemented in a nonracist manner. In order to accomplish all that, I believe we have to restructure the entire system, and what follows is an attempt to make the case for abolition and transformation.

CHAPTER 1

AN INTRODUCTION TO THE RACIAL INJUSTICE OF IMMIGRATION LAW

T HEY SAY A PICTURE is worth a thousand words. Images of US Border Patrol officers on horseback in September 2021 using long "reins" or whips to stop Haitian migrants from entering an encampment on the riverbanks near the Del Rio Bridge, and grabbing some migrants by the shirt, say it all.[1] Nana Gyamfi, executive director of the Black Alliance for Just Immigration, denounced the racist actions as "callous, cruel, and inhumane."[2] To Rep. Ilhan Omar (D-Minn.), the incidents constituted "human rights abuses. . . . Cruel, inhumane, and a violation of domestic and international law."[3] Even the White House press secretary, Jen Psaki, acknowledged that the images were "horrific." Taking the analysis a big step forward, however, Rep. Alexandria Ocasio-Cortez (D-New York) vilified the "immigration system [that] is designed for cruelty towards and dehumanization of immigrants." We can all agree that this corralling of Haitian asylum seekers was racist, but Ocasio-Cortez was right to call out the system because it enabled the abuse.[4] Without a doubt, calling out and punishing the heinous actions of the individual officers are important, but if we are to stop a repetition of such actions in the future, the system needs to be dismantled.

"Abolish ICE" is more than a catchy phrase—it represents a political movement whose most fervent adherents seek to put an end to the US Immigration and Customs Enforcement (ICE) agency.[5] Support for the movement grew in 2018 after Ocasio-Cortez, in her election campaign, advocated abolishing ICE, and when then president Donald Trump separated children from their parents at the border.[6] The movement has developed into a kaleidoscope of different advocacy efforts. There are a variety of views, and there is tension within the Abolish ICE movement. Some proponents want to eliminate all immigration enforcement, while others believe in reforming enforcement to make it more humane.

For more than fifty years, I've represented noncitizens caught up in the US immigration policy and enforcement meat grinder. I've witnessed senseless emotional damage to my clients, their families, and others similarly situated, because of racist and inhumane policies. So the need to abolish ICE is a no-brainer for me. In fact, I count myself among those who call for the abolition of the immigration system altogether. Migrants should have the right to free movement across borders and the right to live free of harassment over immigration status. Our system must be transformed into one that prioritizes our humanity first.

In the chapters that follow, I target specific areas for abolition and transformation. For example, I explain why the deportation of long-time residents who have committed crimes should end. I argue that deporting a noncitizen who lacks proper immigration documents and who has citizen children also makes little sense; in fact, there are millions in that situation who should be freed from the threat of removal. I explain why the current approach to asylum should be turned on its head, and how we should grant asylum to applicants unless the government can prove beyond a reasonable doubt that applicants will not be persecuted. I expose the dysfunction of the immigration courts and outline why they need to be replaced with a new system of humanitarian adjudication that can deal humanely and nimbly with challenging cases. And, finally, I make the case for why immigration detention should be ended: it is both cruel and unnecessary. In essence, by reviewing critical aspects of the current system, I make the case for dismantling ICE. I call for continued disruption until transformation of the system is accomplished.

Let me be absolutely clear about my starting point: immigration laws and enforcement policies are racist. In fact, those laws and policies are the quintessential examples of institutionalized racism. Think only of the foundational immigration laws that began with the Chinese Exclusion Act (1882) and the national origins quota of the Immigration Act of 1924, which favored Western Europeans, and infamous immigration roundups, such as Operation Wetback (1954), which targeted Mexican braceros, who had been issued temporary US work permits to ease labor shortages. In the appendix for this introduction, I provide a quick summary of these and other well-known, and some not-so-well-known, examples of historical racist US immigration laws and enforcement efforts targeting Latin and Asian immigrants: the 1848 shifting of Mexico's northern border by the Treaty of Guadalupe Hidalgo; the recruitment and exploitation of Mexican workers; the Asian exclusion period, which went beyond Chinese to sweep up Japanese, Indians, and Filipinos; the 1986 law against hiring unauthorized workers, which targeted migrants of color; the seemingly race-neutral immigration visa reforms of 1965 and 1976 that severely reduced visas for Mexicans; the US Supreme Court's endorsement of racial-profiling immigration enforcement away from the border; and the so-called "diversity" program that began as an affirmative action program for white migrants.

Congress may have repealed some of those laws and the raids may seem like historical artifacts, but their stench lingers on in the laws and policies that followed. The chapters on detention, deportation, and asylum that follow will cover unfair practices, onerous legal requirements, strange outcomes, and harsh conditions that may appear to be race-neutral on the surface. But peel that layer back, and you'll begin to see that those unfair, onerous, strange, and harsh results have been developed on the backs of noncitizens of color who have been dehumanized, then commodified as "illegal alien."

But first, I highlight the impact of immigration laws on Black migrants, because that topic is all too often ignored.

ANTI-BLACKNESS AS MANIFESTED IN IMMIGRATION LAWS AND ENFORCEMENT

The murders of George Floyd, Ahmaud Arbery, Breonna Taylor, and too many others have ignited a racial justice movement that places defending Black life at the center. The slaying of Black community members by the police, the targeting of Black people and communities of color, and the racist rhetoric spewed by hate groups are continual reminders that anti-Blackness and racism pervade our society and imperil efforts to promote diversity and uphold the rights of all people. As a result, countless individuals and organizations across the country are committed to supporting anti-racism, diversity, equity, and inclusion, declaring that "Black lives matter."

Not surprisingly, immigrant rights organizations are among the groups committed to racial justice for Black Americans. For some immigrant rights organizations, the commitment to supporting justice for Black Americans is consistent with the commitment expressed by others: it's simply the right thing to do in the face of discrimination and police brutality toward Black Americans. For others, fighting for Black rights is a natural part of the battle for immigrant rights because the immigration system is itself racist.[7] Both rationales make sense to me, especially because many victims of the harsh immigration enforcement regime are Black migrants.[8] And for those reasons, many immigrant rights advocates and their allies engaged in the Abolish ICE campaign in parallel with the Defund the Police efforts in the broader racial justice movement.

The treatment of Haitian migrants in September 2021 was emblematic of the intersection of immigrant rights and racial justice. That intersection demonstrates how immigration laws and enforcement policies are strong prima facie evidence and a concrete manifestation of systemic and institutionalized racism. In short, this critical race theory analysis explains why the battle for immigrant and refugee rights should be viewed as an important part of the battle for racial justice. Worse still, being Black outside of US borders, or a Black migrant within our borders, subjects the person to double-barreled racism.

As the racial justice revolution in defense of Black life raged on in the summer of 2020 after the murder of George Floyd, Black immigrants were targeted by the Trump administration in immigration proceedings while the coronavirus pandemic took center stage across the nation and the world.[9] Dozens of Cameroonian activists from the country's Anglophone minority were deported, in spite of clear evidence that they would be tortured or subjected to extrajudicial killings. The action followed Trump's offensive reference, during a 2018 discussion about immigration, to Haiti and African countries as "shithole countries."[10]

This target on Black noncitizens continued into 2021, as the Biden administration failed to end the "deportation flights" of African migrants that had begun under Trump.[11] President Joe Biden attempted a moratorium on deportations for the first one hundred days of his presidency, but a federal judge temporarily blocked the deportation pause, and ICE continued to deport Black immigrants. On its own, however, the Biden administration continued to invoke Title 42, a US health law provision to prohibit prospective migrants' entry to the United States when the surgeon general believes "there is serious danger of the introduction of [a communicable] disease into the United States."[12] The tragedy is that such expulsions returned hundreds of individuals, including children, into hostile and dangerous countries, such as Haiti or Mauritania, at the outset of 2021.[13]

Just to drive home the racist choices under Title 42, consider this: On March 21, 2022, the Biden administration announced a Title 42 exemption for Ukrainian migrants seeking asylum at ports of entry, as it considered new programs to allow displaced Ukrainians to apply for asylum in the United States. On the one hand, the Biden administration welcomed Ukrainian refugees, while on the other it continued to reject Haitian, Black, and brown asylum seekers.

For those who pay attention to the racism in US immigration laws, the first things that might come to mind are the treatment of undocumented Mexican migrants, or the recent hurdles established for Central American migrants seeking asylum. The detention of unaccompanied minors also receives sporadic media attention. Those examples are certainly important, and I summarize some of them below, but first consider some lesser-known examples of racist immigration laws and enforcement policies that particularly impact Black migrants.

Message to Haitians: "Don't Come"

In June 2021, in her first foreign trip as vice president, Kamala Harris announced in Guatemala that the Biden administration wanted to help Guatemalans "find hope at home." For those thinking of making the "dangerous" trek to the United States, she sent this blunt message: "Do not come."[14] Given the severe violence that asylum seekers from Guatemala and other Central American countries are facing at home, Harris's admonition was insensitive and demonstrated a lack of commitment to asylum seekers. That message is reminiscent of the stay-away message that the United States conveyed to Haitians, long before the Del Rio nightmare in September 2021.

Consider the plight of Haitian refugees in the 1980s.

In response to the repressive "Baby Doc" Duvalier regime, which caused political and economic havoc in Haiti in the 1970s, many Haitians fled to the United States seeking refuge. Large numbers sought asylum once they reached the shores of Florida. A backlog developed, so immigration officials implemented an accelerated program to deal with the situation. The program—termed the "Haitian program"—embodied the government's response to the fact that between six thousand and seven thousand unprocessed Haitian deportation cases were pending in the Miami office.

The Carter administration response essentially was to deny asylum and grease the deportation wheels. Arriving Haitians were detained, and there were blanket denials of work permits for Haitians whose asylum applications had been pending. Haitian cases were calendared for hearing, and immigration judges were ordered to speed things up and spend only a few minutes per case. The Immigration and Naturalization Service (INS), the predecessor to today's ICE in the Department of Homeland Security, was fully aware that only about twelve attorneys were available to represent the thousands of Haitians being processed, and that scheduling made it impossible for counsel to attend the hearings. It was not unusual for an attorney representing Haitians to have three hearings at the same hour scheduled in different buildings.

The results of the accelerated program were catastrophic. None of the more than four thousand Haitians processed during the program were granted asylum. In the end, a federal court struck down the accelerated program as a violation of procedural due process. The government was forced to submit a procedurally fair plan for the orderly reprocessing of the asylum applications of the Haitian applicants who had not been deported.

Poverty and infant mortality rates in Haiti ranked the highest in the Western Hemisphere, and the flow of refugees continued. But rather than recognize the crisis and provide assistance, the United States sought new tactics for denying asylum. The government's new strategy was premised on the idea that if the Haitians could be turned away on the high seas before they reached US shores, they could not then seek asylum.

On September 29, 1981, President Ronald Reagan authorized the interdiction on the high seas of vessels containing undocumented aliens from Haiti. The president based this action on the argument that undocumented aliens posed a "serious national problem detrimental to the interests of the United States," and that international cooperation to intercept vessels trafficking in such migrants was a necessary and proper means of ensuring the effective enforcement of US immigration laws.[15] By executive order, the Coast Guard was directed "to return the vessel and its passengers to the country from which it came."[16] Disappointingly, in *Haitian Refugee Center v. Gracey* (1985), a federal court upheld the actions, determining that the president has inherent authority to act to protect the United States from harmful undocumented immigration.

Visa Requirements for African Migrants: Go to the Back of the Bus

US immigration laws have never facilitated significant voluntary immigration from Africa. After the Civil War, in 1870, Congress extended the right to citizenship through naturalization beyond "free white persons" to those of African descent.[17] But the 1917 enactment of a literacy test for immigration became a major barrier to African immigration. In 1924, the national origins quota system was enacted. The law limited the annual number of immigrants who could be admitted from any country to 2 percent of the number of people from that country who were living in the United States in 1890. That meant that the quota for Africans was tiny. Significantly, the 1924 act also designated students as nonimmigrants rather than immigrants, helping to permanently establish in immigration law the notion of foreign students as temporary sojourners. Since students were not classified as immigrants, they could reside in the United States only temporarily and were ineligible to apply for citizenship through naturalization.

Under current immigration laws—largely framed by the 1965 Immigration and Nationality Act, with some revisions in 1990—the primary means of immigration is through family reunification or employment categories. The family categories require a prospective immigrant to have a US-citizen or lawful permanent resident spouse or parent; US citizens also can petition for siblings. Most employment visas are set aside for professionals, corporate executives, outstanding scientists, educators, athletes, and other skilled persons, and investors.

Immigration data make clear that the 1965 act did not facilitate drastic changes to African immigration. In the decade from 1960 to 1969 (before the full effect of the 1965 act could be felt), 3.2 million immigrants became lawful permanent residents of the United States. Of that figure, more than 33 percent (1.13 million) of immigrants were from Europe. Some 358,000 were from Asia, and more than 440,000 were from Mexico alone. Less than 1 percent of the total (23,780) were from Africa, and most were from Egypt (5,581), South Africa (4,360), and Morocco (2,880).

Four decades later, from 2000 to 2009, the numbers were relatively better for Africans attaining lawful permanent resident status. Of a total of 10.3 million immigrants during that period, 759,734 (7.3 percent) were African, compared to 1.3 million Europeans, 3.5 million Asians, and 1.7 million Mexicans. However, of the 759,734 Africans who became lawful permanent residents, many were actually admitted initially as refugees under the 1980 Refugee Act or the 1990 Immigration Act's Diversity Visa program rather than through the provisions of the 1965 act.

The lesson here is that US immigration laws have never been structured in a way that facilitates large-scale migration from Africa. Most immigration categories are set aside for close family relatives of US citizens and lawful permanent residents, and prospective immigrants from Africa cannot readily use family-based categories. Gradually, through refugee and diversity lottery visas, African migrants have settled in the United States. As they slowly become lawful residents and naturalized US citizens, African settlers are able to petition for other relatives through the family-based migration system.[18]

Criminal Law and Immigration

It is a fact that Black and Latinx residents are stopped more frequently by police than whites, not to mention that police are twice as likely to threaten or use force against Black and Latinx people. Couple that with the fact that noncitizens convicted of crimes are then handed over to the ICE deportation machine, and you begin to see the intersection of race and immigration status more clearly. The prison-to-deportation pipeline funnels Black and Latinx noncitizens from the criminal court system into ICE custody. Since immigrants of color are more likely to experience racism in the US criminal justice system, they are more vulnerable to ICE enforcement. That's in spite of the fact that noncitizens are less likely to commit crimes than those born in the United States. The results are stark: Black immigrants make up one in five noncitizens facing deportation on criminal grounds—close to three times their share of the noncitizen population. Thus, a criminal conviction makes deportation very likely for immigrants of color.[19]

Detention

Increased ICE enforcement targeting Black migrants manifests itself in terms of disproportionate detention as well as deportation. For example, Black immigrants represented 7 percent of the total immigration population (about 3.4 million people) between 2003 and 2015 but comprised 10.6 percent of all immigrants in removal proceedings during that time period.[20] In 2020, the number of Haitian families detained by ICE grew significantly at the Karnes County Residential Center in Texas.[21] As the COVID-19 pandemic progressed and ICE released some families, Haitians were less likely to be released. The Haitian population in the Karnes County detention center grew from 29 percent to 44 percent between January and March of 2020.[22]

In 2021, ICE detained asylum seekers from Angola, Benin, Burkina Faso, Burundi, Cameroon, Colombia, China, Cuba, Democratic Republic of the Congo, El Salvador, Guatemala, Guinea, Haiti, Honduras, Mauritania, Mexico, Nicaragua, Nigeria, Russia, Senegal, Somalia, Sudan, Togo, Ukraine, Uzbekistan, Venezuela, and other countries. They included a Sudanese asylum seeker, whose family members were murdered in the Darfur genocide, and a Haitian political activist, who fled after receiving death threats for his political opposition work.

The setting of immigration bond amounts (the ICE bail system) also has a disparate racial impact. According to the Refugee and Immigrant Center for Education and Legal Services (RAICES), in Texas, there is a massive disparity in the costs of Haitian immigrant bonds compared with the bonds for other nationalities.[23] From June 2018 to June 2020, the average bond posted for individuals in ICE detention was $10,500. But bonds required for Haitian detainees averaged $16,700—54 percent higher than for other immigrants. The result: Black immigrants stay in ICE jails longer because of this disparity.

Things did not get better under the Biden administration. During the first couple of years of the administration, Black asylum seekers were detained on average for nearly 4.3 months—27 percent longer than asylum seekers from non-Black majority countries. Black asylum seekers reported racist statements by ICE officers, including derisive explanations that Africans were not released because, according to the RAICES report, they are "inferior."

Conditions in ICE detention facilities were inhumane, to say the least. In July 2021, Black migrant detainees complained to DHS about the conditions at two Louisiana ICE detention facilities: one run by Geo Group, a private prison company, and another by the Allen Parish Sheriff's Office, as noted in a report by the Southern Poverty Law Center.[24] According to the complaint:

> [O]fficials denied Black immigrants basic human necessities, including potable water and necessary medical treatment; physically abused detained persons, including physical abuse of a person in detention while he experienced a mental health crisis; threatened

lethal force against Black immigrants in ICE custody; threatened Black immigrants with punitive solitary confinement in retaliation for peacefully expressing their rights and for their support of the Black Lives Matter movement; and ignored written grievances related to racial tensions between detention officials and immigrants in detention.

Based on an investigation of the facilities, the Southern Poverty Law Center concluded that the detainees were victims of racial discrimination. At different locations, Human Rights First investigators also found that detained Black asylum seekers and immigrants were subjected to horrific anti-Black abuse and mistreatment. ICE officers cut off Black people's hair worn in braids or locks, an affront to dignity and physical integrity with a racially disparate impact. Human Rights First also received reports of racist statements and attacks by ICE and detention center staff. Among the reports were a staff member's comparison of a Black immigrant's work folding laundry to how "[he] and [his] family got whipped back in the day," a statement by staff about lynching Black detained individuals, and a violent assault by a guard who said, "F*** Black people" and shoved a Cameroonian immigrant to the ground.[25]

Police Brutality Against Black Immigrants

Not surprisingly, Black migrants are extremely vulnerable to violence and racism by the police. Consider the examples of Charly "Africa" Leundeu Keunang, Amadou Diallo, and Alfred Olango.[26] Keunang was a forty-three-year-old homeless Cameroonian beaten and killed by the Los Angeles Police Department in 2015.[27] Diallo was a twenty-two-year-old Guinean immigrant shot and killed by New York City police outside his Bronx apartment in 1999.[28] He was shot with forty-one bullets when he reached to grab his wallet (the police claimed they thought he was grabbing a gun).[29] Olango was a thirty-eight-year-old mentally ill Ugandan refugee who was shot and killed by police officers near San Diego in an historically white, conservative neighborhood.[30] His sister had called the police because he was "acting strangely," and rather than providing information about mental health services or seeking any other form of mitigation, the police resorted to violence.[31]

Given those cases, it was upsetting when a *USA Today* reporter called me for a comment on the murder of twenty-six-year-old Patrick Lyoya. The Lyoya family were refugees from the Democratic Republic of Congo who came to America for peace and safety, settling in Grand Rapids, Michigan. They arrived in 2014 after facing years of war and persecution. But in the spring of 2022, in an all too familiar story, Patrick was fatally shot in the back of the head after a struggle with a white police officer during a traffic stop over an issue with his license plate. When the officer asked for Patrick's driver's license, he started to run. After the officer caught Patrick, the two men struggled prior to the fatal shot. My comment to the reporter: this was another tragic example of the "double-barreled racism" faced by Black migrants who are confronted with immigration challenges and US law enforcement.[32]

These four examples demonstrate how Black immigrants suffer from the same structurally racist law enforcement system experienced by Black US-born citizens. Black migrants may be particularly vulnerable to police brutality because their English may be limited or because they may demonstrate behavior unfamiliar to police or other residents.[33] These differences—paired with being Black in the United States—paint a target on the backs of many Black migrants. Due to race, poverty, and class assumptions, Black immigrants' lived experiences tend to become criminalized, inserted into charity narratives (such as with Haiti), or equated to Black American experiences. Such stereotyped categories reflect an attempt to push the Black immigrant to the outskirts of society, and the Black immigrant consequently is often caught in the good-bad binary of immigrants (more often the latter).

In the words of Nunu Kidane, founder and director of Priority Africa Network and herself a native of Ethiopia:

For new Africans in the United States, the challenges of navigating life are no different than what millions of migrants face daily:

managing employment, school, housing, health care, etc. What is special is the "double jeopardy" they face in being Black and immigrant, where few institutions understand the combined challenges let alone provide support and services when they are racially profiled by law enforcement and ICE.[34]

For Black migrants, racial profiling occurs among traditional law enforcement *and* ICE. In addition to facing the violence that may happen during the arrest phase, Black immigrants may also be targeted for abuse while in ICE detention.[35]

INSTITUTIONALIZED RACISM IN THE IMMIGRATION SYSTEM

The evolution of immigration policy, beginning with the forced migration of African workers, and continuing through the infamous Asian exclusionary period and the southwest border enforcement regime, is critical to understanding today's policies and enforcement approaches. We are left with a framework that is inherently racist. The current numerical limitation system, while not explicitly racist, operates in a manner that severely restricts immigration from Mexico and the high visa demand countries of Asia.

The 1965 amendments that emphasized certain family immigration categories and eliminated the national origins quota system represented a welcome change, but the new law was no panacea. President John F. Kennedy originally proposed a large pool of immigration visas to be issued on a first-come, first-serve basis, without quotas for any country. Between 1965 and 1976, Mexico and other countries in the Western Hemisphere faced strict numerical limits on available immigration visas, while the rest of the world enjoyed a definite preference system. After 1976, visas for Mexico were slashed even more.

Today's selection system is disruptive to families and individuals; there is simply no room for many relatives of immigrants because of numerical limitations, and no room for those who are simply displaced workers. They do not qualify for special visas, like those set aside for professionals and management employees of multinational corporations or people in investment categories. Similarly, persons in low-income regions controlled by trade agreements and business globalization find no place in the system, as global corporations relocate to other sites where their production costs are cheaper. As for those affected by climate change in the global south, sadly, that issue is only beginning to get attention.

The system results in severe backlogs in many family immigration categories—particularly for adult unmarried sons and daughters of lawful permanent residents, and siblings or married children of US citizens. For those in some countries, such as the Philippines and Mexico, the waiting periods for certain categories are ten to twenty years! Given the severe backlogs and the continuing allure of the United States (not simply in terms of economic opportunities, but because relatives are already here due to recruitment efforts, or because they sought political stability), many would-be immigrants are left with little choice. Inevitably they explore other ways of entering the United States without waiting. By doing so, they fall into the jaws of the immigration detention and removal laws for circumventing the proper immigration procedures.

Congress has also enacted criminal provisions that go far beyond the civil penalty of removal. For example, the following acts are subject to imprisonment and/or expensive monetary fines: falsifying registration information about the family; smuggling, transporting, or harboring an undocumented migrant (including family members); entering without inspection or through misrepresentation; reentry of a noncitizen after having been removed or denied admission; and making a false claim of US citizenship. Put simply, the act of traveling to the United States by circumventing the current structure can easily result in criminal penalties as well. And immigrants of color from the countries for whom backlogs have been constructed through the systemically racist visa system are most likely to attempt that circumvention. That's a phenomenon that goes as far back as the Chinese exclusion era, when Chinese, like my own father, were forced to make false claims to US citizenship to get here.[36]

Although racism has been institutionalized in the nation's immigration laws and enforcement policies, our inquiry should not end there. We also need to see whether those laws and policies interact with other important institutions in sinister ways that produce discriminatory outcomes. Consider the North American Free Trade Agreement (NAFTA) and the World Trade Organization (WTO). NAFTA has placed Mexico at such a competitive disadvantage with the United States in the production of corn that Mexico now imports most of its corn from the United States, and Mexican corn farmworkers have lost their jobs. The US-embraced WTO, which advocates global free trade, favors lowest-bid manufacturing nations like China and India, so that manufacturers in a country like Mexico cannot compete and must lay off workers. Is there little wonder that so many Mexican workers look to the United States for jobs? Think also of refugee resettlement programs as an institution. When Southeast Asian refugees were resettled in public housing or poor neighborhoods, their children found themselves in an environment that led to bad behavior or crime.[37] Consider the United States' wars and civil conflicts abroad. US involvement in Vietnam, Afghanistan, and Iraq led to involuntary migrants of color coming to our shores. Other racialized institutions that interact with immigration laws and enforcement include the criminal justice system, government agencies in poor neighborhoods, and inner-city schools. In short, actions embraced and fostered by the United States place individuals in predicaments that force involuntary migration, while no pathway to lawful immigration is provided. After arriving in the United States, the migrants are thrust into other institutional settings that can make things worse.

These policies and systems can lead to situations that spell trouble within the immigration enforcement framework. The visa and enforcement regimes may appear neutral on their face, but they have evolved in a racialized manner. When the immigration framework interacts with other racialized institutions, the structure generates racial group disparities. The effects of NAFTA and the WTO help explain why many migrants of color cannot remain in their native countries. The criminal justice system and poverty prey heavily on communities of color, leading to deportable offenses when defendants are noncitizens.

CONCLUSION

ICE should be abolished, and our system transformed, because the foundation of our immigration laws and enforcement policies is racist. These laws and policies have been constructed in a discriminatory manner, and racism is now deeply embedded in that system. In the next several chapters, I'll demonstrate how that racism manifests in critical parts of the immigration enforcement machine and how it has suppressed our humanity.

CHAPTER 2

THE INHUMANE TREATMENT
OF DETAINED CHILDREN

I DIDN'T REALLY KNOW what to expect when I walked into the Border Patrol detention facility at Clint, Texas, on June 17, 2019. As part of an inspection team, I had previously been to an ICE family detention center, which held women and their children. But the Clint facility was devoted exclusively to children under the age of eighteen. My team's assignment at the Clint facility was to interview as many of the 350 children being held about the conditions of their detention. Over the next three days, we interviewed some children who were as young as four and five years old who had been detained for more than three weeks—well beyond the seventy-two hours that Border Patrol officials were authorized to detain children before turning them over to the Office of Refugee Resettlement (ORR), part of the US Department of Health and Human Services. Incredibly, one child who was separated from relatives at the border to fend for herself was two years old.

What we found was shameful and deplorable. With only a couple of exceptions, children weren't offered clean clothes, weren't able to wash the clothes they were wearing, and weren't able to bathe. Toilets were extremely dirty, and some sinks were stopped up. There was not enough soap nor were there enough towels. A pregnant seventeen-year-old had been detained with her toddler for twenty days. She had not received any prenatal care and was stricken with the flu—particularly serious for someone pregnant. Border Patrol guards had made her and her son sleep on the cold floor, without a mattress or blanket. Another teenage mother, who was confined to a wheelchair, was in pain after having given birth to a premature baby in an emergency procedure. She begged the guards for something to wrap her baby in and was handed a dirty towel.

Every member of our team agreed: never before in our lives had we witnessed, or heard of, such degradation and inhumane treatment of children in federal immigration custody, all in the name of immigration border enforcement.

Immigration detention must be abolished. I base that view partially on conversations with clients who have been detained and with attorneys and fellow inspectors, and on reports from other detainees. But my belief primarily comes from what I've seen firsthand.

FLORES SETTLEMENT AGREEMENT

You can blame the Supreme Court for the detention of migrant children. In *Reno v. Flores* (1993), the court approved a Department of Justice policy to detain unaccompanied minors and release them only to a parent, legal guardian, or other related adults.[1] The court left it to a lower court to determine the conditions under which children can be detained. The result was the 1997 Flores settlement agreement, hammered out by attorneys for the children and for the government and which contains these provisions:

- The government is required to release children from immigration detention without unnecessary delay in order of preference beginning with parents and including other adult relatives as well as licensed programs willing to accept custody.
- With respect to children for whom a suitable placement is not immediately available, the government is obligated to place children in the "least restrictive" setting appropriate to their age and any special needs, and stipulates notice of rights.
- The government is required to implement standards relating to the care and treatment of children in immigration detention.

The standard of care and treatment includes basic requirements, such as safe and sanitary facilities, toilets and sinks, drinking water and food, medical assistance, temperature control, supervision, and contact with family members.

The Flores settlement mandates that authorities operate with a policy favoring release to a parent, legal guardian, adult relative, or licensed program. After taking a minor into custody, federal authorities or a licensed program must make and record a prompt and continuous effort toward family reunification and release. They also must maintain up-to-date records, including biographical information and hearing dates, of minors held for longer than seventy-two hours.

Ten years after the settlement was reached, Congress added more conditions. The William Wilberforce Trafficking Victims Protection Reauthorization Act, passed in 2008, requires that after an unaccompanied child is screened by Border Patrol officers, the child must be transferred to custody of ORR, typically within a seventy-two-hour period, for care and further screening. The idea is to place children in the care of an agency set up to safeguard their best interest, rather than with ICE—an agency whose mission is to enforce immigration laws.

That sounds humane, but in reality, ORR detention is still detention. In 2021, about 150,000 unaccompanied minors were held at ORR facilities, and those detention centers are at best challenging for and generally inhospitable to children.

OFFICE OF REFUGEE RESETTLEMENT DETENTION

From October 2014 to July 2018, the federal government received
~~ than 4,500 complaints about the sexual abuse of immigrant
who were being held at ORR-funded detention facilities.
ints increased under the Trump administration's policy
nigrant families at the border. The records of the com-
volved children who had entered the country alone
parated from their parents, detail allegations that
had harassed and assaulted children, specifically
sing minors, watching them as they showered, and

raping them. They also include reports of suspected abuse of children by other minors.[2]

When Pamela Baez spoke for the first time in my introductory migration studies class in fall 2018, she was passionate but matter-of-fact in discussing the psychological trauma experienced by migrant children who had been separated from their parents at the border. I soon learned that, a few months earlier, when Trump's border policy of separating children from their parents was exposed to the world, Pamela had become embroiled in the controversy.

Cayuga Centers, a New York nonprofit where hundreds of separated migrant children were sent, had been awarded $115 million in grants from 2014 to 2018 to house and care for minors in detention.[3] Detaining and housing children, under the Flores settlement agreement obligations, is an expensive proposition for the government. ORR awarded nearly $5 billion in grants over a fifteen-year period, through the unaccompanied alien children program, to various private companies like Cayuga.

Pamela worked for Cayuga Centers and leaked video from inside the East Harlem facility, exposing its inability to care for hundreds of immigrant children who were separated from their families. She appeared on CBS *This Morning* alongside her attorney, Michael Avenatti (of Stormy Daniels notoriety), to discuss her experiences at the facility and the injustice that pushed her to blow the whistle. Pamela told me, "What made me pull out a phone and start recording was knowing that what these kids were going through was causing them great psychological and physical pain." The cell phone footage showed several children eating inside a room. One upset little girl was crying for her mother. Another girl—Jessica—was seen whimpering as she explained to Pamela that she had been separated from her older sister at the border and wanted to see her mother, whom she believed was in Virginia.

Cayuga had become increasingly overwhelmed by the number of children in its care, and staff were unable to provide the children with sufficient medical treatment. The facility was not doing enough to connect the children to their parents. Reunification of the children with their parents, which should have been the number one p…

was an afterthought, according to Pamela. Confronted with the video footage and Pamela's allegations, a Cayuga official admitted that the facility was not prepared to deal with the surge of unaccompanied children being transported to New York by government officials.

Pamela felt compelled to act. "I think that by actually coming out and showing my face will give the courage to other people to actually do the same. Because it's now or never," she said. "This is the time to reunite these families and this is what needs to happen now."[4] Her concern was well-founded. After filing a lawsuit challenging Trump's family separation policy, the American Civil Liberties Union (ACLU) learned that more than two thousand children were separated from their parents. No one at DHS had a plan to keep track of the families who were separated, much less a reunification plan. More than three years after Pamela's warning, attorneys were still trying to reach the parents of 270 migrant children who had been separated at the US-Mexico border under the Trump administration.[5]

The largest ORR-sponsored children's detention center was at Homestead, Florida, where, at its height in 2019, about 2,700 children were detained. Children were housed in prison-like conditions and unnecessarily incarcerated for up to several months without being determined to be flight risks or a danger to themselves or others. Dozens of volunteer lawyers, interpreters, and other legal workers on inspection teams interviewed more than seventy child migrants at Homestead during multiple visits. A fourteen-year-old boy from Honduras said that on two separate occasions he had problems videoconferencing with the social worker handling his reunification, as the company began hiring clinicians and case managers to work long-distance. A Guatemalan girl said she didn't speak any Spanish, only her native Maya language of Q'eqchi', when she arrived, and she had trouble understanding her social worker.[6]

Children complained about noisy, crowded conditions with little privacy. They reported feeling despondent because they had no idea when they would be released. Rules prohibited them from listening to music or writing in a journal. Some reported having suicidal thoughts. Amy Cohen, a psychiatrist who visited the facility, confirmed that the noise level was extremely high, especially in a tent with no soundproofing, where "children are crammed" and teachers had to use microphones to be heard. One child told Dr. Cohen that many of the girls used requests for bathroom breaks as a means to briefly escape the noise and insufferable crowding. But teachers caught onto the ploy and begin refusing the requests. In some other ORR shelters, children were occasionally taken on outings for a change of environment. According to Dr. Cohen, "The children never get out of [Homestead], unless they have a medical appointment."[7]

After intense criticism of the conditions, the Trump administration closed the Homestead facility in August 2019. But, for a while, the Biden administration contemplated reopening the facility.[8]

WELCOME TO CLINT, TEXAS

By the time Peter Schey and Carlos Holguin represented Jenny Lisette Flores before the Supreme Court in 1993, they had been battling on her behalf for several years. In 1984, fourteen-year-old Jenny was arrested as an unaccompanied minor from El Salvador trying to enter the United States illegally. Peter and Carlos were convinced that the real reason for Jenny's detention was that immigration authorities were using her as bait, to lure her parents into a trap, because they did not have immigration papers. That didn't matter to the court, so Peter and Carlos were left to negotiate the conditions of detention that led to the Flores settlement agreement.

In an effort to ensure that the terms of the settlement are met, the federal court authorizes regular inspections of facilities where detained children are held. Over the years, Peter and Carlos conducted many of the inspections themselves, but they often ask for volunteers to be part of the team. Those teams verified many violations of the Flores agreement, such as the chain-link "cages" that held children in South Texas, and agents who made the ridiculous argument that the Flores provision on maintaining sanitary conditions did not necessarily mean that toothbrushes and soap were required.[9] Peter reached out to me and told me that they had information that the Border Patrol at Clint was detaining kids for more than seventy-two hours before turning them over to ORR. When asked if I would travel to Texas to be part of the team to confirm what was happening, I agreed.

While my visit occurred in 2019, years later I continue to process what I experienced. I think often about the children that I interviewed because of what they were forced to endure. I also wonder what has become of them physically and emotionally. One boy, Josue, did settle in Marin County near San Francisco, where his mother lived; the law school clinic was able to assist him, and he seems to be doing OK. I retained some phone numbers of aunts, uncles, and even parents in the United States that the children gave me. I contacted a few of them soon after leaving Clint, and they still had not heard what happened to their children.

One thing the children at Clint shared is consistent with what I've learned from other young clinic clients: They left their home countries out of desperation and were all fleeing some sort of violence and disruption to their lives in their neighborhoods and communities. Many of them had been living with elderly grandparents, while others wanted to reunite with a parent who came to the United States.

The youngest child I interviewed was a four-year-old boy, Jorge, who was with his twelve-year-old brother, Daniel. They were both from Honduras, sweet and gentle, and thinking about Jorge still makes me emotional. When I met them, Jorge wouldn't talk with me. To my untrained eye, Jorge looked like he might be suffering emotionally or physically, so I asked Daniel about him, and Daniel assured me that Jorge was fine. Daniel shared: "He talks. He definitely talks, but he's a little bit shy." I spoke with Daniel for about fifteen minutes and tried to draw out Jorge at the same time, but Jorge still wouldn't engage. I found Nancy Wang, a pediatrician who was part of our team, and explained my concerns. I learned that she'd had the foresight to pack dozens of bottles of bubbles, coloring books, crayons, and other supplies for our work at the facility. She grabbed a bottle of bubbles before we walked back to the interview room. Without a word, Dr. Wang cheerfully sat down, then simply started blowing bubbles. In an instant, Jorge burst into laughter, grinned from ear to ear, began playing with Dr. Wang, and started chatting away. We noticed immediately that he had a severe speech impediment as it was extremely difficult to understand him. But older brother Daniel understood every word that Jorge said, and Daniel explained that he had cared for Jorge since he was nine months old. Their father had abandoned them, and their mother had come to the United States a few years earlier. They traveled all the way from Honduras to be reunited with her in Miami.

Dr. Wang confided that she thought Jorge had more than a speech impediment. For his age, he likely had a learning disability. We were very concerned that the two might be separated by the Border Patrol. So we both wrote special notes to the officials on site, urging that Jorge and Daniel not be separated because the four-year-old was completely dependent on his older brother. A few days after I left Clint, I managed to reach the boys' mother in Miami. Happily, they were eventually reunited and found legal assistance.

If Peter and Carlos were right about the children there being detained for more than seventy-two hours, that would be a violation of the 2008 trafficking victims law. In fact, the vast majority of the children that we interviewed had been detained for more than two weeks. Everyone I interviewed had been at the facility for at least nine days. Some had been held for seventeen to twenty days. They all reported that the belongings they carried to the border were thrown away by Border Patrol officers. We also learned that officers refused to help the children call relatives in the United States to let them know what was happening. Most of the children I interviewed carried pieces of paper with scribbled phone numbers. In fact, I placed calls for all the kids I interviewed, to facilitate conversations with parents or other loved ones who were in the United States. Fortunately, the Border Patrol did not confiscate our cell phones. (On visits to ICE detention facilities in Texas, ICE officials did not allow us to take our phones inside.)

Most upsetting, of course, was the fact that the children were in detention in the first place. Truth be told, when Donald Trump deflected criticism of his handling of the border, including the detention of children and families, by saying that Barack Obama's administration set the precedent for these actions, he was not completely wrong. The George W. Bush administration had largely closed family detention centers, but when the surge of unaccompanied minors and family units occurred in 2014 and 2015, the Obama administration responded by opening or expanding detention facilities. Both the Obama and Trump administrations could have allowed children traveling with aunts, uncles, or grandparents to stay with them and let them be on their way, but they didn't. Children traveling with nonparental relatives were separated from those relatives under the Obama administration, and the children were then classified as unaccompanied minors and subject to the abuse of Border Patrol detention and then ORR detention.

The adult relatives—siblings, aunts, uncles, grandparents—were detained either in an ICE or Border Patrol detention facility, criminally prosecuted for illegal entry, and/or deported immediately. Those criminally prosecuted were subjected to what has come to be known since 2005 as Operation Streamline, under which dozens are prosecuted each day in a kangaroo court-style setting.[10]

In addition to listening to the children, I observed them during the interviews. But a couple of matters didn't fully register with me until days after I returned home. The older children, who were sixteen or seventeen years old, were able to more effectively attend to their personal hygiene. The younger children, who were between four and seven years old, looked markedly different, unkempt and unbathed. I realized that the younger children did not have the benefit of anyone helping them and therefore had not showered or been able to clean their clothes. A couple of girls told me that they felt unsafe going to the bathroom, and I would imagine they were nervous about bathing in a partially public area. According to the Border Patrol, there were laundry facilities, but expecting a young child to be able to navigate this by themself is unreasonable.

One of the most disturbing things I witnessed was how toddlers—including a two-year-old the team encountered—were left to care for themselves. Children who reach the border with an aunt, uncle, older sibling, or cousin are immediately separated from that person at the border—no matter how young the child. Our team of eight had a few small offices and rooms available, along with a larger conference room with a printer. On the way to the printer one morning, I saw something disturbing. Two team members were conducting interviews at opposite ends of the conference room. A six-year-old girl, who was being interviewed by one of the other team members, was crying. My colleague gently took the little girl by her hand and walked across the room to a teen who was being interviewed; the teen had a two-year-old girl on her lap. The teen immediately comforted the six-year-old. I wondered if the teen was the mother of both children, but realized that didn't make sense, because the teen was at most seventeen (the facility was detaining children under the age of eighteen).

Later, at our lunch break, I asked my colleagues about what I had seen. It turned out that the teen, Josefina, who had the two-year-old on her lap, was not the mother of either child. Josefina had been housed in the same room with the girls and had been comforting the toddler and the six-year-old for days, out of a sense of kindness and sympathy. The six-year-old had been separated from an aunt by the Border Patrol at the border days earlier. The two-year-old also was separated at the border from her aunt and had been left on her own. So Josefina had met them in their shared room and made an emotional connection out of compassion; she knew they needed care. Based on what the children housed there told us, they were detained in cramped rooms that slept twenty to fifty, depending on the size of the room. Some had beds. Others had mats to sleep on; a few had nothing.

The children were confined to their rooms all day long, except when the room was being cleaned, when they were out to eat, or when they had to go to the bathroom. Two seventeen-year-old boys reported to me that they were able to go outside to play every day for twenty to sixty minutes. Younger kids reported that they were not permitted to go outside to play on a daily basis. They reported that they could go outside only every two or three days to play. Siblings of different genders were not housed together and could see one another only during meals, and then it was at a distance.

I also interviewed three teen mothers with their infants in their arms—one baby was only five months old. Two of the nursing mothers wore shirts that were stained in the breast area. Although all the mothers said they received three meals per day, the meals never included fruits or vegetables. No special nourishment was provided to nursing mothers.

The absence of nutritious food for all was striking. The Border Patrol personnel we met with the first day greeted us with a "Welcome to Clint, Texas," and bragged about how they provided "three hot meals a day" to everyone. But the facility was set up for children who would be in and out within ten to twelve hours—seventy-two hours max. That's a problem when the children were actually detained for two to three weeks. They were given the same three meals every day: for breakfast, an oatmeal mix with a juicy pouch drink and a cookie or granola bar; lunch was a Maruchan cup of an instant noodles or ramen-type "soup" with another juicy drink; and dinner was a microwaved frozen burrito. No fresh fruits or vegetables were provided. As for the promised three "hot" meals a day, perhaps this meant hot water for oatmeal mix, hot water for ramen, and a zapped burrito technically qualify as hot meals. When asked, all the kids admitted they were hungry. They acknowledged being fed hot food. When we followed up, asking if it was enough, a typical response was "Well, yes, kind of, but sometimes I'm hungry."

We learned that limited medical care was available. In the months prior to our inspection, six or seven deaths occurred in Border Patrol facilities. The children told us that if they felt sick, they would be able to see a doctor or nurse the next day. The rash of deaths in Border Patrol centers must have had some impact. Two of the teen mothers reported that their infants got the flu after arriving in the United States. One case was very serious; the baby had a fever, chills, diarrhea, and vomiting. When a guard saw this, the mother and infant were rushed to a hospital emergency room in El Paso, about twenty-five miles away, and were hospitalized for three or four days before they were brought back.

There was a flu bug going around when we visited the Clint facility. One five-year-old boy who I interviewed was sick with a runny nose and cough. He had not seen a doctor. I reported this to a Border Patrol officer, who said that he would be seen by a doctor the following day. I interviewed one thirteen-year-old boy who had the flu, and a seventeen-year-old boy who was getting over it. They had gotten sick while at the Clint facility and believed that they had caught the flu because they were held in cramped quarters with other people who were coughing or sick.

If a child got the flu, they were transferred to a room specifically for those who had it. On a given day, it could be three children, or fifteen. Many of the guards walked around with surgical masks, as did some of the children. (Recall that this was in 2019, prior to the COVID-19 pandemic. At the height of the pandemic, coronavirus cases surged at immigration detention centers. From April to July 2021, 7,500 new cases were reported as the detained population increased from 14,000 to 26,000.)[11] At Clint, the children with surgical masks on told us that they had been released from the flu room, which is why they were wearing masks. Flu was a problem at other facilities as well. An attorney, who was on the Flores inspection team visiting the Border Patrol facility in McAllen, Texas, the week before, contracted the flu there. She was so sick that she had to be hospitalized for four days. Right after the Clint team arrived in El Paso, she called us from her hospital bed and warned that we should use hand sanitizer constantly and not touch any of the children.

While we did use hand sanitizer and sanitizing wipes, how could we not touch the children we interviewed? Most of us are parents, and we responded to the emotional conversations we had with the children professionally, but also with physical affection. We hugged the children to comfort them. I remember seeing another law professor on the team embracing a four-year-old girl who was sobbing, the girl's legs wrapped around my colleague's waist.

We asked the children about inappropriate touching or abuse by the guards, and there were no complaints. In fact, the guards never touched the children, as far as we could tell. They were likely under orders to not touch the kids, either affectionately or violently, of course. We also heard no complaints about guards yelling at children, though we were disturbed to hear that an agent mocked one for crying about missing his mother. Some children did share that two female agents had been nice to them and seemed to care. I doubt that Border Patrol officers receive any training on counseling children who have been separated from their families and/or about the trauma of traveling across Mexico by foot to reach the US border, and I believe it would be beneficial.

At Clint, the Border Patrol officials did not give us permission to walk around, so we were confined to offices and interview rooms to do our work.[12] Our delegation went to the media a day after we finished our three days of work because we were so troubled by what we witnessed. Our outcry was covered widely by news outlets like the *New York Times*, CNN, CBS News, and *Slate*.[13] When we arrived at Clint, more than three hundred children were detained. We were provided with a list with case numbers and birth dates of the children. A week after we exposed what was happening at the detention facility, the number was magically reduced to about a hundred.

Over the next two weeks, reporters and a congressional delegation were allowed to walk around the Clint facility, and it was apparent that the facility had been cleaned up to some degree. Rep. Judy Chu (D-Calif.), who was one of fifteen members of the congressional group, called me right before going in for ideas on what to look for and what to ask. After the tour, she called again: "I can't believe what we saw. This cannot go on." She later reported:

> It was like a giant steel garden shed with no air conditioning. This is in an area where the temperatures routinely get over 100 degrees. The facility supposedly had air conditioning but we were so hot, we just couldn't stand it. Youth slept on the warehouse floors in cinder block cells. What really was heartbreaking was a toddler who looked so miserable. But, when we got there and waved to him, he came and pressed his face to the glass door. He was just so relieved to see people who were showing care and concern for him.
>
> It makes me so angry that kids are being treated this way. Their world now is just being behind bars. There is no justification for it. They have the right to an asylum hearing. The only reason that they are being detained is because of the policies of the Border Patrol.[14]

I was also moved to tears a couple of years earlier, on a Flores inspection visit to the family detention center in Dilley, Texas, where I spoke with women and their children. Watching families sit through an orientation when they arrived at the facility, I saw lethargic and seemingly depressed children, some of whom were unwell. At the time, my mind juxtaposed a vision of my daughter-in-law and grand-daughter laughing and playing in the comfort of their apartment back in San Francisco. I reflected on what it meant to detain families and drain the life out of the children. Still, at least the families in Dilley had the comfort of each other, and mothers had the ability to bathe their children. But what I witnessed in Clint was shocking—our country was detaining and abandoning the most vulnerable population, leaving them to fend for themselves.

FLORES SETTLEMENT ADDITIONS

Our team's report to the federal court and our media outreach had some impact. Three years after the Clint Border Patrol situation was exposed, Peter Schey, Carlos Holquin, and DHS attorneys announced an update of the Flores settlement agreement with respect to the Rio Grande and El Paso Border Patrol sectors in Texas.[15] The new provisions reflect many of the inspection team's concerns. I'm grateful that the suffering endured by the children we met has been acknowledged. Some of the new provisions include the following:

- *Supplies*: An adequate supply of mats, blankets, undergarments, jackets, sweatshirts, diapers, meals, hygiene products, toothbrushes, toothpaste, baby formula, baby food, and baby blankets will be maintained.
- *Medical care*: 24/7 on-site medical personnel will be available. Referral to local health systems when necessary will be made promptly, and a layered approach to medical support will be used, endeavoring to ensure no single point of failure.
- *Trauma-informed care*: Personnel will take a trauma-informed approach to those in custody, recognizing the potential of trauma in their home countries and on their journey. Personnel will make efforts to foster reassurance, resilience, orientation, recreation, and distraction.

- *Food*: Age-appropriate meals and snacks that meet daily caloric needs will be provided. Food and water will never be used as a reward or withheld as punishment. The food will be in edible condition, not frozen, expired, or spoiled. Clean drinking water will be provided.
- *Temperature*: Facilities will maintain a temperature range of no less than 69° Fahrenheit and no more than 83° Fahrenheit.
- *Sleep*: Sufficient space will be provided for sleep with sufficient mats and blankets. Reasonable efforts will be made to dim the lights between 10 p.m. and 6 a.m. and to minimize noise during those hours.
- *Caregivers*: Fully vetted caregivers of mixed gender will be available at all times.
- *Hygiene and sanitation*: Soap, shampoo, toothbrushes, toothpaste, and towels will be provided. Caregivers will assist children in their hygiene routines, as needed. Soiled clothing will be laundered, but if not possible, clean clothing will be available to replace soiled clothing.
- *Siblings*: Juveniles will be informed that if they are housed separately from a family member, they can ask agents or caregivers to interact with that family member.
- *No family separation*: Children apprehended with adult family members, including nonparents or legal guardians, will remain with that family member during any time in Border Patrol custody.[16]

Missing from these new obligations is what should happen after detention. Pamela Baez's thesis focused not only on minimizing the time of detention but also on ensuring better care during and after detention.[17] The need for better care during detention is obvious, but Pamela pointed out that after the trauma of migration and detention, the children require long-term attention, including legal services, physical health services, mental health services, gang prevention strategies, family counseling, substance abuse counseling, and educational services.

On the surface, the specific new Border Patrol obligations are sound. Of course, many of the items are common sense, so it's hard to understand why it took more than a couple of years to come up with new requirements. On the other hand, it's important to remember that these conditions and obligations relate to how to make things better for the children while in detention. The problem is that the underlying assumption—detention of migrant children—will continue.

CONCLUSION: ABOLISH IMMIGRATION DETENTION

There are plenty of reasons for terminating immigration detention altogether, starting with the poor medical care provided to detained immigrants. There were at least a hundred ICE detention deaths from 2009 to 2019, and another twenty-one in 2020. Those figures may be an undercount, because the ACLU has learned of several deaths that were not counted by ICE, because the victims were released soon after their critical illness was discovered.[18] Beyond the deaths, consider the fact that sexual abuse is common in ICE facilities, and access to counsel is limited, because detention centers are located in remote areas.

Detention is also a waste of money. The United States spent $7.4 billion on immigration detention in 2018. While billions are spent on detention, with more than $800 million going to two of the largest private prison companies alone, the 2023 budget for immigration services to US Citizenship and Immigration Services (USCIS) was only $914 million.[19] USCIS handles immigrant and nonimmigrant visa applications. In July 2022, there was a backlog of 410,000 immigrant visa applicants waiting to be interviewed, and an eight-month wait for tourists and business travelers who would be entering to help the US economy.[20]

Perhaps most importantly, there is no practical need for detention. Before the Obama administration reopened family detention centers, its policy of "catch and release" while awaiting removal proceedings worked. Nearly all those released with some form of monitoring appeared for their hearings. As you'll read in the following chapter, the criminal justice system has already dealt with noncitizens convicted of crimes.[21] You'll hear about folks like Lundy Khoy, Kim Ho Ma, and

John Wong, who were convicted of crimes but always showed up for their hearings (including for removal, in Kim Ho's case) after being released. It is worth underscoring that the vast majority of detainees today have committed no crimes and are survivors who have risked their lives to escape persecution in their homelands. Yet we persist in treating them horrendously in prison-like settings.

Instead of detention, community- and case-management-based alternatives have already proven to work. A formal ICE alternative to a detention program operated from January 2016 through June 2017, with great success. The Family Case Management Program (FCMP) used individualized case management services, so participants better understood the immigration process. The program resulted in compliance rates of over 99 percent with immigration check-in appointments and court appearances. Families enrolled in FCMP did not even wear ankle monitors. Without question, this management program is an important alternative to detention.[22] But the Trump administration terminated the program.

Abolishing detention of migrant children is particularly urgent. The framework that fosters the evils of Clint or Homestead or border cages cannot continue. We can and must do much better.

Great Britain's commitment to eliminating the detention of migrant children is a useful model. In the 1990s, the UK rarely detained families with children. But harsh immigration policies followed, and between 2005 and 2009, the number of children detained with their families was estimated at two thousand per year. But after incorporating the United Nations Convention on the Rights of the Child into immigration law in 2009, and by making policy changes under the Conservative and Liberal Democrat coalition government, the number of detained children substantially plummeted.[23] The number of migrant children in detention fell to one hundred in 2021.[24]

Improvements to the process for unaccompanied asylum-seeking children were part of the UK program to reduce the detention of children. In 2007, a distinct and separate asylum process for children was instituted in Great Britain. The recast Asylum Procedures Directive requires that any representative of a child perform their duties in accordance with the principle of the best interests of the child, and that they shall have the necessary expertise to that end; that interviews with minors are conducted in a child-appropriate manner; and that unaccompanied minors and their representatives are provided with legal and procedural information.

There are reasonable alternatives once we make the decision to end the detention of children. For starters, if they have arrived with relatives—including nonparent adult relatives—they shouldn't be separated. If they are apprehended, release them, or use a non-detention family management program. Set up a system of responsible sponsors or foster families to take responsibility for the children and to expeditiously find relatives who may already be in the United States.

There are plenty of kind and generous families who are willing to step up and help migrant children fleeing violence. In the summer of 2014, when a surge of unaccompanied minors arrived at the US southern border, and eventually in cities including San Francisco and Oakland, I regularly met with community members who wanted to help, to volunteer to receive and assist the children. I am convinced that if you put out the call, many families will jump at the chance to participate in the Refugee Foster Care program for unaccompanied minors, like one that is operated by Catholic Charities in Santa Clara County, south of San Francisco.

Instead of using our financial resources on detaining migrant children and fostering institutionalized abuse, we should imagine humanitarian alternatives to detention that allow children to live freely in a community setting while waiting for their immigration status to be resolved. We need an array of options, some working in tandem. Through our creativity and compassionate commitment, I am confident we can achieve a profoundly improved process. And while we're at it, let's abolish ICE detention altogether.

CHAPTER 3

DEPORTING
AGGRAVATED FELONS

E VERY DAY, ICE DEPORTS individuals who have been lawful permanent residents of the United States since childhood because they have been convicted of aggravated felonies. The removal proceedings are swift because there's no remedy for an aggravated felon. It is notable that deportation comes after a person has served the criminal sentence, so it isn't about avoiding jail time. And deportation comes even though the rest of a person's family (including spouse and children) reside in the United States and are citizens or lawful permanent residents.

This makes no sense to me. These individuals paid their debt to society through the criminal justice system. They are remorseful and rehabilitated. Most have lived in the United States lawfully since childhood. Their crimes are often the result of a brief moment of bad judgment, and the broad aggravated felony classification includes many minor crimes.

The deportation laws that pertain to lawful residents convicted ~~~~y disproportionately on immigrants of color. About 98 ~~~~itizens removed on criminal grounds are from Latin ~~~~n one in five noncitizens facing deportation for ~~~~ck; in fact, Black immigrants (many of whom ~~~~re more likely than other immigrants to be ~~~~viction.[2]

~~~~eir banishment without the opportunity to ~~~~s to be abolished.

LUNDY KHOY AND SEVEN ECSTASY TABLETS

By the time I met Lundy Khoy, she had been ordered deported and had been duped by two lawyers. The Dupont Circle bar where I met Lundy and her sister Linda in 2012 was lively and crowded. Lundy was wearing an ICE ankle monitor to keep track of her whereabouts, and she thought it would be great irony to attend a fundraiser for Detention Watch Network that was being held at the bar. After attending the event for a while, we headed to a Thai restaurant, where we ate and talked for several hours.

At the time, Lundy was in her early thirties, just trying to lead a normal life while awaiting her fate. Having lived in the United States since the age of one, she found it hard to imagine being removed to Cambodia, a country she knew little about and where she had no family. She had started college years earlier, when her life was disrupted. Now she was trying to get back on track to finish college. But after her deportation order, she was no longer a lawful permanent resident and her original school cut off her enrollment. Ironically, she was working as a college enrollment counselor while volunteering for local charities including Habitat for Humanity and the Boys & Girls Club.

Lundy was living in Washington, DC, a few blocks from her sister Linda, who is only eighteen months younger than Lundy. The two had always been inseparable, having grown up sharing a bed and a bedroom until Lundy started college. Linda was always Lundy's best friend and most ardent supporter. They cooked together, went out together, laughed and cried together; they think of each other as soul mates. Back then, Linda frequently joined Lundy in speaking out about deportation policies, and the two were working with community-based organizations in Washington, DC, and Philadelphia to seek a legislative solution for those facing removal. When Lundy felt depressed or worried, Linda provided emotional support to bring Lundy back from that space. Linda could not imagine what her life would be like if Lundy were deported to Cambodia.

Lundy was born in a Thai refugee camp in 1980, after her parents fled the genocide in Cambodia. When she was a year old, she and her family entered the United States as refugees. Her was born in Virginia, just a few months later. Lundy and her parents were granted lawful permanent residence status when Lundy was in kindergarten, but they never filed for citizenship through naturalization because of the expense. The family was not wealthy, but Lundy's parents worked hard to provide a stable life, the children were happy, and they were grateful for their life in America.

Things changed for Lundy one night when, as a nineteen-year-old freshman at George Mason University, she was out having fun with her boyfriend. Perhaps they appeared to be having too much fun, because they were stopped by a bicycle police officer, who asked Lundy if she had any drugs. She answered honestly: "I have seven tabs of ecstasy, but they're not all for me." With those words, Lundy was arrested for possession of an illegal drug and charged with the intent to distribute. Her defense attorney advised her to take a plea deal that would lead to a five-year prison sentence, and she agreed, in part to spare her family the expense and embarrassment of a trial. It was not sound advice for someone in Lundy's position, and the attorney was negligent in not telling her the effect the plea would have on her immigration status. Lundy, in fact, had asked the lawyer about this very issue before taking the deal, as she wrote to me later:

> When I brought up immigration court to my criminal lawyer, at the time he said I had nothing to worry about regarding immigration or getting my citizenship. He said it was unrelated and that I have nothing to worry about. I understood from his advice, there was no correlation and that my guilty plea wouldn't affect my immigration status and/or when I apply for my citizenship. . . . He didn't explain to me that my guilty plea would in fact trigger something with the immigration court and me being at risk of deportation. I believe he was either just clueless about the criminalization to deportation pipeline or he just didn't care to provide quality counsel.[3]

She didn't know how perilous the advice was until years later. Lundy was released and placed on probation after serving only a few months in prison. She developed a great relationship with her probation officer, Melanie, who was very supportive. Lundy paid her court fees, resumed college, and was placed on less scrutinized "relaxed" probation. In the spring of 2004, Melanie called Lundy and asked her to come in. This was no regular meeting. When Lundy stepped inside the office, she was greeted by a grim look on Melanie's face and ICE agents, who were targeting removable aliens on active probation. Lundy was forced to hand over her possessions and stand spread-eagled against the wall; she was handcuffed and placed in a cage inside an ICE van. Along with several others, Lundy was driven about three hours away to the Hampton County Jail, an ICE detention contractor, and served with papers that she didn't fully understand. But she knew that the government wanted to deport her to Cambodia.

Her family managed to find her an immigration attorney. Lundy met with him, and that's when she found out that her plea deal was an aggravated felony for deportation purposes, because it involved a controlled substance. She met her immigration lawyer only once, and the strategy was, she wrote me, to "convince the Judge not to deport me on humanitarian grounds." When Lundy read her lawyer's argument and what he submitted to the court, she was disappointed, as it felt to her to be weak and unconvincing.

Lundy's deportation hearing took place in a trailer at a different jail a few hours away in Farmville, Virginia. When her name was called, she was taken to a private area, where the immigration judge appeared on a television screen. The hearing didn't last long—the judge quickly rejected her attorney's arguments. And because of her aggravated felony, the judge ordered Lundy deported without hearing evidence of her childhood in the United States, her family, her educational pursuits, or her perfect behavior on probation. According to Lundy:

> It felt rushed and it was quick. I remember after the hearing it also felt like the decision was already made before the hearing, like I never really had a chance. Before the hearing, I think I was still holding onto some hope because I thought the Judge would weigh in the fact I've been living in the U.S. since I was one year old, that

I had no ties to Cambodia and that I was a legal permanent resident. So I couldn't imagine a Judge would send anyone to a place they've never been to.

There was no appeal, so ICE began making deportation arrangements, and Lundy had to remain in custody. In ICE detention, she realized that her situation was not unique; she met a Bosnian woman in her twenties and an Israeli mother, both convicted of drug-related crimes, both of whom were later deported. Meanwhile, Cambodia wasn't rushing to issue travel documents for Lundy. Linda constantly called ICE, demanding Lundy's release. Before Lundy or any other Cambodian could be removed, a passport needed to be issued. After nine months, ICE finally released Lundy, pending the issuance of a Cambodian passport. To this day, for reasons unknown, as other Cambodian deportees were handed passports, Cambodia seemed to delay coming up with a passport for Lundy. Of course, if Lundy had been born in the United States, like Linda, or if her parents had become naturalized citizens before Lundy turned eighteen, she would have been a US citizen and deportation would have been averted altogether.[4]

After Lundy was released from ICE detention, she tried to get her life together. She managed to reenroll in college and get a job, but all the while she was nervous and worried that at any moment ICE would come knocking on her door with a Cambodian passport and her deportation ticket. Lundy spoke with other lawyers who said there was nothing they could do. Her parents were filled with shame and anxiety. Lundy felt isolated, with no sense of community.

An old college friend, who was outraged at Lundy's situation, introduced her to an acquaintance who was a documentary filmmaker, and they convinced Lundy to tell her story. The result was a short, beautifully done nine-minute film that caught the attention of Mia-Lia Kiernan, a community activist who reached out.[5] The fact that Mia-Lia and others were advocating against Cambodian deportations was eye-opening to Lundy; the group became a comforting community for her. They encouraged Lundy to join them, and eventually Lundy became invested, deciding to tell her story as often as she could get an audience to listen to the injustice of her situation.

By the time we met in 2012, Lundy was still desperate, and the deportation order had been hanging over her head for a decade. I was on the board of Southeast Asia Resource Action Center, in Washington, DC. One of the projects that SEARAC and I have long worked on focuses on the craziness of deporting lawful permanent residents from Cambodia who first entered as refugees when they were infants and toddlers. Until 2002, the United States did not remove noncitizens to Communist-dominated countries, but as part of the early post-9/11 era, the George W. Bush administration strong-armed Cambodia into agreeing to accept deportable Cambodians who committed criminal offenses in the United States. In exchange for signing the agreement, Cambodia would receive US foreign aid.

The repatriation agreement with Cambodia was done without fanfare. (As an aside, I found out about the agreement from an undergraduate student at the University of California, Davis, in 2002. Keo Chea told me that her brother was going to be deported. Like Lundy and so many others, Keo's family entered the United States as Cambodian refugees when she and her brother were toddlers. I told Keo that, in my experience, the United States did not deport Cambodians. In fact, a year earlier, the Supreme Court decided a case involving a Cambodian refugee, Kim Ho Ma, who had been in immigration detention after being ordered deported. The question in the case was whether he could be detained indefinitely, given the fact that there was no "realistic chance" that Cambodia, which had no repatriation treaty with the United States, would accept him. The Supreme Court ruled that after six months, a person with a deportation order should be released from immigration detention if removal is unlikely.[6] The ruling was the reason that Lundy was released after nine months of ICE detention. But not long after the Supreme Court decision, Cambodia signed the repatriation agreement, and Kim Ho Ma and Keo's brother were deported.)

After I met Lundy, she asked whether I thought anything could be done in her case. We discussed a different Supreme Court case, from a couple of years earlier, involving a noncitizen who got bad advice from a criminal defense attorney on a plea bargain. In *Padilla v. Kentucky* (2010), the court ruled that criminal defense attorneys have to advise noncitizen clients about the deportation risks of a guilty plea. In that case, the defense attorney incorrectly told Jose Padilla that he "did not have to worry" about whether a guilty plea to a marijuana charge would affect his immigration status. Since the decision, competent criminal defense attorneys know that they better warn noncitizen clients about potential deportation consequences of any conviction or plea bargain. The "don't worry" advice that Padilla received was strikingly similar to the words that Lundy heard from her own defense attorney. However, the court also held in *Padilla* that the ruling did not apply retroactively.[7]

I spoke with Lundy about the prospect of a pardon from the governor of Virginia; the deportation statute expressly provides that a pardon by the governor or the president protects a noncitizen convicted of crimes of moral turpitude or aggravated felonies from deportation. By the time I took on Lundy's case, I had worked on a few cases where a pardon request was successful given strong community and family support, coupled with exemplary behavior, such as that of Eddy Zheng, who became a community leader working to help at-risk youth.[8]

Lundy and I decided that a pardon request was worth a shot. So Lundy enlisted the help of her supporters to put together a pardon application to Virginia governor Terry McAuliffe, because that's where her conviction took place. The application was compelling, filled with glowing testimonials of Lundy's exemplary character, her commitment to family, her positive contributions to the community, and her work ethic. The challenge was that there are two types of pardons in Virginia: an absolute pardon, given strong evidence that the person never committed the crime, and a simple pardon, in which the person is worthy of a second chance. I wrote to Governor McAuliffe's staff and explained why Lundy needed an absolute pardon:

> Ms. Khoy was charged with deportation as an "aggravated felon" under 8 U.S.C. § 1227(a)(2)(A)(iii). The basis of that charge was her conviction on February 23, 2001 in Arlington County of possession with the intent to distribute a controlled substance under Section 18.1–248 of the Virginia Criminal Code. As Ms. Khoy points

out in her letter to the Governor, the conviction was based on her possession of seven ecstasy tablets as a 19-year-old college student.

Under 8 U.S.C. § 1227(a)(2)(A)(vi), the aggravated felony ground of deportation no longer applies if the alien has been granted a "full and unconditional pardon" by the President of the United States or by the Governor. Therefore, under Virginia's pardon structure, it does appear that Ms. Khoy needs an "absolute" pardon to avoid deportation. I understand that an absolute pardon is only granted when the person was "unjustly convicted and is innocent." We believe that Ms. Khoy has made the case that she was "unjustly convicted" because she was never fully apprised of the immigration consequences of the criminal charges before she pled guilty. See Padilla v. Kentucky, 559 U.S. 356 (2010) (criminal conviction is unjust when defense counsel failed to correctly advise noncitizen defendant). The conviction is further "unjust" because the additional punishment of deportation is grossly disproportionate to the original offense, especially since Ms. Khoy has completely satisfied the criminal punishment that was imposed by the Arlington County Circuit Court.

We respectfully request that the Governor exercise his pardon power by granting Ms. Khoy an absolute pardon of her February 23, 2001 conviction.

But Governor McAuliffe balked. He signed a fancy-looking document on May 4, 2016, declaring that "Lundy Khoy is a fit subject for clemency having provided evidence of a commendable adjustment and having received a favorable recommendation by the Virginia Parole Board" and was therefore granted a simple pardon, which provides official forgiveness. We came close to winning the case, but it wasn't enough to expunge Lundy's criminal record.

While awaiting deportation, Lundy met and fell in love with A. J. Acosta. They married, and Lundy gave birth to their son, Gabriel, in 2015. They initially lived in Virginia, but after Donald Trump was elected president in 2016, they were worried about his anti-immigrant actions and rhetoric, so they moved to Spokane, Washington, to be closer to the Canadian border. A.J. figured that if Trump's enforcement efforts reached Lundy, the entire family would flee to Canada.

In the meantime, Lundy continued speaking out about her case. She and Linda constantly spoke with reporters and made public appearances. Lundy's story appeared in the *New York Times* and the *Washington Post*, and she was interviewed on CNN. She even appeared on *Full Frontal* with Samantha Bee.

While in Spokane, Lundy paid close attention to Virginia politics. On November 5, 2019, voters in Arlington, Virginia, elected a progressive prosecutor, Parisa Dehghani-Tafti, who ran on a restorative justice, decarceration platform. She defeated a long-serving, lock-them-up-and-throw-away-the key district attorney. A few days later, Lundy contacted Jay Stansell, whom she had met during her antideportation campaign (Jay had represented Kim Ho Ma). She asked Jay whether Dehghani-Tafti's election could make a difference in the case.

Jay and I have communicated occasionally about Lundy's case over the years. In early 2019, we talked about a possible motion to reopen Lundy's case on a statutory ground that would involve her citizen husband filing an application for her. But when Lundy told Jay about Dehghani-Tafti's election, he decided to pivot strategies. As a longtime criminal defense attorney, he knew that newly elected progressive prosecutors were making headlines across the country helping to overturn old convictions and reducing sentences that were wrong or unjustified. Jay warned Lundy about being overly optimistic, but he thought that the election really could be a game changer.

Jay practiced in Seattle, so he knew he had to recruit lawyers in the DC-Virginia area to assist. Through an old college roommate, Jay met two attorneys at Baker Botts, an international law firm, who knew the new district attorney personally; they agreed to take on the case pro bono. The team made a rarely used motion to vacate Lundy's conviction based on the argument that she did not "knowingly and voluntarily" enter a guilty plea in 2000. Importantly, prosecutor Dehghani-Tafti agreed to support the motion, and her office submitted its own legal arguments supporting Lundy's position. The original criminal court judge in Lundy's case had long since retired, so the papers were filed with a new judge in Arlington County, who granted the motion and set aside Lundy's conviction completely.

But the case wasn't over yet. The deportation order was still in force, and the only way it could be changed was by the immigration court itself. A motion to reopen the deportation case had to be filed, and even if the case were to be reopened, it was not certain that an immigration judge would terminate the deportation order after so much time had elapsed.[9] So Lundy's team turned to a longtime Washington, DC, immigration attorney, Jim Tom Haynes, who immediately agreed to help. Haynes convinced the federal agency to support a motion to reopen the deportation case in order to terminate the proceedings. With all that before the immigration court, the motion to terminate was granted, and Lundy's deportation nightmare ended.

Afterward, Jay admitted: "Huge relief. I was holding my breath, afraid we won the battle but the case would die before some sticky IJ [immigration judge]. . . . A wonderful victory for such a lovely person and her lovely family . . . Really one of the highlights of my career."[10]

In spite of the hell that Lundy has been through, she considers herself lucky. For whatever reason, the Cambodian government never issued a travel document, and that bought time for Jay and the new legal team to act.

KIM HO MA—MR. DANGER-TO-THE-COMMUNITY

Kim Ho Ma wasn't so fortunate.

Kim Ho Ma was a happy man on July 9, 1999. After more than two years in state prison, and several more months in the custody of immigration authorities, he had been released. His words at the time were filled with relief: "I can work. I pay taxes. I just want to live the American life."[11] Within three years, however, the United States would deport Kim Ho to Cambodia—a place he had left as a toddler, a place where he was unable to speak the language, a place that was a completely foreign environment to him.

Kim Ho was born in Cambodia in 1977, in the midst of the Khmer Rouge regime's sinister oppression and genocide. From 1975 to 1978, two million people—30 percent of Cambodia's population—perished during the "killing fields" genocide of the Pol Pot regime. Kim Ho's mother had been sentenced, at eight months pregnant with Kim Ho, to dig holes at one of Pol Pot's work camps. The idea was to teach her humility. When she collapsed from exhaustion, she expected to be killed. Instead, the guards walked away. When Kim Ho was two, his mother carried him through minefields, fleeing the Khmer Rouge, first to refugee camps in Thailand and the Philippines, and eventually to the United States. By then, Kim Ho was seven.

Kim Ho's first home in America was a housing project in Seattle, where he and other Cambodian refugees had the misfortune of being resettled in the middle of a new war—one between Black and Latino gangs. Both sides taunted Kim Ho and his friends, beating them up for fun. Still affected by the trauma she had experienced in Cambodia, and preoccupied with two minimum-wage jobs, his mother did not understand what was happening to her son. Determined that they would not be pushed around, Kim Ho and his friends formed their own gang.

In 1995, at age seventeen, Kim Ho and two friends ambushed a member of a rival gang; Kim Ho was convicted of first-degree manslaughter. With no previous criminal record, Kim Ho was sentenced to thirty-eight months. Earning time off for good behavior, Kim Ho served twenty-six months, but was released straight into the custody of immigration officials.

Like Lundy, he was ordered deported because of his aggravated felony. The law directed ICE officials to deport Kim Ho within ninety days, but they were unable to do so because the United States and Cambodia did not have a repatriation agreement. ICE refused to release Kim Ho because of his former gang membership, the nature of his crime, and his planned participation in a prison hunger strike. ICE argued that he was a danger to the community.

Enter Jay Stansell.

At the time, Jay was a young, passionate federal public defender in Seattle. Jay filed a petition for a writ of habeas corpus to get Kim Ho out of custody because immigration authorities were unable to

deport Kim Ho. A panel of five federal judges in Seattle ordered officials to release Kim Ho and about a hundred similar individuals. In
their view, the Constitution forbids post-removal-period detention,
unless there is "a realistic chance that [the] alien will be deported."
Since there was no "realistic chance" that Cambodia, which had no
repatriation treaty with the United States at the time, would accept
Kim Ho, he was released on July 9, 1999. Although the government
appealed, within two years, the Supreme Court narrowly endorsed
Kim Ho's release; by then he was rehabilitated and living a model life.
Through the struggle, Kim Ho and Jay became friends.

Things changed for Kim Ho when the Cambodian government
was strong-armed by the US government into signing a repatriation
agreement in March 2002 to facilitate the return of deportable Cambodian refugees. He was among the first deported on October 2, 2002.
Shortly after Kim Ho's flight to Phnom Penh, Jay wrote:

> I cannot write this in "reporter" mode, so I must take a breath and
> speak from my heart. [Kim Ho] bore the weight of "The Ma [Su-
> preme Court] Decision" and . . . sat there in the Supreme Court
> hearing his precious freedom dismissed [by the government] as
> expendable. [Yet, the Court ruled in his favor], and it was a mo-
> mentous victory for all of us who worked for the rights of all hu-
> man beings. . . .
>
> And still, throughout this, Kim knew that he would someday be
> deported, and now he has been.
>
> Over the course of his three years of freedom, Kim Ho spent
> a lot of time with me and my family. . . . He became a son and a
> brother to me and my wife. A big brother to our now 10 and 6
> year old boys. A fan at Adam's baseball games, a wrestling partner
> for Toby. A gentle friend and kind soul. . . .
>
> . . . On September 19, 2002, I received a call that the INS was
> sending Kim Ho a "bag and baggage [deportation] letter." [He
> would be] banished from the United States. . . . I will frame it as
> a monument to 130 years of cruelty to immigrants in the United
> States, and as a reminder of the courage of Kim Ho and all immi-
> grants who step forward in the struggle for justice.[12]

By the time Kim Ho was convicted of manslaughter, he had become a lawful permanent resident of the United States. He is one of thousands of longtime lawful permanent residents to have been deported because of aggravated felonies since that term was introduced to the immigration laws in 1988. As previously emphasized, they have all served their time in jail, so deportation is not a way to avoid serving a criminal sentence. Most have spent nearly their entire lives as lawful residents and have families who remain in the United States. They have straightened out their lives and have job opportunities. But all of that is ignored. As Kim Ho's and Lundy's cases illustrate, aggravated felons have virtually no deportation relief available in immigration court. Issues of rehabilitation, remorse, family ties, community service, and employment history are irrelevant.

It wasn't always like that.

TIMING IS EVERYTHING—A SECOND CHANCE FOR JOHN WONG

Prior to 1988, lawful permanent residents and refugees could be deported for engaging in criminal activities that included crimes involving moral turpitude, drug offenses, prostitution, or certain firearms offenses. Besides obvious crimes like murder, rape, and aggravated assault, moral turpitude crimes included theft, robbery, burglary, passing bad checks, credit card scamming, and perjury, and acts involving recklessness or malice. Under immigration laws at the time, there were two categories of deportable noncitizens convicted of moral turpitude crimes: A noncitizen would be deportable for one conviction if the crime had been committed within five years of entry and the person had been sentenced to confinement for one year or more. A noncitizen would be deportable for two crimes involving moral turpitude at any time after entry, irrespective of how much time had passed. Thus, a noncitizen could be deported for two crimes involving moral turpitude, even if the crimes occurred many years apart. In fact, one of my first clients—Juan Alvarez— was placed in deportation proceedings for two petty thefts that were committed twenty years apart. Paradoxically, if a noncitizen had only a single conviction for something serious, such as murder, committed more than five years after admission, deportation was not triggered prior to 1988.

A separate ground for deportation existed in relation to drugs or marijuana; only one conviction was necessary, including a conviction for simple possession of marijuana.[13]

John Wong was one of my clients in this pre-1988 period. I first encountered John when I was a legal services attorney in San Francisco's Chinatown. Because of convictions for gang-related crimes and for the sale of heroin, he was deportable for two crimes involving moral turpitude and separately for his drug conviction.

John's path to criminality was not unique. He was born in Hong Kong on March 27, 1956, the fifth of six children. His parents, originally from mainland China, immigrated to Hong Kong after World War II, when the Communist Party took over. As tailors, they owned a small business making suits. As such, they were able to buy property and had the time and money to provide for their children. They were doing fine in Hong Kong, but their lives changed when John's aunt, who lived in the United States, convinced John's parents that the United States offered a better future, full of opportunity for their children. She filed immigration papers for John's parents, and they sold their possessions and left Hong Kong.

The family arrived in San Francisco in 1963, when John was only seven years old. They settled in San Francisco's Chinatown, where John's aunt owned a restaurant. John's parents worked twelve- to sixteen-hour days in the restaurant, mostly washing dishes. They were grateful for the opportunity to work and earn money but found themselves too tired to spend much time with their children. Their search for other work was hampered by their inability to speak English. Eventually, both of John's parents were able to use their tailoring skills to find work at a sewing factory, and they moved the family into a two-bedroom apartment.

Life was dramatically different in the United States for the Wong family. Because language barriers resulted in limited job opportunities for the parents, the family had much less income to spend. John's parents simply could not support the family in the same way they had in Hong Kong. Like John, other immigrant children faced cultural and identity conflicts. At school, the American-born Chinese (ABC) children would pick on the foreign-born kids. As early as kindergarten, John assumed a tough-guy persona in response to bad treatment from the ABC kids. He would get into frequent fistfights with the ABCs.

With little supervision and a group of friends who were struggling to fit in, John gradually lost interest in school. On a typical day, he would go to school only to meet friends and cut classes. They started stealing from local stores for fun. Smoking, drinking, and fighting became a regular occurrence in the neighborhood. John was arrested a few times, and he started hanging out with his friends even more; cutting classes in high school became the norm. It soon became clear to his parents that they could not control him, and they decided to allow the juvenile authorities to take over.

The other kids in juvenile hall were of different races and they were bigger than John. John was forced to stand up for himself, because he was constantly picked on. By the time he was released, John was tougher and less adjusted to life on the outside. Though John never joined one of the neighborhood's gangs, he continued low-level criminal behavior. By the age of nineteen, he had been convicted of armed robbery and was sentenced to three years' incarceration.

John confirmed the well-worn cliché observing that "if you're not a criminal and you're sent to state prison, you become a criminal." He made friends with other Asians, and they would watch each other's backs. These friends exposed John to drugs. Eventually, he learned to avoid the fighting, and after serving three years in state prison, he was released and moved to San Jose, California, south of San Francisco.

John spent six months at a halfway house. He was required to report to a parole officer periodically. He remained drug-free and crime-free during this period, and he received training in electronics and landed a job at General Electric. After his parole ended, John quit his job with General Electric and returned to San Francisco. Back in his old neighborhood, he reverted to hanging out with old friends, using drugs, and getting into fights. John left prison with a drug addiction and had become more prone to criminal behavior.

Just two years after being released from state prison, John was sentenced to two years in federal prison for possession with intent to distribute heroin. Unlike at state prison, in federal prison John was in the company of many nonviolent white-collar criminals whose influence led him to reconsider his life trajectory. He completed his high school general equivalency diploma (GED) while serving time, and he attended a drug rehabilitation program while being regularly tested for drugs. The program was in a minimum-security area, where John was able to meet "a lot of good people." While John was in federal prison, his mother passed away. He was filled with remorse about what he had done and how he had missed being with those he loved. He told me later, "It hurt me a lot. I would always return from jail badder and badder." Released again at the age of twenty-five, John decided to do things right.

John's resolve to stay out of trouble was strengthened by his new role as a husband; he had married his girlfriend right before going to federal prison. An old friend helped him get a job as a city hall clerk for minimum wage. After a year, John was accepted to the city's mechanic's assistant program. The two-year training led to work with the municipal railway service of San Francisco. John was determined to stay clean for himself and his family.

But John's criminal past finally caught up with him. Immigration authorities arrested him and started deportation proceedings. John was shocked. He had been in the United States for more than twenty-five years. He thought: "I did my time; I don't deserve getting deported."[14]

Timing is everything. Prior to 1996, discretionary relief from deportation was available for longtime lawful permanent residents, such as John, who had been convicted of serious crimes. After serving their time in prison, they could apply for a waiver of deportation to the immigration court if they had been residents for at least seven years. In deciding whether to grant a waiver, immigration judges would weigh the good things about the person's life against the bad. Was the person rehabilitated and remorseful? Was the family supportive? Was a job waiting? Was there other support from the community, church, or friends? What was the likelihood that the person would commit a crime again?

Waiver relief was not automatic. Someone with a sporadic employment record, a lengthy and very severe criminal record, and long involvement in the drug culture, might be denied.[15] A conviction for sexual abuse of an eight-year-old niece might be so serious that a favorable exercise of discretion was not warranted, even in the face of good factors or outstanding equities such as longtime US residence, relatives in the US, and a solid work history.[16] However, someone convicted of possession of twenty-one pounds of marijuana with intent to distribute could still get a second chance from an immigration judge if the applicant had been married to a US citizen for many years, had citizen children who were dependent on him, or faced the imminent breakup of his marriage if deported, and if he had an otherwise clean criminal record.[17]

This was the context in which John Wong's deportation hearing was held. John was clearly deportable because his drug conviction was a matter of record. However, because John was able to apply for a waiver, an immigration judge could weigh his good equities—a stable marriage and employment history—against the serious drug offense and the armed robbery conviction. Since his initial immigration to the United States at the age of seven, John had never returned to Hong Kong. He had no relatives or friends in Asia and would have had an extremely difficult time adjusting to life in Hong Kong. His life, his home, his work, and family were in the United States. John had become the sole provider for and caretaker of his elderly father. He was married with children. Dozens of support letters from friends, family, supervisors, and coworkers, as well as from his parole officer and a court-appointed psychologist, were submitted. In the end, John Wong was granted relief by an immigration judge who was impressed with his rehabilitation and the likely hardship to himself and his family that would result from his deportation. He was given a second chance to establish a law-abiding life in the United States.

That was in 1985. John made good on his pledge to the judge, that he would stay out of trouble. Years later, he became a naturalized citizen. He worked with the local transit authority for more than forty years, until he retired in 2021 at sixty-five in the midst of the pandemic. He is married and has three adult daughters, all of whom are college graduates with good jobs. His family is his inspiration—he has stayed away from drugs and worked hard to keep his life on track.

The fact that John's case took place in 1985, and particularly that it was reviewed before 1996, made all the difference in the world. The second-chance statute for serious offenders was still in force.

INTRODUCING THE "AGGRAVATED FELON"

In 1988, as mentioned previously, Congress decided to add a more scary-sounding term to the list of criminal grounds for deportation: "aggravated felony," which included murder, rape, drug trafficking, sexual abuse of a minor, and firearms trafficking. With that change, noncitizens—including longtime, lawful permanent residents—convicted of a single aggravated felony, any time after admission, became deportable. The new aggravated felony ground for deportation overlapped with other deportation provisions. For example, drug convictions that were now aggravated felonies remained independent grounds for deportation under the provision pertaining to drug crimes. Similarly, any person who was convicted of two crimes involving moral turpitude was still deportable, irrespective of whether one or both crimes were aggravated felonies.

The list of aggravated felonies, expanded several times since 1988, is so broad that my old friend Dana Marks, who has served as president of the National Association of Immigration Judges, considers the category a "misnomer that includes many offenses that are neither aggravated nor felonies." Beyond murder, rape, and serious drug offenses, some fairly minor offenses are included. For example, selling ten dollars' worth of marijuana or "smuggling" a baby sister across the border illegally are aggravated felonies for deportation purposes. A crime classified as a misdemeanor under state law might be regarded as an aggravated felony under the federal immigration law. Several offenses are classified as aggravated felonies if a sentence of one year in prison is imposed; they include theft, burglary, perjury, and obstruction of justice.

Although the aggravated felony ground for deportation became part of the law in 1988, until 1996, a long-term, lawful permanent resident convicted of an aggravated felony could still ask an immigration judge for a second chance. In other words, the John Wong–type of discretionary waiver relief could be sought in immigration court. Based on evidence of remorse, rehabilitation, and hardship, an immigration judge could cancel deportation for someone labeled an aggravated felon. That all changed in 1996.

No More Second Chances for Aggravated Felons

The introduction of the aggravated felony concept in 1988 signaled a major shift in how policy makers looked at noncitizens convicted of crimes. In 1990, Congress barred state criminal court judges from making a Judicial Recommendation Against Deportation. (Until 1990, a state court judge could make a recommendation that was binding on immigration authorities, that, in the interest of justice, a noncitizen should not be deported because of a state court criminal conviction.)

Later, in 1996, debate over major reform focused heavily on immigrant criminality, increasing categories of deportation and "streamlining the removal process."[18] In a statement resembling Donald Trump's later rhetoric in 2015, that Mexican migrants are "bringing drugs and crime" to the US, Sen. Orrin Hatch (R-Utah) argued, "Frankly, a lot of our criminality in this country today happens to be coming from criminal, illegal aliens who are ripping our country apart. A lot of the drugs are coming from these people."[19] This conflation of "illegal alien" with pervasive crime was enough to affect the treatment of all noncitizens convicted of crimes—even those who were long-term, lawful permanent residents.

The Illegal Immigration Reform and Immigrant Responsibility Act of 1996 eliminated the John Wong second-chance waiver relief. In its place, a new provision permitted immigration judges to "cancel removal" only for certain noncitizens guilty of crimes, and the noncitizen must have been a lawful permanent resident for at least five years and have resided in the United States for seven years. Most significantly, the provision held that anyone convicted of any aggravated felony was ineligible for the cancellation of removal. The aggravated felony category, which began as additional grounds for crime-based deportation, became a convenient marker for barring eligibility for relief. That means that for people like Lundy Khoy, Kim Ho Ma, and John Wong—all aggravated felons—judges no longer can consider whether the person is rehabilitated and worthy of a second chance. There's no weighing of the good against the bad. There's no consideration of remorse, family, or community. All that is now irrelevant. In essence, a single bad act that may have taken a few minutes to commit controls the outcome, even though the rest of a person's life is exemplary and crime free.

A deportation order is now preordained once there is an aggravated felony conviction. That's why Kim Ho Ma was deported. That's why Lundy Khoy's order of deportation loomed over her head for more than twenty years. And but for the fact that John Wong's case took place before 1996, I would have been foreclosed from introducing evidence of his life, and he would have been ordered deported to Hong Kong. His productive work and family life in the United States would have never occurred, because he would not have received a second chance.

Even federal judges have acknowledged that "[f]ew punishments are more drastic than expelling persons from this country when their family members are residents."[20] But the federal courts have no power to intervene because the law is the law. The sweeping, mandatory deportation scheme governing aggravated felony deportation often includes misdemeanors involving short prison sentences. The category "includes many crimes that bear little . . . relation to an actual threat to public safety."[21] The law results in automatic deportation for convictions as minor as petty theft, urinating in public, or forgery of a check for less than twenty dollars.[22] And it doesn't matter if the person immigrated as an infant or toddler and grew up in the United States. This system of deporting longtime lawful residents of the United States should be abolished.

PROPORTIONALITY: DOES THE PUNISHMENT FIT THE CRIME?

One way to justify limiting the removal of lawful noncitizens convicted of crimes is by viewing the situation through the lens of proportionality. In other words, does the punishment fit the crime?

Deportation is not a get-out-of-jail-free card for noncitizens. Lundy Khoy, Kim Ho Ma, and other noncitizen aggravated felons facing deportation have already gone to jail and, as the saying goes, "paid their debt to society." Kim Ho's removal to Cambodia, without regard to his rehabilitation or the hardship on his family, raises a serious question of whether the punishment fits the crime. After serving the prison sentence, is the added punishment of deportation proportional to the crime committed?

The 1996 elimination of the John Wong-type discretionary waiver relief embodies a zero-tolerance policy for aggravated felons. In reality, Kim Ho is punished three times for his crime: First, he served his sentence in prison for manslaughter, and second, he was deported from the United States. But as a deported aggravated felon, in what amounts to a third punishment, Kim Ho is permanently barred from returning to the United States—exiled from home and family. This triple punishment simply is not proportional to the crime. If Kim Ho had been a citizen, he would not have been deported. His prison time would have satisfied our societal interest in punishment through the criminal justice system. But because Kim Ho was a noncitizen, two immigration penalties were tacked on. Juxtaposing the penalties for citizens versus noncitizens exposes the absence of proportionality. The removal of any lawful permanent resident in that situation is simply unjust, especially when the vast majority of those affected are long-time residents of color. Short of ending this practice, a more proportional approach to the removal of noncitizens convicted of crimes needs to be implemented.

When I chaired the San Francisco Immigrant Rights Commission, Anoop Prasad, a legal services attorney who has advocated for proportionality, provided important insight to our body. He noted that the fundamental problem with our criminal deportation system is that it judges people based on their worst acts alone, the worst fifteen minutes of their lives. The system blocks evidence about a client who has turned his life around: who has finished college in prison, has become a firefighter, or whose mother will be heartbroken if he is deported. All the immigration judge will see is the crime the client committed at age sixteen.

European courts take proportionality in the deportation context seriously. For example, in *Nasri v. France* (1995), the European Court of Human Rights blocked the deportation of a thirty-five-year-old Algerian national who had several convictions—including for theft, assault, and participation in a gang rape:

> [R]emoving the applicant from his family and sending him to a country with which he has no ties would expose him to suffering of such gravity that to do so might be regarded as inhuman treatment. In a democratic society which adheres to the principle of respect for the dignity of the human person, a measure of such severity cannot be proportionate to the legitimate aim of maintaining public order.[23]

Using a proportionality approach, the European Court considered several psychological evaluations and the possibility that Nasri would be tortured back in Algeria, along with the fact that his "family relationships would be made impossible" if he were deported. The commission concluded that deportation would be a disproportionate punishment and unjustified.

In *AR (Pakistan) v. Secretary of State for the Home Department* (2010), the deportation of an asylum applicant who had been granted indefinite permission to remain in the United Kingdom was upheld, but not until the applicant had been given two warnings following several criminal convictions and unsuccessful participation in drug rehabilitation programs. The question, in the words of the Court of Appeal in the United Kingdom, is "whether deportation is proportionate, given due weight to the public interest and to the right to family life."[24] And the "task of deciding whether deportation is or is not proportionate typically involves weighing up conflicting factors." In deciding that the deportation was proportionate, the Court of Appeal considered the criminal record and the warnings that had been issued. The court considered the applicant's children. The applicant and his wife had divorced, and their three children lived with their maternal grandparents. As in the *Nasri* case, the court was well aware of the fundamental right to family life under the European Convention on Human Rights. However, the applicant had not maintained close contact with his children—in part because of his intermittent time in prison—and therefore the public interest in his deportation was stronger.

Some immigration judges and criminal justice officials support a call for proportionality when it comes to the deportation of immigrants convicted of crimes. Immigration judge Dana Marks criticized the current system as a "blunt instrument" that does not "serve the public and private interests."[25] She argued that immigration judges should have the discretion to consider the "individual circumstances unique to each case." Paul Grussendorf, a former immigration judge in San Francisco and Philadelphia, is also troubled by the aggravated felony bar to discretionary relief no "matter how old or minor the offense."[26] He agrees that immigration judges need the discretion to weigh "the age of the conviction, the severity of the offense, evidence of rehabilitation, [and] family ties in the United States."

Robert Johnson, a past president of the National District Attorneys Association, had assumed that mandatory detention and deportation would result from "only the most heinous crimes," but he learned that aggravated felonies include offenses like "possessing marijuana, shoplifting or getting in a fight at a sports game."[27] While US citizens often get their cases dismissed after completing a treatment program, immigrants do not get that chance. Johnson thinks that the criminal justice system would be more efficient and just if prosecutors knew that immigration judges would consider the individual factors, including "U.S. military service, rehabilitation and family ties, to determine if it is in the best interests of the United States to let someone remain in the country." Similarly, Steven Jansen, a former criminal prosecutor from Detroit, uses the language of proportionality, writing that our system strives for "case outcomes that reflect a balance of punishment, compassion and concern for victims and community" including for offenders who are not citizens of the United States.[28]

Yet, the outcomes in deportation cases do not meet those goals. Jansen argues that as "problem solvers," prosecutors understand that "crime prevention and community safety demand a more nuanced [and balanced] approach." Jeff Rosen, the former district attorney for

Santa Clara County, California, believes that immigrants who commit minor offenses "should be prosecuted, held accountable and then allowed to earn the right to continue on a legal path to citizenship."[29] He argues that deportation in some cases is "a grossly disproportionate punishment" that would "tear a family apart" and is a damaging and costly aspect of this automatic deportation policy.

These critiques of "automatic deportation" call for a more holistic, proportional approach to deportation.

Reinstating the waiver relief that was available to noncitizen aggravated felons prior to 1996 would be better than nothing. As in John Wong's case, the immigration judge is in a good position to assess evidence of rehabilitation, remorse, family, support, and prospects for the future. But even that remedy had problems—beyond the fact that most noncitizens are unrepresented and don't have the capacity to gather the necessary evidence to win their cases. Proportionality and fairness would be better promoted if immigration judges had more assessment tools or alternatives to immediate deportation available to them. Even during the pre-1996 era, the immigration court had only two options: deport or grant relief—nothing in between. In either scenario, the noncitizen had no further contact with government officials after the order was enforced.

Deportation does not have to be the only option. We should implement a system that addresses the concerns of both the proponents and opponents of deportation of those who have committed an aggravated felony. I believe that we can come up with ideas, premised on a belief that individuals are capable of changing their lives, that can satisfy the deportation-minded while striving to meet the goals of proportionality.

INSTITUTING A PAUSE BUTTON

A simple option is simply to hit a pause button on removal proceedings and place the person under temporary probation. Monitor the person's behavior. Deportation proceedings could be placed on hold pending an opportunity to assess the person's chances at rehabilitation. That would provide an opportunity to assess whether deportation would be proportionate or not.

The criminal justice system provides some examples of alternatives that could be implemented during the deportation pause. Some options are available prior to trial, while others may be considered after a finding of guilt. Consider the use of probation office reports and recommendations, pretrial diversion programs, group therapy, anger management, drug rehabilitation programs, and community service options. Some jurisdictions have adopted restorative justice or relational justice programs that have an underlying premise that may be particularly appropriate to consider as an alternative to the deportation of refugees. If one assumes that an immigrant- and refugee-receiving country (i.e., the United States) bears some responsibility to assist in the adjustment of newcomers to their new culture, then a program that responds to criminal behavior in a manner that seeks to repair damage to the community and/or to encourage the person to take responsibility for their actions on the road to rehabilitation is worthy of consideration.

Even the probation officer or department entity, which are such critical parts of the criminal justice system, offer ideas to consider. Probation is a post-conviction process that serves as an alternative to incarceration. Probation helped Lundy Khoy and, eventually, John Wong. Its fundamental purpose is the reformation of the defendant in the society in which they must eventually live. The defendant is released under the supervision of a probation officer and is subject to reasonable court-imposed conditions.

Probation office reports are critical to the process. A probation report is a written account of the probation officer's investigations, findings, and recommendations regarding the defendant's fitness for probation. The purpose of this report is to assist the sentencing judge in determining an appropriate disposition of the defendant's case after conviction. Besides offering information on the basic facts of the case and crime, the report can include details on the defendant's prior criminal conduct, social history, family, education, employment, income, military service, and medical and psychological history, as well as an evaluation of factors relating to the disposition, recommendations, including a reasoned discussion of aggravating and mitigating factors affecting sentence length, or whether imprisonment was even necessary.

In diversion programs, criminal cases are "diverted" out of the criminal justice system prior to a conviction. In such programs, courts generally require offenders to participate in a treatment or rehabilitation program in lieu of being incarcerated. Criminal charges are dropped upon successful completion of diversion programs, sparing defendants from the stigma that comes with a criminal conviction. Either the prosecution or defense counsel may offer diversion to defendants. Defense counsel may ask a judge at a defendant's first court appearance to order an evaluation for diversion. A defendant referred to diversion meets with a probation officer, who conducts an investigation and prepares a report regarding suitability for diversion. A recommendation may specify the type of program most suitable for the defendant.

Requiring defendants to perform community service is another alternative. In such cases, courts assign offenders to work, uncompensated, for nonprofit organizations or governmental entities instead of serving jail time. Requiring community service holds offenders accountable and encourages a more positive connection with the community. Local community service coordinators or probation officers administer community service orders. The orders often involve work in community centers. Community service is usually imposed in conjunction with other forms of punishment, such as probation, fines, or restitution.

In another option, courts may order offenders out of their homes for fixed terms, placing them in group living arrangements, such as residential treatment facilities. Under this scheme, clinical and counseling staff provide offenders with regular mentoring, counseling, and treatment for drug abuse. The goal is for residents to learn to become self-sufficient, contributing members of society.

The world of corporate fraud prosecutions uses a time-out tool that could be a useful model for deportation cases. In response to corporate crimes, federal prosecutors have adopted strategies to manage the complexity of prosecutions and to foster better behavior on the part of corporations. Prosecutors can elect to defer prosecution, in cases where the corporation cooperates with investigations and takes remedial actions to change its illegal behaviors. This culminates in a deferred prosecution agreement (DPA) between the government and the corporation—essentially a form of probation, or "pretrial diversion." The government suspends charges against the company during the pause. In other words, it's a temporary probationary period.

The time-out period of a DPA is generally from one to two years. In return, corporations undertake reforms and pledge active and complete cooperation with the ongoing investigation, and they pay substantial civil penalties and victim restitution. Companies will often be required to engage the services of a monitor or examiner during the diversion period to review and report on compliance efforts. If the corporation meets all the terms of the agreement, prosecutors dismiss the charges.

Mary Jo White, former US attorney for the Southern District of New York, believes that DPAs are useful "as a means to force companies to behave and reform themselves."[30] For example, in agreeing to pay a $1.2 billion criminal penalty for hiding safety defects from the public, Toyota was subjected to three years of monitoring by the Department of Justice while a prosecution for wire fraud was deferred.[31]

DPAs provide tremendous rehabilitative incentives to the corporations, since billions of dollars may be involved and the careers and lives of officers, board members, employees, and shareholders are at stake. The adaptability of deferred agreements to deportation cases involving noncitizens convicted of crimes is obvious. Why not monitor and impose conditions on such individuals for a reasonable period of time to see if rehabilitation is possible? Why not provide government attorneys or immigration judges with the authority to implement such conditions?

The use of DPAs in the removal context makes better sense than straight removal. Deferred agreements would reduce the necessary resources that are expended by the government in the full removal process, allow ICE to monitor the person's behavior for a reasonable amount of time, provide a remedy for deserving cases, and serve an important public policy in keeping families together. DPAs would give the government the opportunity to monitor a lawful permanent resident who may have made one mistake, but who appears to be rehabilitated or on the road to rehabilitation.

When the federal government announced a deferred agreement in a case against America Online (later AOL), it stated that the agreement was designed to "achieve a result that minimizes the collateral damage to shareholders and employees while imposing an appropriate punishment and protecting the rights of victims."[32] This reluctance to cause extensive economic harm to the public, and the goal of minimizing "collateral damage," is relevant in removal cases of longtime lawful permanent residents of the United States who have committed deportable crimes.

What is gained by deporting a person who is rehabilitated, remorseful, and integral to family and community? Removal in that situation can result in economic, social, and psychological harm to family and community. The use of a DPA in those circumstances would provide a way to monitor the person and, if the conditions are met, a family and community could be saved from serious damage.

Using the deferred model is a way to adopt a rehabilitative approach to justice, where relationship-building is a central theme. The use of DPAs in the aggravated felon removal context would provide space for the voices of the noncitizen and their family and employer, as well as those of members of the community. Societal justice is about repairing relationships between individuals and institutions, and between individuals and communities. Focusing on restoring relationships is time well spent, in terms of reducing recidivism.

We can be creative when it comes to the types of conditions that would be included in removal DPAs. Regular check-ins with ICE deportation officers, or even with cooperating community-based organizations, can be used. Many ex-offenders facing removal already are required to check in with probation officers. Conventional approaches, such as probation office reports and recommendations, pretrial diversion programs, group therapy, anger management, drug rehabilitation programs, and community service options can be included. However, informal networks—such as family, friends, neighbors, and employers—can be made part of the process. A program that responds to criminal behavior in a manner that seeks to repair damage to the community and/or to encourage the person to take responsibility for their actions on the road to rehabilitation can be part of the goal.

A REHABILITATIVE, RELATIONSHIP-BUILDING APPROACH TO JUSTICE

As mentioned, focusing on restoring relationships is time well spent, in terms of reducing recidivism. In contrast to the incapacitation view of justice, a view of justice as the state's duty to protect the public from future harms by perpetrators, relational justice is premised on a belief that individuals are capable of change. This approach is particularly relevant in the deportation context, in which the noncitizen aggravated felon has already served and completed a sentence for the criminal offense. The deportation setting is, therefore, properly viewed as all about the individual's future. That is where guidance and encouragement to become reincorporated into the community make great sense.

Relational justice recognizes that conventional criminal justice institutions (i.e., courts, police, probation departments, community agencies) should not solely be responsible for the outcome. "Informal networks," including family, friends, neighbors, employers, and perhaps even victims, must step up to make the process work.

Relational justice incorporates a set of values that needs to be ingrained in the system if the system is to work properly. It seeks to preserve a person's sense of being valued as a human being, with hope for the future. It begins by treating those in the system with courtesy, dignity, and respect. It looks for unspoken signs that a person may need an explanation and reassurance.

The current removal process for aggravated felons who have grown up in the United States contains none of these components or values. Relief is altogether foreclosed for them. Information on their lives, their families, their community, and their rehabilitation are deemed irrelevant. The immigration laws have made deportation part of the criminal justice process.

The idea behind many of these options is not just that removal may not be appropriate or proportional but that rehabilitation is a real possibility that should be promoted. In the removal setting, rehabilitation is a possibility that ought to be encouraged, given the circumstances of many noncitizens of color—such as Kim Ho Ma and John Wong—who have resettled in challenging environments. The benefits to the individual are obvious. But the family, the community, and the entire society also stand to gain from a constructive rehabilitative approach.

CONCLUSION

After twenty years of worry that she could be deported at any moment, Lundy Khoy was able to avert deportation. It took the help of some creative lawyers with a lot of resources, and the lucky fact that, for whatever reason, the Cambodian government dragged its feet in issuing a passport. John Wong was able to avoid deportation because a remedy was available in immigration court that permitted him to introduce evidence of his rehabilitation and other positive changes in his life. Kim Ho Ma wasn't so fortunate, nor were thousands of other lawful permanent residents convicted of so-called aggravated felonies who never had a chance to present evidence that they deserved a second chance.

In spite of bad and expensive lawyering in her initial criminal and deportation cases, Lundy came across other attorneys who finally came through. It is gratifying to have played a small role in helping Lundy, and it was meaningful when she shared that we had allowed her to "have faith in attorneys again." But it is unfortunate and telling that it had to take the heroic efforts of Jay, the Baker Botts attorneys, and Jim Tom Haynes to achieve a just, proportionate result. The grim reality is that the vast majority of individuals with aggravated felony convictions don't have access to legal assistance for pursuing a governor's pardon or attacking the validity of the conviction. It shouldn't take that type of access, but it does. For that reason, deportation of permanent residents convicted of crimes should end. As underscored, these individuals have already paid their debt to society by fulfilling their obligations to the criminal justice system.

Short of abolishing all automatic deportation, a system open to weighing the potential for rehabilitation needs to be instituted. John

Wong's triumph over a history of criminal activities and transformation into a hardworking, law-abiding, stable family man is a tribute to his diligence, maturity, and strong values. His triumph also is a tribute to the good judgment of an immigration judge who saw fit to grant John a second chance. That good judgment was possible prior to 1996.

Of course, no one can perfectly predict what an individual will do with a second chance; there are too many variables that affect behavior. However, a blanket rule against second chances is too harsh. The zero-tolerance approach to aggravated felons results in an outcome—deportation—that is, in too many cases, disproportionate to the crime. We should implement alternatives to deportation, such as probation or diversion. Providing alternatives to the zero-tolerance approach to criminal immigrants is not synonymous with being soft on crime. It's synonymous with seeking justice and promoting rehabilitation to avoid future criminality.

Why push ourselves to end deportation, or to at least come up with alternatives to deportation and reinstitute immigration judge discretion? Because our basic humanity demands that we look beyond the poor judgment of individuals who acted imprudently for a few moments, and that we recognize the potential for reform and rehabilitation, and the value in providing a second chance. Deportation separates families. Deportation forecloses the benefits that we can all gain from a life that has changed. It's hard to see a benefit from the deportation of Kim Ho Ma.[33] It's hard to see what our society would have gained from expelling Lundy Khoy or John Wong. Immigration judges and prosecutors committed to just results see the need for nimble approaches and increased discretion, rather than enforcing the status quo, which can be unnecessarily harsh on individuals and their families. We can help position these individuals to do better and, in the process, help their families and our communities as well.

CHAPTER 4

DEPORTING ANTONIO SANCHEZ

*The Failure of Prosecutorial Discretion
and Cancellation of Removal*

E VERY DAY, UNDOCUMENTED noncitizens like Antonio Sanchez,
who have lived in the United States for decades without incident, and who have US-citizen children and often two jobs,
are deported from the United States.[1] They are cheerful role models
for their kids, taking an active part in their soccer teams and their
schools' PTAs. They are sometimes churchgoers, helping their friends
and neighbors, and lead an honest life except for the occasional park-
ing ticket. The legal basis for their deportation is simple: they are living
in the United States without authorization because they either overstayed their visas or entered the country without inspection.

Immigration laws enacted in 1996 provide an avenue for relief
for folks like Antonio. Cancellation of removal can be granted by an
immigration judge if the person has resided in the United States for
at least ten years and has demonstrated good moral character. However, the statute also requires a showing that removal would result in
"exceptional and extremely unusual hardship" to the person's spouse,
parent, or child who is a US citizen or legal permanent resident.[2] That
hardship requirement is an insurmountable hurdle for the vast majority of applicants like Antonio.

For decades, immigrant rights activists have argued that millions
of individuals like Antonio simply should be granted legalization or
amnesty for social, economic, and human rights reasons. Although
Congress came close a couple of times in the last twenty years, it has
not happened. The last time a legalization program was enacted Ronald Reagan was president, when about three million noncitizens got

green cards. A broad legalization program today could potentially benefit ten to twelve million.

Presidents including Barack Obama and Joe Biden have responded to the difficulties of meeting the requirements for cancellation of removal, and they addressed the congressional failure to pass a legalization law, by issuing enforcement guidance to ICE officials. Using "prosecutorial discretion" guidelines, the presidents hoped to send a message to ICE agents to de-prioritize the removal of people in Antonio's situation. But unfortunately, my experience with Antonio's case demonstrates how these enforcement guidelines are often ignored and illustrates the problems with the cancellation of removal law.

LORENA'S FATHER, ANTONIO SANCHEZ

On the night before Antonio Sanchez was forced to leave the United States, in late September 2011, I stopped by his home to say goodbye, to answer any last minute questions he might have, and to do my best to console his family. The fifty-five-year-old Mexican immigrant had not been in Mexico for more than twenty-five years, and leaving his wife, Zoila, his twenty-one-year-old daughter, Lorena, and his thirteen-year-old son, Antonio Jr., was the biggest challenge he had ever faced. The usually stoic, peaceful man had tears in his eyes as we reviewed the process of his departure and the documents he would need to sign and submit to the US consulate in Mexico City in order for his family's bond money to be refunded. In his soft-spoken, humble tone, he explained how he rejected the entreaties of acquaintances who advised him to abscond; he did not want to be a fugitive—what example would that be for his family? He always played by the rules and never cheated at anything. Even his entry to the United States more than a quarter century earlier came at a time when crossing the border was a simple task of walking along a path near San Diego. Border Patrol officers simply turned and looked the other way at certain times of the year when they knew that seasonal workers were coming to harvest crops that needed attention.

Antonio's daughter, Lorena, a smart, energetic college senior who handled most of the communications with me over the monthlong period I represented her father, was somber that evening. She and her mother were crying, but her kid brother was not. Antonio Jr. maintained a blank face for the hour or so I visited with them, not saying more than a word or two, sitting emotionless at the dinner table as he listened to the conversation. Lorena whispered to me that Antonio Jr. had not cried and she knew that he was holding a lot inside. About a week earlier, in one of Antonio Jr.'s soccer games, he drew a penalty red card for kicking an opposing player who had stumbled—a violent act so uncharacteristic that the entire family was stunned and left the field ashamed.

The next evening, Lorena called me from the airport after she hugged her father goodbye outside the TSA security area. Her mother fainted from the traumatic experience and was being driven back home by family friends. Antonio Jr. decided not to go to the airport, preferring to stay home, ensconced in his bedroom.

A few weeks later, on November 22, 2011, my wife and I were finishing dinner, half listening to highlights from the Republican presidential primary debate on national security, broadcast from DAR Constitution Hall in Washington, DC. My ears perked up when the moderator, CNN's Wolf Blitzer, posed a question on immigration policy. While candidates including Mitt Romney and Michele Bachmann espoused a hard line of deporting all undocumented immigrants, Newt Gingrich pivoted and announced:

I do not believe that the people of the United States are going to take people who have been here a quarter-century, who have children and grandchildren . . . separate them from their families and expel them. . . . [L]et's be humane in enforcing the law without giving them citizenship but by finding a way to create legality so that they are not separated from their families.

"Wow!" I cried out to my wife. "That's Antonio Sanchez he's talking about."

The forced removal of Antonio provides important lessons about the thousands of deportations of mostly Latinx migrants, living in the United States without authorization, that take place every year.

My representation of Antonio centered on navigating the administrative process for requesting prosecutorial discretion from Department of Homeland Security officials. But the story also includes the efforts of his previous attorneys, who tried to convince the Board of Immigration Appeals to recognize the hardship that his family would face. Antonio's case and the experiences of others pursuing similar processes reveal disquieting evidence of inconsistencies and frustratingly harsh results. Sympathetic applicants, like Antonio, highlight the challenges encountered in exercising prosecutorial discretion during the deportation process, the need for cultural and procedural reform of immigration policies, and, ultimately, the need for new remedies, including a different approach to cancellation of removal.

CAN YOU HELP MY FATHER?

In the course of my academic and community work, I often get invited to speak at various community meetings and events related to immigration law and policy. At those events, I meet many individuals who are members of groups that engage in activism on behalf of immigrants and immigrant communities. One such group, Responsibility, Integrity, Strength, Empowerment (RISE), comprises students from Berkeley High School in Berkeley, California. In the summer of 2011, I received a series of emails from this group asking to meet about the possibility of working together on projects related to deportation. But in particular, they wanted to discuss the pending deportation of the father of one of their members.

On August 29, 2011, several students from the RISE program—mostly high school students—arrived at my office with their sponsor, Adriana Curley, a counselor at Berkeley High School. We briefly discussed their ideas, including making a presentation at the United Nations about deportation and having a retreat to educate other young people in the San Francisco Bay Area about the facts and issues associated with deportation. However, the students' main desire was to talk about the pending deportation of Lorena's father, Antonio Sanchez, which was scheduled in less than a month.

Lorena, a member of RISE, appeared calm, but was filled with despair. A former student at Berkeley High, Lorena was about to start her senior year at the University of California, Berkeley. She explained the details of her father's situation. He entered without inspection twenty-five years earlier. He had no criminal history, not even anything minor. She and her brother, Antonio Jr., were both born in the United States. Like her father, Lorena's mother, Zoila, also was undocumented.

Four years earlier, ICE agents had come to the hotel where Antonio was employed as a kitchen helper and arrested him. The family managed to scrape together the money to bail him out and to retain a private attorney. Antonio was placed in removal proceedings, and months later at his hearing an immigration judge granted his application for cancellation of removal and a lawful permanent resident (green) card. But ICE officials appealed the judge's decision and prevailed, and as a result, Antonio was ordered deported. According to his attorneys, no other appeals were available to her father.

Lorena and the other students wanted to know how this could be happening to Antonio in light of the Morton Memo, which purported to de-prioritize noncriminals in immigration enforcement. Lorena asked: "Can you help my father?"

THE MORTON MEMO

On June 17, 2011, ICE director John Morton had issued the important memorandum on the use of prosecutorial discretion in immigration matters. Prosecutorial discretion refers to the agency's authority to not enforce immigration laws against certain individuals and groups. The memo called on ICE attorneys and employees to refrain from pursuing noncitizens with close family, educational, military, or other ties in the United States, and to instead spend the agency's limited resources on persons who pose a serious threat to public safety or national security. The memo reaffirmed many of the principles and policies of previous guidance on this subject but went a step further in articulating the expectations for and responsibilities of ICE personnel when exercising discretion.

Specifically, the memo provided a non-exhaustive list of relevant factors that ICE officers should weigh in determining whether to exercise prosecutorial discretion. Several of these factors had a direct bearing on Antonio's case, including these:

- the agency's civil immigration enforcement priorities
- the person's length of presence in the United States, with particular consideration given to presence while in lawful status
- the person's criminal history, including arrests, prior convictions, or outstanding arrest warrants
- the person's immigration history, including any prior removal, outstanding order of removal, prior denial of status, or evidence of fraud
- whether the person poses a national security or public safety concern
- the person's ties and contributions to the community, including family relationships
- the person's ties to his home country and conditions in the country
- whether the person has a U.S. citizen or permanent resident spouse, child, or parent
- whether the person or the person's spouse suffers from severe mental or physical illness[3]

The memo further pointed out:

[ICE] has limited resources to remove those illegally in the United States. ICE must prioritize the use of its enforcement personnel, detention space, and removal assets to ensure that the aliens it removes represent, as much as reasonably possible, the agency's enforcement priorities, namely the promotion of national security, border security, public safety, and the integrity of the immigration system.

The memo went on to provide examples of those for whom prosecutorial discretion was not appropriate: gang members, serious felons, repeat offenders, and those posing national security risks. Importantly, and most relevant to Antonio, the memo noted that prosecutorial discretion can be exercised at any stage of the enforcement proceedings, although exercising it earlier is better to preserve government enforcement funds.

The Morton memo was greeted with fanfare. Some four hundred thousand pending deportation cases would be reviewed to cull out low-priority cases for termination of proceedings. In my view, the stage was set for suspending the deportation of model individuals like Antonio.

Lorena hinted that she was not confident that Antonio's current attorneys, Angela (Angie) Bean and Jesse Lloyd, had done their best to advocate for her father or if they understood the effect of the Morton Memo. She wanted to know if I would be willing to review their work and possibly intervene to help her father.

I knew both Angie Bean and Jesse Lloyd. In fact, Angie was a former student of mine and had been practicing immigration law since the 1980s. Jesse had been a student at UC Davis School of Law during the time I taught and directed all clinical programs there. He participated in the immigration law clinic at Davis, and although he was not directly one of my students, the clinic instructors thought highly of Jesse. In my opinion, Jesse and Angie were more than competent and likely did a good job on Antonio's behalf. However, I was concerned about the reaction they received from local ICE authorities when they mentioned prosecutorial discretion as outlined in the Morton Memo. Knowing Angie and Jesse would likely be forthcoming with me, and how dire the situation was, I agreed to help.

Lorena presented several convincing reasons that persuaded me to help her father avoid deportation. First, from her description, he seemed to deserve favorable treatment. Second, I was interested in having firsthand experience with the implementation of the Morton Memo. Third, just a few weeks prior to meeting Lorena, I assisted Abigail Trillin of Legal Services for Children in terminating proceedings in a sympathetic case involving a young, undocumented teen whose parents also were undocumented immigrants. In that case, the local ICE attorney who facilitated the termination seemed fairly open-minded, even prior to the issuance of the Morton Memo. As it turned out, whatever confidence I developed from handling that case did little good in preparing me for my experience on behalf of Antonio.

LORENA CINTRON

When we first discussed her father's case, I realized we had met before. Lorena told me she had heard me give a couple of presentations in the past, including with Educators for Fair Consideration (later renamed Immigrants Rising), a nonprofit organization that raises funds for and provides grants to Development, Relief, and Education for Alien Minors Act (DREAM Act) students in college who required financial aid. Lorena had worked with the organization periodically, and largely based on what she had heard me say at those presentations, she sought my help.

Lorena shared that her biological father died in a car accident when she was just two years old, and Antonio Sanchez became her stepfather when she was six. In high school she was studious, taking several Advanced Placement classes, and she earned a spot at UC Berkeley. She was one of the few Latinas in most of her classes and confided to a school counselor that she sometimes felt like she was fighting society's negative "stereotypes" about Latinx students. Her desire to prove these stereotypes wrong was motivating. In addition to her academic achievements, Lorena had a passion for soccer and was selected to be part of the varsity team as a high school freshman. She was voted most inspirational player on her high school team and served as captain of both her high school and club soccer teams. Her prowess in the sport helped Lorena get hired as a part-time coach in youth soccer leagues, which allowed her to earn money to pay her own expenses and alleviate some of the financial stress on her parents. In spite of her busy schedule, Lorena found time to volunteer in the community, play the violin, form a Latina psychology group in high school, and intern for Team-Up for Youth, a nonprofit that helps low-income youth participate in sports.

ANTONIO'S BACKGROUND

Antonio was born in 1955 in a small town in the state of Guanajuato, Mexico. He grew up poor—often lacking food, clothing, and housing—and attended the local elementary school through the third grade, the highest level of education that the school offered. He then attended three more years of school in a town that was five kilometers away, walking two hours each way because the family could not afford to pay for the van ride. At the age of eleven, he had to stop school and begin working to help put food on the table.

The population of Antonio's hometown—Valle de Santiago—was about five hundred residents, and the only work available was in the agricultural fields. Some years later, his father decided to try his luck in Mexico City to earn more money. In 1975, the entire family moved to join their father in Mexico City, where Antonio found work in a stationery store making minimum wage—more than what he made in the fields.

While there, Antonio met Laura Gomez and fell in love, and after three years of dating, they decided to get married and start their own family. Even after marrying, Antonio still felt an obligation to help his parents and siblings with expenses, so he continued to share part of his salary with them. His dream was to build a house with his wife and raise children in an environment where they could obtain a good education—an environment very different from his own childhood. Unfortunately, the couple learned that Laura was unable to have children, but they continued to strive for their dream of earning enough money to build a home. But good work was difficult to find.

Like so many others, Antonio looked to the United States to pursue his dream. In 1985, he crossed the border with his father-in-law and ended up in Oakland, California. He soon found work as a potato packer for a produce company, earning only $120 per week. Six months later, he found a better job working the graveyard shift in the kitchen of a Holiday Inn (later purchased by Hilton Hotels). Antonio had worked the 11 p.m. to 7 a.m. shift for ten years when he was given the opportunity to work the day shift. He maintained that shift until August 2007, when he was arrested by ICE.

Although the pay was modest, the hotel kitchen job provided medical benefits. In addition to working there, in the early 2000s, Antonio took part-time work at a pizza parlor to supplement his income. In total, he averaged seventy-two hours of work a week to provide for his family's needs. By the time the BIA ruled against him in 2010, Antonio had worked in the hotel kitchen for almost twenty-five years.

After his first trip to the United States, Antonio returned to Mexico a couple of times. His last entry to the United States was in 1987, with Laura, and he had resided in the country continuously since then. In September 1993, the couple decided to buy a house in Oakland, with the idea that they would adopt a child. Both continued working, but in 1994 Laura began getting sick. Her illness became so debilitating that she was unable to work. Eventually Laura's lungs and heart were affected, and she died in January 1995.

Having been married to Laura for seventeen years, Antonio was devastated by her death. He discouraged his parents and siblings from traveling to the United States because of the difficulties and dangers of crossing the border. He was alone in the United States, living in pain.

After some time, he met Zoila, a widow with two young children. She and Antonio eventually married in March 1996. The new couple felt fortunate to have been brought together when each was in such great pain and need. Zoila's two children, an older son, Donaldo, and Lorena, were quite young when Antonio became their stepfather. He loved them and was deeply committed to them.

In preparing for Antonio's deportation case, Angie Bean gathered supporting documents from Antonio's friends and neighbors that described him as a humble, caring, and well-respected member of the Berkeley community. Antonio and Zoila had successfully integrated into the neighborhood and established roots. Antonio was described as a good neighbor, a good worker, and a regular churchgoer. He was the godfather to a disabled boy, and Reverend A. M., executive director of a local church organizing group, noted that Antonio and his family "participated in many community activities in our organization" and that the clergyman was "grateful for their leadership, responsibility, and commitment to the community."[4]

Antonio's commitment to the community extended well beyond religious boundaries. L.A., a union representative, wrote that Antonio "has been an active Union member . . . for 22 years. He has always helped his co-workers with problems, attended Union meetings, and worked together with management to resolve any issues as they came up."[5] Antonio also was deeply involved in PTA meetings, school activities, and community athletic and cultural programs. Other parents in the community expressed: "Mr. [Sanchez] is an active, honest, respectful, and quietly supportive member of our community soccer programs. He and his wife are truly role models for his children as well as their teammates." Antonio's service to the community through many outlets made him a role model for other children and adults. For example, parents in the community described Antonio as "a very responsible person, dedicated to the well being of his family, deeply involved in community and family activities, PTA meetings, school reunions[,] and church issues." The PTA council president added, "I feel strongly that Mr. [Sanchez] is a stabilizing factor in our community. We need more men like him, who are loyal and loving to their families." Another Berkeley parent noted, "Year after year, [Antonio] volunteered with me in events held for the local church and Berkeley Unified School District where our children attended. As part of his nature, [Antonio] goes out of his way to motivate our Latino population and even organizes cultural celebrations at our church and local senior centers."

ROBERTO'S CASE EXAMPLE

As I mulled over Antonio's story and excellent supporting letters in the context of the Morton Memo, I could not help but compare him to Roberto, an undocumented sixteen-year-old boy whom I met through Abigail Trillin. A few weeks before I met Lorena, I spoke with Abigail, the managing attorney of Legal Services for Children, about Roberto, who was in the middle of removal proceedings. A couple of years earlier, Roberto had been handed over to ICE authorities after he took a plastic pellet gun to school to show his friends. He was forced to spend Christmas at a juvenile facility hundreds of miles away from his family, while awaiting deportation to Mexico, the country he had left at the age of two. Although the "gun" was not dangerous, and Roberto made no effort to conceal it, it triggered his high school's zero-tolerance policy, and he was reported to the police. Roberto was suspended from school for five days, and a judge sentenced him to informal probation for one year. He successfully completed his probation without incident. Although his parents were also undocumented, ICE did not arrest them.

Roberto lived with his family in a tight-knit community in San Francisco's Richmond District. He was soft-spoken and deeply contemplative, the eldest of four children, with two younger sisters, ages ten and six, and a six-month-old baby brother. His younger sister and baby brother were both born in the US and thus had citizenship. Roberto's father, a proud taxpayer, supported the family by working over ten hours each day, taking only Sundays off to be with his wife and children. Roberto's mother raised the children and actively participated in the local community and the church, which the whole family regularly attended for Sunday services. Rev. Francisco Gámez described Roberto as "very active in the Church."

As the oldest child, Roberto took on a central role in caring for his younger siblings and was actively involved in their day-to-day lives. He helped his sisters prepare for school and got them out the door in the morning, and he helped his ten-year-old sister with her homework on a regular basis. Several times a week, the task of preparing dinner fell to Roberto.

Roberto enjoyed the responsibility of helping his parents care for the family. The entire family was very close, often sitting for meals together, sharing household chores, and looking out for each other. One of Roberto's teachers, who had witnessed many disciplinary incidents at school, stated unequivocally that Roberto's parents were more actively involved in the process of Roberto's incident than any other parents she had ever seen.

Roberto also maintained an active social life. He had many friends and spent several weekday afternoons each week with them at the Boys & Girls Club. On Friday afternoons he participated in a leadership and civic responsibility workshop at the club.

At the time of the incident, Roberto was attending Mission High School, where he was highly regarded by his teachers and the principal. They described him as a "successful" and "trustworthy student," with "good attendance" and as a "critical thinker and debater" who had "a great awareness of current events."[6] They said he was an "intelligent and insightful young man," who was surely destined to attend college upon graduation from high school.

Roberto maintained an excellent grade point average, receiving many As over the course of his high school career. He was a model student, and his teachers all stated that he was an active participant in class who often helped his classmates. Roberto was actively involved in school physical education and sports programs. As a freshman, he played for the soccer team, and ran cross-country as a sophomore.

Seven of his teachers and the school principal wrote letters in support of Roberto. Their statements were clear and concise: Roberto was exactly the kind of student their high school sought to cultivate. They unanimously believed that deportation was not only an inappropriate and disproportionate response to the incident, but that it would send a message that ran counter to their efforts as educators. The assistant principal said that, because of the immigration implications of Roberto's case, the school had changed its policy and would no longer report that type of offense to the police.

Based on these facts, Abigail, Michael Dundas (a law student), and I put together a packet of information requesting that the local ICE chief counsel, Leslie Ungerman, terminate removal proceedings. The immigration judge agreed to a continuance while the request was pending. Finally, Ungerman agreed to cancel removal proceedings, and the case was dismissed.

From my perspective, this made sense, especially after the Morton Memo was issued. Roberto presented no public safety threat and had no criminal record. The dismissal of the case freed up ICE and immigration court resources. Roberto's removal would have separated him from his parents and US-citizen siblings.

As I mulled over Antonio's case, there were very similar policy reasons for terminating deportation efforts against him as well: family ties, lengthy residence in the United States, excellent community support, and a clean criminal record.

THE CANCELLATION CASE THREE YEARS EARLIER

Based on my conversations with Angie Bean, and after reviewing Antonio's file, it was clear that Angie did a great job representing Antonio Sanchez. Angie is experienced, smart, and knowledgeable about the law, and she is a strategic thinker who is respectful of her clients and committed to following through on every logical angle. Angie was particularly motivated in Antonio's case because her daughter and Lorena had been teammates on a club soccer team for years. Angie had known Lorena, Antonio, and the rest of the family for years. This was personal for Angie.

Antonio was arrested in the Hilton Hotels kitchen where he was working on August 29, 2007. Although no one knows with certainty, it seems that ICE was operating on an explicit tip about Antonio. When the agents arrived, they asked for him specifically; he offered no resistance. Fortunately, he was eligible for release on bond, so after a few days in custody, his family posted bond and he was released. Lorena was about sixteen at the time, and Angie told me that "[Lorena] grew up real fast" during that stressful period, going to visit her father in ICE custody.

Angie took full advantage of her personal knowledge of Antonio's family, employment, and community background. By the time his removal proceedings finally took place, on May 14, 2008, his length of residence, citizen children, clean record, and work history made him seemingly eligible for cancellation of removal and the grant of lawful resident status.

Angie knew that the big challenge in any cancellation of removal case is the hardship requirement. The documents supporting Antonio's cancellation application—including many affidavits from friends, neighbors, and acquaintances—were impressive. Antonio Jr.'s fourth-grade schoolteacher, M.C., wrote about what a good student Antonio Jr. was, and how Antonio was involved in the school's PTA and English Learner Advisory Committee, and how he served as a role model. Another of

Antonio Jr.'s teachers, K.K., wrote of how Antonio was a "supportive and positive presence on our campus and in [Antonio] Jr.'s life, in the classroom, at home, and on the soccer field."[7] A soccer parent, R.G., wrote that the desire of "Mr. [Sanchez] and his wife [Zoila] . . . to support their daughter [Lorena] led them into every aspect of parent support: from attending parent meetings, to bringing refreshments, to carpooling, to being substitute sideline officials, and fundraising."

Other school parents said the couple was involved in the school and supported their children's education, that the family had their priorities right, and that they were good solid people—people who would be role models for other Latinx families. S.E. and M.E., fellow parishioners at their Catholic church, wrote that "Antonio is a very proper gentleman that is always looking to help others in need." A coworker, C.T., observed, that while many at first glance would regard Antonio as "just a dishwasher," he proved to be the hardest worker in the workplace, maintaining cleanliness and order not just for the sake of his job, but because he genuinely cared for the people he worked with.

As the language of the cancellation statute makes clear, hardship on Antonio's US-citizen children had to be "exceptional and extremely unusual." In his personal statement (later reiterated in his hearing testimony), Antonio talked about how Antonio Jr.'s birth in 1998 completed their "happy family." He was "very proud" of how well his children were doing in school, and how he supported "them in everything that will bring benefit to their lives; and we keep them in a healthy environment so that they will triumph in the future." He pleaded for permission to remain in the United States "to help my children move forward, and to show that we are a responsible family of good people, and that we can contribute much to the United States." Antonio Jr.'s handwritten statement noted, "My dad always takes me to school and soccer practices, and church. Also, we go to the library; in our free time we play and go to parks." Antonio Jr. was ten years old at the time.

Lorena's statement in support of her father's cancellation application was written when she was a high school senior. She described his strong work ethic, his loving and caring nature, and the values that he had instilled in her:

I met my father when I was six years old. To be exact, I met him on Mother's Day in 1996. He took my family . . . out to dinner to celebrate this special day. I remember being really thrilled to go to a fancy restaurant and eat dinner like typical families do. My mother and my birth father came to America, "the land of opportunity," to build a better life for their children. Unfortunately, my father died in a car crash in 1992 . . . when I was about [two] years old. . . . In 1996, my mother married [Antonio Sanchez] whom I not only consider to be my father, but also my hero. He provided my family with what we lacked; support and unconditional love from a father figure. . . .

. . . He is extremely passionate about his children and loves playing baseball and soccer with us. He is fully dedicated to my family and is always taking my younger brother and [me] to school, soccer practices, and church. Although he is quiet compared to my mother in [sic] the sidelines, his presence and support means the world to me. I find myself playing better when my father is watching my games because I want to show off my moves and prove to him that I am a good soccer player, like he is in baseball.

I have absorbed my father's persistence and I have taken advantage of all of the opportunities that he never had. . . . Thanks to my father's unconditional love and support I have made it this far and I have accomplished many goals in my life.

The day that my father was apprehended by Homeland Security, I cried and cried. It was the first day of my senior year and this was the very moment that my family dreaded for so long. Although my family has gone through many obstacles, none of them have been as difficult as seeing my father in a San Francisco court cuffed and escorted by a Homeland Security officer. . . .

. . . I fear that I will come home one day and not see my father there. I am scared that I won't get the chance to hold my father and tell him how much I love him when I graduate from high school. My father is seen as a criminal for coming into this country but in my eyes, he truly is a hero and a survivor. . . . I beg you Judge [Loreto S.] Geisse, with all of my heart, to give my father permission to stay in this country legally.[8]

Angie Bean's strategy at the removal hearing made sense. Not only did Antonio need to testify on his own behalf, Lorena and Antonio Jr. would need to testify as well. To support the hardship claim, Angie called as witnesses a high school counselor and the director of the East Bay Asian Youth Center, who knew both Lorena and Antonio Jr., as well as Lorena's high school guidance counselor and the PTA council president.

The day of the hearing, things went well. The judge, Loreto S. Geisse, had been an immigration judge for almost four years, having previously worked for the chief immigration judge of the Department of Justice's Executive Office for Immigration Review. She had also worked as a trial attorney with the Office of Immigration Litigation, also in the Department of Justice. Judge Geisse had a reputation among immigration attorneys for being fair. She was open to receiving all the evidence offered by Angie, and she thought that the actual testimony of Antonio and Lorena was not necessary for the record, since the information contained in the written statements of the other prospective witnesses was not contested by the government.

At the hearing, the government challenged Antonio's application on the grounds that the hardship evidence was insufficient, but also on the moral character requirement. The government attorney claimed that Antonio used a false birth certificate to get his hotel job. However, Judge Geisse dismissed the government's allegation because the documents submitted were deemed unclear, and Antonio was never prosecuted for using a false birth certificate.

After considering all the evidence, Judge Geisse issued her decision on September 12, 2008, granting the cancellation of removal application. Judge Geisse found that the exceptional and extremely unusual hardship requirement was met because of the likely effect that Antonio's removal would have on Lorena and Antonio Jr.

> [Lorena] relies on the respondent and her family to support her financially and certainly emotionally. She has a loving and close relationship with her stepfather and believes that if he were removed [to] Mexico not only would she suffer emotionally and not only would her grades suffer as evidenced by her previous experience as a senior

in high school, but also she would very likely [,] at minimum[,] have to stop playing soccer, which is an important part of her life. And secondly, she might even have to stop school because of her inability to be able to continue going to school while assisting her mother. . . .

With respect to [Antonio Jr.], this Court notes that he is 10 years old, [and] on the verge of adolescence, which is a significant time in a child's development. He has a close and loving relationship with his father, who serves as a positive role model. . . . [H]e is reaching a point in life where he needs his father even more to assist him going through adolescence. He appears to be doing well in school and is actively involved also in soccer, and much of this is due to his father's involvement in his life.

. . . As for respondent's wife, she has had a difficult life, being widowed with two young children and having to provide for her family, this does not minimize the hardship to them as it would indirectly affect the respondent's US-citizen qualifying relatives. Therefore, based on the record as a whole, this Court believes respondent has met the exceptional and extremely unusual hardship to establish eligibility for cancellation of removal.[9]

Unfortunately, the victory was short-lived.

APPEAL TO THE BIA AND THE AFTERMATH

The grant of cancellation by the immigration judge was a glorious, magnificently hopeful moment for Antonio and his family. The family was elated. It would mean lawful permanent residence status for Antonio. It would mean that his family could go back to their normal life—likely even better than before. Antonio could resume his work at the Hilton, but now with lawful immigrant status, he might be able to get an even better job. Perhaps, at some point, he and his family could figure out a way to help Zoila regularize her status. The tremendous weight of living in the shadows without proper immigration status was lifted. The possibilities were endless.

This was a glorious moment for Angie Bean as well. The primary goal of immigration lawyers is to secure a visa or immigration status of some sort for their clients. When a client is undocumented, the best outcome is to obtain lawful permanent residence status for the person. You cannot do much better than getting a grant of cancellation of removal for an undocumented client who faces deportation. This was a big relief for Angie; the added pressure of representing a family friend had been enormous.

Unfortunately, the government had other things in mind for Antonio and, by extension, his family. Something about Antonio's case was hard to swallow for the ICE attorneys who handled and reviewed the case. Was it the purported use of a false birth certificate back in 1987? Were they really not convinced of the great hardship that Lorena and Antonio Jr. would suffer if their father was deported? What would the government have to gain from appealing the case? For whatever reason, the government decided to appeal Judge Geisse's decision to the BIA.

Apparently, in 2008, appealing the grant of cancellation was an important priority, even though Antonio had lived in the United States for almost twenty-five years and had no criminal history, had an excellent work history, had strong community support, and was civically engaged and had two US-citizen children who loved him and relied on him. Ronald LeFevre, the ICE chief counsel for San Francisco at the time, made the decision to file the appeal. LeFevre had a reputation among local immigration attorneys as being harsh and unhappy with any government "loss," and for being willing to file time-consuming appeals on even the most sympathetic cases. Years earlier, a group of immigration lawyers filed a complaint with the Department of Justice about LeFevre's callous behavior. He saved his job by apologizing and promising to be better, but he slid back to his old ways. I recall inviting him to speak in one of my classes, and he admitted to my students with a wry smile that his wife "can't believe how unreasonable I am toward noncitizens facing deportation."

Perhaps those who made the decision on the part of the government to appeal the case felt vindicated, or maybe even happy, when the BIA reversed Judge Geisse's decision more than a year later, on January 14, 2010. Although the government appealed Judge Geisse's decision in part on the grounds that Antonio was not deserving of favorable discretion because of the alleged use of a false document, the BIA reversed the decision because the "Immigration Judge erred in concluding the respondent met his burden in establishing the requisite hardship." So the BIA ordered that Antonio be removed.

As wrongheaded as I may regard the ICE decision to appeal Antonio's cancellation case, or as insensitive as the BIA's treatment of the case may feel to me subjectively, the actions taken by LeFevre and the BIA find support in the BIA's guiding cases on cancellation relief. In Antonio's case, the BIA made it clear: the exceptional and extremely unusual hardship standard for cancellation of removal applicants is a high threshold. The BIA felt that neither Lorena nor Antonio Jr. suffered from health issues nor compelling educational needs. The fact that Lorena might not be able to complete college if Antonio were removed did not constitute exceptional and extremely unusual hardship. And the BIA found that ten-year-old Antonio Jr. would not suffer hardship that is substantially beyond what would ordinarily be expected as a result of a parent's removal.

Even though Angie Bean sought review of the BIA's decision at the federal Ninth Circuit Court of Appeals, the effect of the BIA's decision on Antonio and his family was immediate. His job at the Hilton was terminated, which meant the loss of health-care benefits for everyone in his family. The family could no longer make payments on the house where they were living, and they were forced to move to a more dangerous, low-income neighborhood. Worst of all, the family became demoralized. Their joy and hope on September 12, 2008, turned to despair on January 14, 2010. Help from the court of appeals would not be forthcoming; the court had ruled that since no "constitutional or legal claim" was raised, the question was purely a matter of administrative discretion over which the court had no jurisdiction. Hope for a future together was lost, and Antonio awaited news of when he would be deported.

Antonio did not hear from ICE authorities for more than a year after the BIA decision. He was informed in early July 2011 that he had to depart by September 24, 2011. If he failed to heed the order, he would be subject to arrest and forcibly removed, in addition to being considered in violation of the terms of his bond conditions that were set when he was released on bond in 2007. That was the background when Lorena and the RISE students came to see me in late August 2011.

INVOKING THE MORTON MEMO

I suppose it is human nature to dislike someone looking over your shoulder or second-guessing your professional efforts and judgment, and I suspect that most lawyers hate being second-guessed about their strategy or advocacy. When Lorena told me that Jesse Lloyd at Angie Bean's office had submitted an application for a stay of deportation on August 12, I was curious whether and how Jesse may have incorporated the elements of the June 17 Morton Memo in the request.

When I called Jesse, I was relieved to find that he did not seem the least bit defensive about my call and the fact that Lorena had asked me to make an inquiry. He seemed open to my questions and answered them forthrightly. He easily put himself in Lorena's shoes and understood why she might talk to me about the case. Jesse immediately shared copies of the stay of deportation request and most of the case file. Jesse, and later Angie herself, welcomed my participation. In reviewing Jesse's work, I noted that he had indeed argued that the Morton Memo should guide the local ICE director's actions on the stay request. Jesse and Angie agreed that having a new attorney—me—enter at this point might strategically help, and certainly not hurt, the chances for getting the local ICE field office director to reconsider the case.

I also turned to Zach Nightingale, another former student of mine, who has built a stellar reputation as an immigration attorney. He agreed that since Antonio's case had already gone through the immigration court and the BIA, I would have to deal with the ICE field office director, Timothy S. Aitken, rather than ICE attorneys. Aitken was the officers' commander.

Zach's advice was to update all the information on the family before approaching Aitken and to contact anyone and everyone I knew at DHS in Washington, DC, who might have some influence over the implementation of the Morton Memo.

Students helped me prepare a hundred-plus-page prosecutorial discretion packet, and we filed it with Aitken's office. I emailed the packet to a number of individuals at DHS whom I knew or who were recommended by others. The list included Ivan Fong, general counsel for DHS; Traci Hong, of the DHS Office of Civil Rights and Civil Liberties; and Kelly Ryan, of the DHS Office of Immigration and Border Security. We also contacted Martha Flores, director of constituent services for US senator Dianne Feinstein (D-Calif.).

Although most of these individuals responded to my entreaties, Kelly Ryan was the most positive, taking notes, asking me to keep her informed, and cc'ing others at DHS each time she returned my emails. At one point she asked me to contact Paul Gleason at the Office of the Principal Legal Advisor of DHS. Gleason also returned my calls, took interest in the case, and led me to believe that he was in contact with Aitken's office. At no point did any of these contacts in Washington, DC, express criticism of the merits of Antonio's case. In fact, I found their comments to be positive, and our conversations always left me feeling hopeful. Additionally, Martha Flores of Senator Feinstein's office also was engaged and quite interested in Antonio's case. She submitted an official inquiry about Antonio's case with the DHS legislative liaison office in Washington, DC. I also arranged to have Antonio's daughter Lorena speak with Flores about the case.

In short, I engaged in a flurry of direct, serious conversations and email exchanges about the case over an intensive three-week period. I truly felt that something positive was about to happen for Antonio, in large part because of the interest expressed in the case from Washington, DC.

THE FINAL DECISION AND HUMANITARIAN PAROLE

In spite of these efforts, Timothy Aitken denied the request in a fax dated September 16, 2011:

Dear Mr. Hing:

Reference is made to your request for Deferred Action filed on behalf of your client, [Antonio Sanchez].

As you are undoubtedly aware, deferred action status is an action of administrative choice, and in no way can it be construed as giving an alien unlawfully in the United States an entitlement to such relief. The deferred action program has always been, and continues to be, an internal procedure of the Agency, which, the Field Office Director can initiate as soon as he perceives an alien's expulsion would be inappropriate. After a careful review of your client's case, I decline to grant such action.

Sincerely,
Timothy S. Aitken
Field Office Diretor [sic]

With several days remaining before Antonio had to leave, I renewed my attempts to get DHS officials in Washington, DC, to intervene. I also attempted to convince Leslie Ungerman, the ICE chief counsel, to support a motion to reopen the removal proceedings; if proceedings were reopened, she could take over jurisdiction of the case and terminate proceedings under the Morton Memo. She declined. Martha Flores of Senator Feinstein's office reported that, to her surprise, she could not get the DHS congressional liaison office to intervene. However, from DHS in Washington, DC, Paul Gleason informed me that I should contact Aitken again. The implication was that someone from the ICE Ombudsman's Office in DC had contacted Aitken and asked him to reconsider his decision.

When I finally reached Aitken again by phone, I asked if he would reconsider his decision, especially given the favorable tone of the Morton Memo for cases involving individuals like Antonio. Aitken was unmoved and told me:

I've always exercised discretion. The June 17 and August 18 memos and announcements from D.C. didn't say anything new that I have not already been doing; they didn't change anything; they didn't change my marching orders; 25 years residence doesn't mean anything; Sanchez just happened to be under the radar. The public expects us to enforce immigration laws. No one has told me the Sanchez case is a low priority case; resources have always been expended on these kinds of cases. I also won't consider an extension

of time for him to attend [Lorena]'s graduation. If I did that, then what about the next kid?[10]

The answer was "no." The Sanchez family was devastated. I was surprised and extremely disappointed by the outcome. The sense I had from my conversations with the officials in Washington was that they were sympathetic about the case. Yet whatever methods of intervention they engaged in did not help. So, Antonio, sadly but dutifully, left the country on the evening of September 23, 2011.

The nightmare of Antonio's forced departure has a postscript. A few days before the departure, a college scholarship mentor with whom Lorena had been in contact attempted to reach DHS secretary Janet Napolitano on Antonio's behalf. It seems that he had met the secretary a couple of years earlier at an American Law Institute gathering, where he spoke and thought she might remember him from. The mentor also encouraged Lorena to draft a personal letter to Secretary Napolitano, mentioning the mentor by name. The mentor was able to obtain a fax number for Napolitano and the email address of her assistant.

On September 20, 2011, the mentor emailed Lorena's letter to Napolitano's secretary with the following message:

> Dear Janet [Napolitano], please look at this urgent letter from [Lorena Cintron] and hold off the imminent departure of her father on Friday. . . . The disruption and hardship to her and her family are severe and the determination [by the] San Francisco [ICE office] seems incompatible with the President's recent policies. [Lorena] is a U.S. citizen, scholarship student at [college], and young leader who wants to become a lawyer and who [sic] we admire and want to help.

Unfortunately, while Napolitano may have had some interest in the case, the interest was not manifested until after Antonio departed. Days after the departure, January Contreras and Carrie Anderson of the US Citizenship and Immigration Services (USCIS) ombudsman's office contacted the mentor, who in turn put them in touch with me.

They expressed surprise that Antonio had not been granted prosecutorial discretion in accordance with the Morton Memo and encouraged me to file an Application for Humanitarian Parole on behalf of
Antonio—which would allow him to return to the United States—
largely based on the psychological trauma Antonio Jr. was suffering
because of his father's deportation. Both Contreras and Anderson
offered a hopeful, supportive tone.

The section of the parole application that focused on Antonio Jr.
contained a school history from his counselors that was supplemented
by two separate psychological evaluations:

> [Antonio] Jr. is suffering grave hardship because of his father's de-
> parture and his mental health is likely to deteriorate even more
> with continued separation.
>
> Prior to Mr. [Sanchez]'s forced departure from the United States,
> [Antonio] Jr. began suffering emotionally from the prospects of sep-
> aration from his father. Soon after Mr. [Sanchez]'s arrest and the
> institution of removal proceedings, [Antonio] Jr.'s health steadily
> declined. The individuals closest to [Antonio] Jr.—his parents and
> sister—saw the effects first hand. [Antonio] began getting migraine
> headaches that disrupted his daily routine. His sister [Lorena] could
> see that [Antonio] Jr.'s migraines were "severely painful and often
> lead him to feel nauseous, forcing him to vomit." The emotional
> and physical effects on [Antonio] Jr. became "more frequent and
> extremely" frightening. Without employment authorization after
> the BIA reversed the Immigration Judge's decision, Mr. [Sanchez]
> lost his job and employment benefits. The family lost their home
> to foreclosure because of the drop in income and had to move to
> a "rough" neighborhood, where the family saw that [Antonio] Jr.
> became "exposed to gangs, drugs, violence, and countless other
> negative influences that were not present in [their] old neighbor-
> hood." [Antonio] Jr. himself was "constantly worried about my
> family being destroyed if my father is deported."[11]

Also included in the Application for Humanitarian Parole was an
analysis of Antonio Jr.'s and Zoila's psychological state based on a

number of interviews and tests conducted by two psychologists. Dr. Yvette Flores interviewed Antonio Jr. and his mother in early October. She determined that Antonio Jr. was "suffering from depression and anxiety." The severing of his relationship with his father provides the background for Dr. Flores's conclusion:

> Prior to his departure, Mr. [Sanchez] spent a lot of time with [Antonio], taking and picking him up from school, going to his practices and games, and helping him with homework. Both [Antonio] and his mother indicated that Antonio tucked him in at night. [Antonio] indicated that he felt very secure with both of his parents. Now that security is gone.
>
> [The mother] expressed worry that [Antonio] comes home from school and isolates in his room. He does not want to socialize with friends or acquaintances. He does not communicate much and appears sad and withdrawn. . . .
>
> The doctor's study also determined that:
>
> In the past [Antonio] was offered counseling at school but declined to continue. When asked if he would consider talking to a counselor again, he stated, 'what good will that do? It is not going to bring my dad back to the [United States].' . . . [Antonio] indicated that he feels angry a lot of the time; he can manage it most of the time, but not always. [Antonio] presented with symptoms of depression.
>
> . . . A continued separation from his father can promote a worsening of [Antonio]'s depression, which can interfere with his academic and social functioning. . . . The secure foundation he experienced in early childhood has been shattered. He is clinically depressed and experiences symptoms of anxiety.
>
> There is no evidence of lying or malingering in [Antonio]'s account. In fact, he tried to minimize his distress. . . . Antonio is suffering greatly. I strongly recommend mental health counseling to prevent the onset of serious behavioral problems.

Shortly after Dr. Flores's assessment, Antonio Jr. met with another clinical psychologist—Dr. Robert Kaufman—to participate in another

round of psychological tests. Dr. Kaufman highlighted what Antonio Jr. discussed with him:

- Obvious pride that a counselor at school has observed [his father] as being generous to other parents during open school night
- An active and highly involved life with his father
- "Help" with school assignments and "how his father would be there for his bedtime routines every night, including routinely tucking him in even as an early adolescent"
- No history of significant problems in the family, despite the tragedies noted in the history. Prior to the immigration problems, life at home was stable and happy, with his parents getting along well. [Antonio] [Jr.] himself was also doing well in elementary school, attaining solid grades, and establishing good friends.
- He misses the feeling of at least one of his parents being at home.
- [Antonio] [Jr.] experiences the added stress from all of this and says it's now hard to keep focus on his school work and hard to keep up with assignments.
- [Antonio] [Jr.] can report becoming impatient with himself, disappointed that he can't get things done, and sometimes he will just "blank out," not picking up on what's going on around him.
- [Antonio] Jr. has "episodic headaches [and] developed migraines about two years ago [and] cannot predict when he will have a headache."

After conducting a series of tests and interviews with Antonio Jr. and with the other key people in his life, like his school counselors and family, Dr. Kaufman determined that Antonio Jr. had suffered greatly from the deportation of his father and was showing more and more signs of anxiety and depression that were interfering with his day-to-day life. If the situation did not change, his frustration and anger could increase and manifest in maladaptive ways, including

increased aggression and involvement with drugs or alcohol. Antonio's deportation had created a large hole in Antonio Jr.'s development.

In spite of the evidence of psychological trauma that had been suffered and anticipated by Antonio Jr., the request for humanitarian parole for Antonio also was denied.

HISTORY OF PROSECUTORIAL DISCRETION IN DEPORTATION CASES

When I started practicing immigration law at the San Francisco Neighborhood Legal Assistance Foundation as a young law graduate in 1974, experienced lawyers at boutique immigration law firms advised me to stay on top of the law, to be honest, and to be forceful when necessary, and to march into the Immigration and Naturalization Service (INS) district director's office and push him to do the right thing, even if the law was not on my side. In other words, my older colleagues were well aware of the vast discretion held by the district director. It was not called "prosecutorial discretion" back then, but in those days when the district director had the power to issue an order to show cause to start a deportation case, he could also stop expulsion at any time.

I recall speaking with INS district director David Ilchert in the 1980s about two sisters from the Philippines. This was during a time when the backlog in the sibling immigration category for Filipinos was already quite substantial. Corazon Ayalde became a US citizen several years after she immigrated to the United States as a registered nurse to work in a public hospital devoted to caring for senior citizens. When her sister Cerissa, who had remained in the Philippines, became widowed without children, the pair longed to be reunited. Cerissa obtained a tourist visa to the United States to visit, and soon after arriving, Corazon filed an immigration family petition for her sister. Cerissa was particularly concerned, because Corazon had been ill, and was slowly becoming worse; Cerissa wanted to remain in the United States so that she could care for her sister. They had heard that there was a backlog in the sibling category, but shortly after the petition was filed, immigration authorities mistakenly sent them a notice that Cerissa should come into the local office to complete the adjustment of status process to obtain lawful permanent resident status. Believing that God had answered their prayers, Cerissa carefully completed the paperwork and fingerprint card, obtained photos for her green card, made an appointment for an interview, and appeared, accompanied by her sister, at the local INS office.

When they arrived, however, the INS agent informed them that a mistake had been made: no visa was available, and Cerissa would have to leave the country and wait in the Philippines until an immigrant visa became available. She was given a notice to appear for a deportation hearing. Disheartened, the sisters came to my legal aid office. I prepared an argument based on detrimental reliance on the government's own mistake—a logical argument, but not one with great authority at the time. But before the immigration court hearing, I presented the facts of the case to Ilchert. After holding the case for several weeks, he called me in and told me that he would simply suspend going forward with the deportation case until Cerissa's priority date for a visa was reached. Years later, Cerissa's permanent residence was granted. Corazon told me she felt her "heart being lifted to heaven" as the sisters were permitted to remain together and did so until Corazon passed away a few years later.

Another one of my clients was not so fortunate. The case began with a call from a caseworker at a local community agency: "Do you have time to come to our next staff meeting to explain the visa preference system and grounds of deportation?" I was on the phone with Vera Jones, a veteran counselor at the International Institute who worked with noncitizen students on English-language skills and advising newcomers on life in the United States. The case involved a student from Eritrea who had come to the institute for help with his student visa.

Only about six months into the job, I was no expert, but if the staff at International Institute wanted a summary of the immigration preference system and the grounds of deportation, I could certainly accommodate. I also learned that when you're a legal services attorney in a neighborhood law office, you are quickly considered an expert in your particular field by staff at community-based organizations and neighborhood residents.

The International Institute staff had varying degrees of experience. Monica Abello had been a counselor for about two years (eighteen months longer than me). Vera had been around for more than five years and the rest of the staff for less than a year. I shared an outline of the immigration visa preference system and the grounds of deportation that I had prepared, but it was clear that they wanted to discuss a person whose case Vera had referred to me: Fethawit.

In 1975, Fethawit Tewelde was one of my first clients. He was a student from Eritrea who had been denied an application to change schools, from Fresno State University to San Francisco State University. He was also suffering from a rare heart condition that made it imperative that he avoid high elevations. (Though Fresno has an elevation of only three hundred feet, San Francisco was much better for Fethawit because it lies at sea level.) The problem was that Fethawit had started taking classes in San Francisco before he filed his transfer application. The INS scheduled an in-person interview with him to review the transfer application. According to Fethawit, the INS interviewer took the application for change of status from Fethawit, listened to his story, took the doctor's letters, jotted down some notes, then told him, "You'll receive a decision by mail, but it doesn't look good."

A few weeks later, the denial letter from the INS adjudicator arrived. It read, "If being at a high elevation is a problem, then take a boat back to Eritrea." That administrative denial was part of my rude introduction to the world of agency discretion, which I have encountered all too often over a fifty-year span representing immigrants and citizens before the INS and DHS. When Fethawit came to me with the letter, I could not believe its insensitivity. I still recall Fethawit's pained breathing, caused by a combination of his disease and his distress over the decision when he recounted the situation.

Although only a few months into my career as an immigration attorney, I had already met INS district director Ilchert and thought that he would surely reconsider his officer's denial if I presented the facts to him personally. After a twenty-minute conversation, he told me, "Students have to learn to play by the rules. If you don't like the opinion, you can appeal to DC." The administrative appeal I filed on

Fethawit's behalf didn't do much good. The dismissal was perfunctory, and eventually Fethawit had to depart. However, his example certainly served as a stark, early lesson in the vagaries and harshness of agency decision-making.

A few years after that incident, Leon Wildes, a noted New York immigration attorney, reported on his formal findings of what practitioners had always suspected: the INS actually had an official, albeit secret, process for keeping certain cases that presented sympathetic factors—such as family, community support, length of residence, age—on hold indefinitely. Although various INS regimes enforced deportation provisions fairly rigorously, at times the equities or political ramifications presented by certain cases would move even the most hard-nosed INS enforcement agent. This program was exposed in the midst of the government's attempt to deport John Lennon, the legendary member of the Beatles.

After the Beatles broke up, Lennon and his wife, artist Yoko Ono, traveled to New York in August 1971 to seek custody of Ono's daughter by a former marriage to a US citizen. At the time of Lennon's entry to the US, INS authorities were aware that he had pleaded guilty to possession of one half ounce of hashish in Great Britain in 1968. US officials temporarily waived what was deemed to be a ground for exclusion, the prior conviction. Lennon's temporary visa was eventually extended to February 29, 1972. During his stay, he performed at rallies organized to protest the United States' involvement in the Vietnam War. His activity irritated President Richard Nixon, who ordered immigration officials to remove Lennon from the United States. Soon after Lennon's visa expired, in March 1972, deportation proceedings were instituted against Lennon and Ono. Although the couple had filed applications for lawful permanent residence in the US, INS officials did not act on the applications, choosing instead to seek deportation, based in part on the British drug possession conviction, which they had earlier ignored. Lennon and Ono retained Leon Wildes for assistance.

While the proceedings were pending, Wildes sued the INS, arguing that Lennon and Ono should be allowed to remain as a matter of discretion. As part of the lawsuit, Wildes filed a Freedom of Information

Act request and discovered the existence of the "nonpriority program." Nonpriority status was an administrative halt to deportation that effectively placed a deportable noncitizen in a position in which the person was not removed because the case had the lowest possible priority for INS action. Traditionally, the status was accorded to noncitizens whose departure from the United States would result in extreme hardship to the individual or family.

The deportation proceedings came in the midst of the frantic search for Ono's child. When the father absconded with the girl and could not be found, Wildes argued that the sympathetic situation involved in Ono and Lennon's search for the child justified their application for the newly discovered nonpriority status.

What Wildes unearthed about the government's nonpriority program was surprising to many. He was allowed to examine 1,843 cases and found that nonpriority status could apply in virtually any circumstance where a grave injustice might result from removal. Nonpriority had been granted to aliens who had committed serious crimes involving moral turpitude (including rape), drug convictions, fraud, and prostitution. Nonpriority had been given to avowed Communists, the clinically insane, and the medically infirm. It did not matter if individuals faced multiple grounds for deportation. Family separation, age (whether elderly or young), health, and economic issues were important factors that officials usually considered.

After the revelation of the existence of the secret nonpriority program, the INS formalized the process publicly, publishing guidelines for requesting "deferred action" from INS authorities. Local INS district directors had the authority to grant a deportable person deferred action, permitting the noncitizen to remain in the country indefinitely. The primary considerations district directors used in deciding whether to grant deferred action included these:

1. the likelihood of ultimately removing the noncitizen, including physical ability to travel, or availability of relief
2. the presence of sympathetic factors that might lead to protracted deportation proceedings or bad precedent from the INS perspective

3. the likelihood that publicity adverse to the INS will be generated because of sympathetic facts
4. whether the person is a member of a class whose removal is given high priority, e.g., dangerous criminals, large-scale smugglers of noncitizens, narcotic drug traffickers, terrorists, war criminals, or habitual immigration violators

Deferred action in the deportation context today is thus manifested in the exercise of prosecutorial discretion by DHS officials.

PROSECUTORIAL DISCRETION AND THE DREAM ACT STUDENTS

The DREAM (Development, Relief, and Education for Alien Minors) Act was first introduced in Congress in 2001 by a bipartisan group of legislators that included Dick Durbin (D-Ill.), Orrin Hatch (R-Utah), Luis Gutiérrez (D-Ill.), and Richard Lugar (R-Ind.). Various versions of the legislation would provide lawful permanent residence status and a pathway to citizenship to certain undocumented individuals (up to age thirty or thirty-five, depending on the legislative version) of good moral character who graduated from US high schools, arrived in the United States as minors, and lived in the country continuously for at least five years prior to the bill's enactment. If the individuals completed two years in the military or two years at a four-year institution of higher learning, they would obtain temporary residency for a six-year period. Eventually, the individuals could qualify for lawful permanent residence and ultimately US citizenship. The subsequent Morton Memo was in large measure a result of lobbying efforts by DREAM Act students and their supporters (including members of Congress) to convince President Obama to grant deferred action to DREAM Act students after a version of the act failed to pass the US Senate in December 2010.

The DREAM Act reached the Senate floor in mid-September 2010 with support from both parties and the White House. At a September 21 press conference, Secretary of Education Arne Duncan declared, "It is no surprise that a common-sense law like the DREAM Act has always been supported by both Democrats and Republicans. There is no reason it shouldn't receive that same bipartisan support now."[12] As Congress became hyperpoliticized during the first two years of the Obama presidency, the DREAM Act suffered from an erosion of bipartisan support. When Senate Majority Leader Harry Reid (D-Nev.) included the DREAM Act in the defense authorization bill in September, the bill failed the cloture vote 56–43 without garnering a single Republican in favor of its passage. Republican senators Orrin Hatch and Bob Bennett, both of Utah, voted in favor of adding the DREAM Act to the defense authorization bill in 2007 but voted against the measure in 2010. Likewise, Sen. John McCain (R-Ariz.), who cosponsored the DREAM Act in 2005, 2006, and 2007, voted against it in 2010.

The DREAM Act faced a substantial political challenge. The legislation occupied a tenuous middle ground: liberals accused it of being too limited in scope and conservatives charged that it is too far-ranging. Kristen Williamson, a spokesperson for the Federation for American Immigration Reform, a conservative group, asserted that many Republicans viewed the DREAM Act as "amnesty disguised as an educational initiative."[13] Critics of the DREAM Act alleged that the measure rewards lawbreaking and creates a greater incentive to defy immigration laws. With the 2010 midterm elections on the horizon, Republicans also accused congressional Democrats of capitalizing on the DREAM Act "to motivate Hispanic voters in the upcoming elections."

On the other side of the aisle, many liberal Democrats believed that broader immigration reform was still possible and opposed the DREAM Act's piecemeal approach to reform. Marshall Fitz, director of immigration policy at the Center for American Progress, explained, "The expectation that we will only get one shot at an immigration debate during a legislative session suggests that moving forward on a piece like DREAM means it is to the exclusion of other equally worthy pieces."[14]

However, after the November 2010 elections, the prospects for broader immigration reform grew dimmer. Democrats lost their majority in the House of Representatives for the next Congress. In the lame-duck congressional session after the elections, the House passed the DREAM Act with a 216–198 vote on December 8. With Republicans (most of whom opposed the bill) taking over the House and increasing their number of seats in the Senate from 42 to 47, the chances of the bill being passed were slim for at least the next two years. The DREAM Act became a top priority of Senate Majority Leader Harry Reid, who had won a tough reelection fight with the help of Nevada's large Latinx community, which strongly supported the DREAM Act. The bill garnered a majority of Senate votes, 55–41, but failed to advance because sixty votes are required to overcome a filibuster.

Four months later, after the new Congress had assembled and Republicans had taken control of the House, twenty-two senators sent a letter to President Obama asking for deferred action for undocumented immigrant youth who would have qualified for the bill. Led by Senators Durbin and Reid, the Senate reminded the president that

> the exercise of prosecutorial discretion in light of law enforcement priorities and limited resources has a long history in this nation and is fully consistent with our strong interest in the rule of law. Your Administration has a strong record of enforcement, having deported a record number of undocumented immigrants last year. At the same time, you have granted deferred action to a small number of DREAM Act students on a case-by-case basis, just as the Bush Administration did. Granting deferred action to DREAM Act students, who are not an enforcement priority for DHS, helps to conserve limited enforcement resources.[15]

Similarly, Congressman Gutiérrez also protested that the president had the power to stop deporting immigrants with "deep roots" in the United States.

The White House and DHS announcements that accompanied the Morton Memo in the summer of 2011 make clear that DREAM Act students were the primary intended beneficiaries of the memo. On August 18, 2011, DHS secretary Napolitano explained that "it makes no sense to expend enforcement resources" on young people who pose no threat to public safety.[16] Senator Durbin, a primary DREAM Act sponsor, praised the announcements:

The Obama Administration has made the right decision in changing the way they handle deportations of DREAM Act students. . . .
These students are the future doctors, lawyers, teachers and, maybe,
Senators, who will make America stronger. We need to be doing all
we can to keep these talented, dedicated, American students here,
not wasting increasingly precious resources sending them away to
countries they barely remember. The Administration's new process
is a fair and just way to deal with an important group of immigrant students and I will closely monitor DHS to ensure it is fully
implemented.[17]

An August 18, 2011, *Los Angeles Times* headline blared: "Dream
Act Students Won't Be Deportation Targets, Officials Say." But the
broad language of criteria set forth in the Morton Memo made clear
that other aliens subject to removal, like Antonio, were intended to be
covered under the policy as well. The policy's design was well received
by immigrant rights groups and immigration lawyers. "[G]overnment
officials and advocates now have a new tool for doing the right thing,"
according to some advocates. Congressman Gutiérrez applauded the
announcement: "Focusing scarce resources on deporting serious criminals, gang bangers, and drug dealers and setting aside non-criminals
with deep roots in the US until Congress fixes our laws is the right
thing to do and I am proud of the President and Secretary Napolitano
for standing up for a more rational approach to enforcing our current
immigration laws."[18] The American Bar Association was pleased that
ICE would "exercise its prosecutorial discretion to close low priority
cases" not limited to DREAMers.[19] The ACLU "tentatively praised"
the announcement, waiting for "the details."[20]

In the months that followed the Morton Memo and White House
announcements of prosecutorial discretion on low-priority cases,
the practical reality of the implementation of the Morton Memo began to surface. When I spoke with my contacts in Washington, DC,
about Antonio's case, the message I received was that his really was
a low-priority case that should be covered by the memo. But it turns
out that while his request was being rejected, other low-priority cases
were being denied as well.

The available data revealed that relatively few immigrants facing deportation had their cases closed. On May 29, 2012, ICE officials announced they had considered 232,181 cases of immigrants not held in detention.[21] Authorities identified 20,608 possible cases for administrative closure (less than 10 percent), though about 12,000 of them had been held up awaiting criminal background checks. The May 2012 update was DHS's third report on the process. Each time, the percentage of cases found eligible for administrative closure in the prosecutorial discretion review fell. In a March 5, 2012, report, 8 percent were eligible for closure, 6.2 percent of cases reviewed between March 5 and April 16 were eligible for closure, and just 6 percent of those reviewed from April 16 to May 29 were eligible. In all, about 7 percent were found eligible for administrative closure.

In a membership survey by the American Immigration Lawyers Association, those denied prosecutorial discretion included a longtime resident with no criminal history, no prior removals, and US-citizen relatives (Detroit); a longtime resident with no criminal history, no history of fraud, strong community ties, and US-citizen relatives, including a spouse with a severe illness (San Francisco); and an elderly person who suffered with health problems, with no criminal history, no prior removals, and US-citizen relatives (New York). On the other hand, those granted prosecutorial discretion included a longtime resident with no criminal history, strong community ties, US-citizen relatives, and few ties to the home country (New York); a person present in the United States since childhood with no criminal history and with US-citizen relatives (Detroit); and a person present in the United States since childhood with no criminal history, no prior removals, a US high school graduate, with few ties to the home country (Seattle). The lack of consistency across the country in the application of prosecutorial discretion was apparent.

Field office director Aitken's my-marching-orders-haven't-changed response to me was certainly disappointing. However, the AILA survey of attorneys in other parts of the country yielded similar disturbing reports. In the Arlington, Virginia, and Washington, DC, area, ICE officers stated that the June 17 memos "don't mean anything. If we can arrest you, we will arrest you."[22] In Atlanta, ICE attorneys and officers stated that "they d[id] not intend to comply with the June 17th memos absent specific rules to do so." In Boston, two of the congressional offices reportedly confirmed that "ICE is very reluctant to implement the memos and that their offices have been flooded with [prosecutorial discretion] requests." The offices further asserted that "[a] stay of removal was granted only after congressional intervention at the [ICE Headquarters] level." In Dallas, an ICE attorney recounted that the ICE Office of Chief Counsel had expressed that they were presently exercising prosecutorial discretion and thus did not have to make any changes to their protocol.

In Detroit, ICE refused prosecutorial discretion requests even in "very meritorious cases," and one attorney was informed that, among other rationales, prosecutorial discretion was not forthcoming because "resources have already been expended in litigating the case."[23] This reason may have been in the back of Aitken's mind when he denied Antonio's request. In Los Angeles, one attorney claimed that less discretion was being exercised after the June 17th memo. In Orlando, Florida, an attorney declared that ICE was "not heeding the memo and does not consider it binding." Finally, another attorney, in Miami, communicated that ICE Enforcement and Removal Operations has described their status as "business as usual."

Clearly, part of the problem with the lack of consistency in the implementation of the Morton Memo was resistance from ICE employees and the ICE union. In January 2012, the *New York Times* reported:

> [W]hile virtually all of the agency's lawyers and supervisors have received training, the union representing about 7,000 field agents is refusing to let its members attend the sessions. . . . The union president, Chris Crane, says the strategy is preventing agents from enforcing the law. In October, he told Congress the policy was too confusing for agents to understand and would lead to "victimization and death," for reasons that were unclear.[24]

Crane took his grievances to the hard-right media, complaining on Fox News's *Lou Dobbs Tonight* show that his bosses were endangering lives and abdicating their law-enforcement duties.

A few days after the Morton Memo was issued, the ICE union issued its own press release in which Crane warned:

> Any American concerned about immigration needs to brace them-selves for what's coming. . . . The desires of foreign nationals ille-gally in the United States were the framework from which these policies were developed. . . . [T]he result is a means for every per-son here illegally to avoid arrest or detention; as officers we will never know who we can or cannot arrest.[25]

One year later, in August 2012, ten ICE agents filed a lawsuit against DHS secretary Napolitano alleging that the prosecutorial dis-cretion policies announced in the Morton Memo prevented them from doing their job and "defending the Constitution."[26] The lawsuit was funded by the anti-immigrant organization Numbers USA, and the lead counsel was Kris Kobach, the architect of several anti-immigrant state laws, who would later become chair of a short-lived commission established by President Donald Trump to find alleged voter fraud by noncitizens in the 2016 presidential election.

Although the Morton Memo of June 17, 2011, did result in the termination of some deportation proceedings involving DREAMers, the removal of many DREAMers with no criminal backgrounds con-tinued. For example, Ramon Aguirre, who had entered the United States at the age of seven and became a talented artist in high school, was deported even though he had a four-year-old son.[27] Cesar Mon-toya faced deportation after being stopped for driving without a li-cense. In Denver, Colorado, a recent high school graduate who was brought to the United States as an undocumented seven-year-old by his mother was first told that he would be granted prosecutorial discretion, but the local ICE chief counsel later said that there was a "mix-up" and the young man would not be receiving prosecuto-rial discretion.[28]

Also, DREAMers who had criminal records, but arguably not se-rious ones, were removed. Twenty-two-year-old Yanelli Hernandez was removed to Mexico in January 2012 because she was undocumented and had convictions for driving under the influence and for forgery.[29] Records indicate that Hernandez, a factory worker with mental problems, had attempted suicide twice. When denying her request for prosecutorial discretion, the Detroit ICE field office director wrote, "The removal of individuals with final orders of removal, as well as criminal aliens, is an ICE civil immigration enforcement priority. Ms. Hernandez was never lawfully present in the United States."

DREAMers and their supporters were disappointed in the Morton Memo results and called on President Obama to do more. On June 15, 2012, to make his intent very clear to ICE officials in the field, the president specifically announced that DREAMers would be granted deferred action and employment authorization for at least two years. Not coincidentally, his decision came after a weeklong protest and sit-in at his campaign office in Denver. Under the directive, deferred action would be granted on a case-by-case basis to individuals who met the following criteria: they came to the United States when they were younger than sixteen and are currently under age thirty-one; they have continuously resided in the United States for at least five years; and they are in school, have graduated from high school, have obtained a GED, or are honorably discharged veterans of the armed forces. In addition, the individuals may qualify if they have not been convicted of a felony, significant misdemeanor, or multiple misdemeanor offenses, or do not otherwise pose a threat to national security or public safety. By the time Donald Trump took office, in 2017, about eight hundred thousand DREAMers had been granted permission to live and work under the Deferred Action for Childhood Arrivals (DACA) program.

While prosecutorial discretion memos from Washington, DC, provide solutions for some deportable noncitizens and hope for countless others, my experience with Antonio's case and my survey of others make clear that relying on guidance from the federal government can be problematic. The inconsistencies that flow from various decision makers' idiosyncrasies and biases doom prosecutorial discretion as a reliable solution for the millions of undocumented noncitizens seeking a peaceful, productive existence.

HISTORY OF SUSPENSION/CANCELLATION

The harsh language dismissing the hardship to Lorena and Antonio Jr. used by the Board of Immigration Appeals (BIA) in Antonio Sanchez's case illustrates the need for statutory changes to the hardship requirement. In reversing the immigration judge's grant of cancellation of removal, the BIA reiterated that the "exceptional and extremely unusual hardship" standard for cancellation is a very high threshold.[30] This was not always the case. Prior to 1996, the relief was called "suspension of deportation" and could be granted by the discretion of the immigration court if deportation would result in "extreme hardship" to the respondent or to their lawful resident or US-citizen children or spouse.

Under the old law, the mere fact that a suspension client had a US-citizen child was not necessarily decisive on the extreme hardship issue. However, in many cases, the US-citizen child would be forced to return with deportable parents to their country of birth, so the possible effects of uprooting a citizen child who is assimilated into US society was important. The older the child and the more assimilated, the greater the possibility of satisfying the extreme hardship requirement. Thus, having school-age citizen children was generally sufficient to meet the hardship requirement. In the suspension-of-deportation era, courts realized that sometimes a citizen child might not accompany the deportable parent back to the native country, and the hardship-due-to-separation rationale would be sufficient.

But things became quite different after the law changed in 1996. The BIA is simply unfazed by things like family separation, as we saw in Antonio Jr.'s situation, in which the BIA concluded that the ten-year-old would likely not suffer hardship "substantially beyond what would ordinarily be expected as a result" of Antonio's removal. The BIA is equally unmoved even when citizen children will in essence be forced to relocate along with a deported parent. In *Matter of Monreal*, the respondent was a thirty-four-year-old citizen of Mexico who had lived in the United States for twenty years.[31] He argued that his eight- and twelve-year-old children would suffer exceptional and extremely unusual hardship if he was removed because they would have to accompany him to Mexico. The children would have to leave their school, friends, and other relatives behind—forcing them to settle in an unfamiliar country, with fewer education opportunities and poorer economic prospects. But the BIA ruled that the hardship requirement was not met. Similarly, in *Matter of Andazola*, the BIA ruled against a thirty-year-old Mexican single mother of two US-citizen children who had lived and worked in the United States for seventeen years. The immigration judge granted cancellation, ruling that the children, six and eleven, would face "complete upheaval in their lives and hardship that could conceivably ruin their lives."[32] On appeal, the BIA reversed the judge's decision, concluding that even though the children had lived in the United States for their entire lives, they would "likely be able to make the necessary adjustments" to their future lives in Mexico. The BIA held that the respondent had not shown that her US-citizen children would be deprived of all schooling in Mexico.

Antonio and his children fell prey to the institutionalized, racist approach that the BIA has taken toward undocumented Mexicans in the United States, irrespective of their length of residence, the presence of citizen children, model community behavior, and exhibiting a good work ethic.

CONCLUSION

After Antonio's departure, I continued to communicate with his daughter, Lorena. Her words and her family's experience continue to fuel my efforts to combat the injustice of deportation and removal, especially when the well-being of other family members also is at stake. Here's one email from Lorena about seven months later:

April 17, 2012, 7:07 PM: Email from Lorena Cintron

Dear Professor Hing,

. . .

These past months without my father have been a blur. Again, I cannot help but thank you for your support throughout my dad's case. I know you tried your best, we all did, nonetheless, my dad often brings you up and reminds me that there are good people in this world that want to help families like mine.

Father:

I try to speak to my dad as much as possible. Lately, we've fallen off mainly due to his unreliable phone service. This can be very daunting for my mother and I who assume the worst at times. We've gone through periods of about a week or so without speaking to my father. Sometimes we don't even know where he is, what he's doing, if he's eaten, or if he's home safe. This is extremely heart-wrenching.

According to my aunt, my dad has lost a lot of weight and has been getting ill often. I want to assume that his weight loss is due to poor nutrition and depression. When my dad is sad he tends to sleep for long periods of time. I continue to encourage him to eat healthy and exercise . . . daily. He's very responsive but we all understand that it's nearly impossible for my entire family in Mexico to eat healthy on a regular basis. If my family in Mexico is not eating healthy, neither is my dad.

Overall, my father appears to be doing worse than he was when he first left. This is very concerning to me and I try my best to lift his spirits whenever I speak to him on the phone.

Mother:

My mom is struggling. I've never seen her so low. She's recently been very upset at everything and everyone, including myself. She often withdraws from me for a few days and comes back whenever she feels ready to talk a bit. She's exhausted—both on a mental and physical level. My mom has taken over my dad's responsibilities and let me tell you—she's doing an amazing job. I have yet to figure out how she's managing to work and take care of our home responsibilities on top of caring for my younger brother. She's a true soldier and I admire her in every way possible.

I help her in the best way I can but I realize that everything I do is not enough because she is missing her husband, her soulmate. I cannot imagine what she is feeling as a mother and wife.

Younger brother:

I'm happy to report that my brother is doing very well in school, soccer, and his music. He's matured a lot since my dad's been gone but seems to be a bit more reserved and quiet. He's gotten a lot more moody lately as well but helps out after complaining for a bit about how he just wants to finish his homework.

He's a talented boy. A math genius and soccer star. He doesn't cry at all nor does he ever speak about my dad unless I ask him what my dad talked to him about over the phone. His answers are simply a "yes" or "no." He NEVER mentions my dad about anything and I'm almost certain that he doesn't speak about our situation to any of his friends/teachers.

I try my best to communicate with him despite the awkward big sister–younger brother dynamic. I've recently demanded him to inform me about my mom's well-being. See—just recently my mother has lashed out about how she just wants to disappear from the world. My brother spends the most time with my mom and although he never asks how she's doing, he lies in bed with my mom and watches movies with her. He won't ask her why she's sad all the time but he sits with her and listens to her cry without ever saying a word.

[Antonio] Jr. will be a Freshman [in high school] and hopes to play for the soccer team. He plays the guitar in his room for hours and often speaks about becoming an architect so that he could build a home for my parents.

As for me, I am doing okay. I find myself with little time for my studies/law school preparation since I've boosted my hours at work and at home helping my mom with our family duties. My grades are fine. I've been receiving A's on almost all of my papers and exams, minus a few quizzes. My attendance has dropped since I've been carless and on-call whenever my mom is dealing with a mental breakdown.

I attended my first psych appointment just yesterday. I was referred to a psychiatrist but cancelled my appointment because I'd rather focus on a huge project that I have due this Friday. For the first time in my life, I feel that I am in serious need of medical/psychological support.

I don't play much soccer but I try to run whenever I feel the need to clear my mind. I never expected things to get worse, but they are, and lately things seem to just continue to fall apart. Our cars are no longer insured and now unregistered. We are able to pay our rent but have little time to breathe and rest since we all have boosted our work hours. I just get really sad and cry now. I am anxious to see my dad and I can't seem to control my emotions lately.

I often flip through my dad's case documents in search of an answer. What did we do wrong? What did we miss?! Can we still get him to come back? If so, how? I just cannot comprehend what's happened and what is currently happening to my family. I am happy that graduation is less than four weeks away but I cannot help but feel sad because I know that my dad will not be there to watch me walk the stage. I owe this moment to my dad and it's just frustrating to know that he is just not going to be there.

. . .

Thank you for your time and I hope to hear from you soon.

Kindest Regards,
[Lorena][33]

I don't know if Antonio's deportation could have been prevented since administrative options were exhausted, and going to the media wasn't possible because the family feared that Zoila's employer would learn of her status and terminate her employment. Antonio's family and I were relying on the good faith of ICE to implement the Morton Memo policies. I continue to learn, after years of handling cases, observing the agency, and talking with other practitioners, that relying on administrative good faith is foolish, given the range of factors that can affect the exercise of discretion, including the likely enforcement backgrounds of various decision makers, their explicit racial prejudice, or their reliance on institutional practice that is structurally racist. These last words to me from Director Aitken are emblematic of that structural racism:

> The public expects us to enforce immigration laws. No one has told me the Sanchez case is a low priority case; *resources have always been expended on these kinds of cases.* I also won't consider an extension of time for him to attend [Lorena]'s graduation. *If I did that, then what about the next kid?* (Emphasis added)[34]

He was right. Resources have always been expended on these kinds of cases—namely, on Mexicans living in the United States without immigration documents. And yes, what about the "next kid"—the next citizen child of a Mexican person without papers? The deportation of individuals like Antonio has become ingrained in the system of enforcement that the "public expects" officers like Aitken to follow. The institutionalized racism against Antonio was apparent in the BIA's decision against him as well.

How could immigration laws be revised to provide relief for someone like Antonio? We could eliminate or take a different approach to the hardship requirement for cancellation; for example, recognizing that potential family separation automatically qualifies. There is currently a "registry" provision in the law that provides that a person of good moral character who entered the US by 1972 can automatically qualify for lawful permanent residence. Why not update the cutoff date? Or, as in criminal law, where a statute of limitations bars the bringing of most criminal charges after a number of years have passed, we could have a statute of limitations on removal after a few years of residence. Also as in criminal law, if the person facing removal wins at the immigration court level, we could bar the government from appealing the case to the BIA.

Any of those changes in the immigration laws would have helped Antonio. However, a humanitarian legalization program for folks like Antonio via broad congressional legislation is, ultimately, the best answer. Individuals like Antonio, who have resided in the United States for years, should not be deported. The current approach, mixing prosecutorial discretion and cancellation of removal, needs to be abolished. Those avenues yield results that are wholly inconsistent and demand evidence of hardship that are unrealistic for average individuals who are simply working and steadily contributing to the well-being of their families.

CHAPTER 5

GIVING THE BENEFIT OF
THE DOUBT TO ASYLUM SEEKERS

ALWAYS EXPERIENCE EXTREMELY mixed emotions on my visits to counsel asylum seekers in Tijuana and Nogales. On the
one hand, I am so touched by the gratitude expressed by the
individuals and families, whether it be for the explanations of asylum law and procedure or for the meals that I help to serve. They
are uniformly good people, primarily from Central America but also
from Haiti, Mexico, and countries in other parts of the world: Africa,
Eastern Europe, the Middle East, and South America. On the other
hand, my students and colleagues from the law school clinic have to
be honest with asylum seekers about the challenges they face ahead.
We realize that the people we've advised, at places like the Kino Border Initiative or Al Otro Lado, are more likely than not going to be
denied asylum. That's tragic, because we know that most of the migrants have real fears of persecution.

The United States has a legal and moral obligation to protect those
fleeing persecution.[1] However, the hurdles erected at the US southern border to thousands of asylum seekers and the political tactics
of governors from Texas, Florida, and Arizona sending busloads of
migrants to sanctuary jurisdictions signal that the path to asylum is
not a smooth one. In fact, the legal and procedural hurdles for asylum
have evolved into a process that has become so strict that US obligations to protect asylum seekers have been ignored for the vast majority of applicants. Rudina Demiraj and Chanpreet Kaur are among the
many asylum seekers who will help explain why the current asylum
system needs to be abolished.

"LET ME INTRODUCE YOU TO LUZ"

I never met Luz Cardoza-Fonseca, but I represented her at the federal Ninth Circuit Court of Appeals in 1985. All I knew about her was from the file her attorney, Dana Marks, handed to me, saying, "Let me introduce you to Luz." Luz was from Nicaragua, and she feared political persecution from the Daniel Ortega regime, which had overthrown the government Luz supported. Hers would be one of the first tests for asylum based on the Refugee Act of 1980. Within two years, Dana and I would celebrate the biggest case of our careers on behalf of Luz—a precedent-setting decision by the Supreme Court.

In 1985, I was considering leaving academia and had started working part-time for the respected boutique immigration law firm of Simmons and Ungar, in San Francisco. Milt Simmons and Don Ungar had built a reputation for being smart, creative, community-minded lawyers who attracted big cases and always seemed to win. I looked forward to working with them.

Don and Milt added several great attorneys over the years, and by the early 1980s, Dana Marks was one of them. Dana primarily concentrated on employment and business immigration visas but had agreed to take on Luz's asylum case pro bono. Luz had entered the United States on a tourist visa in June 1979. Within a month of her arrival, the Nicaraguan president, Anastasio Somoza, was overthrown by the Sandinista National Liberation Front, and a five-person national reconstruction group, which included future president Daniel Ortega, took over. Luz overstayed her visa in the midst of the political turmoil in Nicaragua, and when immigration officials initiated deportation proceedings, she sought asylum.

When Dana began representing Luz, the remedy available was called "withholding of deportation" for those who could demonstrate a "clear probability of persecution."[2] But Congress passed a new law in 1980 right before Luz's first hearing. The "withholding" remedy remained, but a new specific "asylum" provision was added for those who could demonstrate a "well-founded fear" of persecution.

Dana thought that Luz should be granted asylum because Luz feared persecution due to her political opposition to the new leftist government in Nicaragua. Dana presented evidence that Luz's brother had been tortured and imprisoned because of his political activities. Both Luz and her brother testified that they believed the Sandinistas knew that the two of them had fled Nicaragua together and that even though she had not been active politically herself, Luz would be interrogated about her brother's whereabouts and activities. Luz also testified that because of her brother's status, the government would learn of her own political opposition to the Sandinistas. Based on these facts, she claimed that she would be physically harmed if forced to return.

The immigration judge denied asylum, stating that Luz had not demonstrated a "clear probability of persecution."[3] Without much analysis, the immigration judge borrowed the "clear probability" language of withholding relief and applied the same standard to the new asylum relief. To the judge, the new "well-founded fear" of persecution standard for asylum was the equivalent of the "clear probability" standard for withholding. In short, the judge ruled that the amount of evidence needed to win an asylum claim was equivalent to that required in a withholding of removal claim. But the new law had created a second, separate remedy (asylum) for applicants fearing persecution, and that suggested to Dana that Congress contemplated a different level of proof for asylum when it used the term "well-founded fear."[4] Dana appealed the case to the Board of Immigration Appeals (BIA) to no avail. In a curt decision, the BIA agreed with the immigration judge: Luz had failed to demonstrate a clear probability of persecution and did not qualify for asylum.

There is a universal truth inside and outside of the law: words matter.

Determined to prove that Luz should be granted asylum, Dana appealed to the federal Ninth Circuit Court of Appeals. By then, a few years had passed, and when the case was scheduled to be argued before the Ninth Circuit Court of Appeals in 1985, Dana asked me to step in. I had several Ninth Circuit cases under my belt by then and had represented Peter McMullen successfully in the immigration court and at the Ninth Circuit. Peter was a former member of the Provisional Irish Republican Army who tried to leave the PIRA, only to have them place a target on his head. The *McMullen* case established that under 1980 Refugee Act modifications, "withholding of removal" was mandatory if the applicant proved that persecution was more likely than not.[5] In Luz's case, the question was how much proof was necessary to qualify for asylum rather than withholding, and we felt that there was good reason to argue that the amount of proof necessary was different for asylum. After all, the 1980 law introduced the words "asylum" and "well-founded fear," so we agreed that the new words deserved their own definitions. In establishing a new asylum remedy, Congress was aware of the clear-probability standard of proof for withholding that required applicants to demonstrate that it was more likely than not that they would be persecuted. However, Congress did not use "clear probability" language for asylum, opting to use "well-founded fear" instead. That formed the crux of our argument, that applicants for asylum can meet the well-founded-fear standard of proof even if they cannot demonstrate that it is more likely than not that they will be persecuted.

THE *STEVIC* DECISION—WHAT DOES "CLEAR PROBABILITY" MEAN?

Timing is everything. A year before I represented Luz at the Ninth Circuit, the Supreme Court decided a case that reviewed the meaning of the "clear probability" standard for withholding. In *INS v. Stevic* (1984), the court ruled that an application for withholding of deportation should be granted if it is supported by evidence establishing that it is "more likely than not" that the applicant would be subject to persecution.[6] The Supreme Court defined "clear probability" to mean "more likely than not." The court also hinted that the standard for asylum was probably "more generous."

Then, on March 1, 1985, three months before my appearance at the Ninth Circuit, the BIA issued a precedent decision that helped frame my argument before the court rather nicely. In *Matter of Acosta* (1985), the BIA for the first time ruled on what amount of proof would be necessary for an applicant to qualify for the new asylum provision and failed to recognize that Congress must have created a new asylum remedy separate from the withholding relief for a reason. Even with the benefit of the Supreme Court's analysis in *Stevic*, the BIA concluded that the new "well-founded fear" standard for asylum was no different than the "clear probability" standard for withholding. That was in spite of the fact that under the new 1980 Refugee Act, there were now two separate provisions (withholding and asylum) with separate requirements (clear probability and well-founded fear). So when I appeared at the Ninth Circuit, I asked the judges rhetorically, "Why would Congress use clear probability of persecution for one category and well-founded fear of persecution for the other if Congress meant the same thing?"

The Ninth Circuit agreed that by establishing two different remedies, Congress intended that the proof needed for asylum must be different from that needed for withholding. The judges ruled that the BIA had applied a standard that was "too strict" for Luz and ordered the agency to apply the more generous standard.[7] But the government attorneys refused to give up on their argument. They appealed to the Supreme Court, insisting that "well-founded fear" of persecution somehow means the same thing as "clear probability."

THE SUPREME COURT'S LANGUAGE LESSON

When the Supreme Court agreed to hear the case, Dana and I enlisted help from Susan Lydon and Kip Steinberg. Susan was my deputy at the Immigrant Legal Resource Center, where I volunteered as the executive director. She was brilliant and had clerked at the Ninth Circuit. Kip was one of Dana's partners at Simmons and Ungar who specialized in deportation defense; he was smart and active in the National Lawyers Guild. Of course, we had Don Ungar as a resource as well.

As we wrote the legal brief and prepared for the argument before the Supreme Court in the fall of 1986, it was clear to us that this was a case of international as well as national importance to asylum seekers. Although the United States had agreed to international refugee standards in 1967, it took more than a decade for those standards to be incorporated in US immigration laws, in 1980. We felt that we had to educate the Supreme Court on those international obligations in our court filings, so we cited international law standards and experts throughout our legal briefs, even though US courts generally ignore international law.[8] Dana, who wanted to argue at the Supreme Court, made the best of that opportunity before the justices, emphasizing international approaches to refugees and the meaning of "well-founded fear."

The strategy worked. In the spring of 1987, the Supreme Court announced that the plain meaning of "well-founded fear" and the structure of the law clearly demonstrate that the definition of "well-founded fear" is intended to be generous. Winning asylum does not require a showing of 50 percent likelihood of persecution. Justice Stevens's majority opinion added: "There is simply no room in the United Nations' definition for concluding that because an applicant only has a 10% chance of being shot, tortured, or otherwise persecuted, that he or she has no 'well-founded fear' of the event happening. . . . [I]t need not be shown that the situation will probably result in persecution, but it is enough that persecution is a reasonable possibility."[9]

We were thrilled with that language and overjoyed at the outcome. We felt that the decision made sense given the humanitarian purposes of asylum law. Today, the *Cardoza-Fonseca* case is often cited by the federal courts, immigration judges, and immigration attorneys. To me and many others, the implication of the "10 percent" language is that strong evidence of likely persecution is not required, and that applicants should be given the benefit of the doubt.

THWARTING *CARDOZA-FONSECA* AND THE HUMANITARIAN INTENT OF ASYLUM

While the *Cardoza-Fonseca* case has made a positive difference in the lives of thousands of asylum seekers, unsympathetic asylum officers, immigration judges, federal courts, and policy makers have thwarted the generous humanitarian intent of the case.

The data on asylum applicants show that many immigration judges don't think about the well-founded fear standard the way I do. The Transactional Records Access Clearinghouse (TRAC) at Syracuse University collects all sorts of immigration data, including asylum approval and denial rates for immigration judges. Consider the variation in asylum approval rates among immigration judges across the country.[10] In the Atlanta Immigration Court, for example, none of the immigration judges in that court has an asylum approval rate of greater than 8.5 percent. Atlanta immigration judge Earle Wilson has a 98 percent denial rate. In Baltimore, Judge Denise Slavin approves asylum applications at a rate close to 90 percent, but another judge, Phillip T. Williams, approves less than 33 percent of his asylum cases. My co-counsel in *Cardoza-Fonseca*, Dana Marks, who understands the humanitarian purpose of asylum, became an immigration judge in San Francisco and had a 91 percent approval rate before her retirement. But also in San Francisco, Judges Michael Yamaguchi and Anthony S. Murry only approved 4.5 percent and 4.9 percent respectively. Does the quality of asylum claims in the same city vary that much from judge to judge? Doubtful. More likely than not, the judges look at the same cases differently. Perhaps even more worrisome, consider Judge Sunita Mahtabfar in El Paso and Judge John F. Walsh in Los Angeles, each with a 1.2 percent approval rate.

CREDIBILITY AS A PRETEXT

One way that immigration judges find their way around their humanitarian responsibilities to asylum seekers is by concluding that the applicant is not credible.

Having represented refugees and asylum seekers from all over the world for more than half a century, I can attest that the vast majority of those fleeing persecution don't hand-carry documents proving why they fear persecution. Given the ubiquity of cell phones today, remarkably, some of our clients have retained threatening text messages. Still, most asylum applicants arrive with only their stories of past persecution or threats of future harm.

After *Cardoza-Fonseca*, the BIA recognized that asylum applicants presenting only their stories might still qualify. In *Matter of Mogharrabi*, the BIA acknowledged "the difficulties faced by many aliens in obtaining documentary or other corroborative evidence to support their claims of persecution."[11] Therefore, the BIA concluded that an applicant's "own testimony in an asylum case may be sufficient, without corroborative evidence, to prove a well-founded fear of persecution where that testimony is believable, consistent, and sufficiently detailed to provide a plausible and coherent account of the basis for his fear."

The case, from the 1980s, involved an applicant who feared persecution in Iran, primarily because of an altercation he had with an official agent of the regime of the Ayatollah Khomeini. The applicant testified that while he was in the United States in February 1981, he went with an Iranian friend to the Iranian Interests Section at the Algerian Embassy. He wanted to document his continuing student status in order to continue receiving funds from relatives in Iran. He took copies of his passport and an arrival-departure document that was provided by US officials when he entered the United States. When he presented the copies to a student who was working at the embassy, he was told that the originals were required. According to the applicant, he was informed that the originals were necessary because students who did not have them had probably submitted them to US immigration officials in connection with asylum applications. The student-employee was insistent, and the applicant's friend asked to see the supervisor. The supervisor appeared, but further trouble ensued. The student apparently grabbed the applicant's friend's neck, but the supervisor separated them. The student then told the applicant's friend that he and "his kind had better keep their eyes and ears open because 'their day' would come soon." [12] In response, the applicant told him that "he and his kind had robbed Iran of all that was worth living for and that they were nothing more than religious fascists stuffing their pockets with the nation's wealth." According to the applicant, the student then drew a gun, and he and his friend ran out the door. The applicant testified that there were cameras all around the room recording these events. A witness for the applicant testified at the hearing that he had accompanied the applicant and his friend to the Algerian Embassy, although he had waited in the car and did not go inside with them. This witness testified that when the applicant and his friend returned to the car, they were nervous, and a couple of people were following them. The applicant felt that he was now known to Khomeini officials and, as a result, had good reason to fear persecution if he was returned to Iran. The applicant also testified that he had participated in anti-Khomeini demonstrations in the United States.

The BIA granted asylum because the applicant's account was "plausible, detailed, and coherent." There was "nothing in the record" to suggest that the applicant "was not credible." The irony of the *Mogharrabi* decision is that while it stands for the important principle that an applicant without more than a credible story can be granted asylum, adding more evidence "in the record" can create a credibility problem for decision makers looking for a way to deny.

Years ago, I was an advisor to independent filmmakers Michael Camerini and Shari Robertson, who produced the PBS documentary film *Well-Founded Fear*. Given unprecedented access to the federal asylum offices in New York and New Jersey, the filmmakers were able to film dozens of asylum interviews and to interview asylum officers. After we won the *Cardoza-Fonseca* case, Dana, Susan, Kip, and I had high hopes that the percentage of successful asylum applicants would surge after the decision, but it did not. The film *Well-Founded Fear* helps explain why. The film revealed a corps of officers failing to apply the deferential standard announced by the Supreme Court. Instead, the officers all seemed completely focused on questions of credibility. In my view, that focus provides a convenient, but improper, way to impose a more-likely-than-not or even a beyond-a-reasonable-doubt standard of proof.

Consider the words of one asylum officer from the film, Kelvin:

> I [did not grant asylum]. I found him not consistent. There were things in there that were inconsistencies [in] his testimony. There was a time when he said he was brought by two men into a van and drove around town for two hours, during which time he was beaten. And then this is where the inconsistency was. He said, "No, no, no, there was three of them. . . . One was driving and two were in the back with me." So that was enough for me. Now, some people might say, in fact, I told [another asylum officer] about this case. We frequently share . . . We have a case and talk to other asylum

officers about it, and he said, "That's cheap." I don't think it is. But, you know, that inconsistency again; if that was in another case, maybe I wouldn't have clung onto it; I may have saw past it. But for some reason, in this case I didn't. That's because I found him not to be credible.

. . .

This may be the 450th time that I've interviewed a similar case, because I've had this experience; I'm seeing it totally different. Totally different story. You sat in on one case that I had, and I made a credibility determination. First he said there were two people in the van, then he said there were three, and I determined that this person wasn't credible, aside from the horrible story that he was detained and beaten, and I do that every day. And I've referred people [to the immigration judge], women who have told me that they were raped and that they've been abused. And I didn't do that because they didn't fall within the framework of what it takes to get asylum. I did it because I found that they weren't credible. . . . And I know in the beginning, as I said earlier, that I used to grant a whole lot more, but after you do this for a while you become much more critical, and you become much more, very aware of inconsistencies, and I hope that's what it is, right? I mean, I know that it could just be the fact that you're just very jaded. And how do you know where one begins and the other ends? If I admitted that I was jaded, wouldn't I then be saying that I shouldn't be doing this job anymore? So I say that I have a more acute understanding of credibility issues.[13]

Kelvin's words are troubling. He admits that a different officer disagrees with his assessment ("that's cheap," meaning that's a poor excuse for doubting the story). Kelvin admits that he might overlook the same "inconsistency" in a different case. He has interviewed so many similar cases ("450th") that he might be "jaded." His approach is not deferential. In fact, his approach is at the very least inconsistent, and that's a problem for someone charged with the responsibility of making a life-and-death asylum decision.

One of the more sympathetic asylum officers in the film, Mary-Louise, confides:

> How do you decide whether someone is telling the truth or not? It's not simple. You're never sure; that's the problem. If you are pretty sure that it's not the truth, then at least you're in the comfortable position that the decision is based on something that's real. But, in a case like this, when it's just plain fuzzy, I have to talk to somebody else about it, to get another perspective. That's life; it's real life. We're dealing with real people, in real situations; yes, they stay fuzzy forever. And we still have to make a decision, based on fuzziness!

"Fuzziness"? Does she mean inconclusive? If so, I believe that should be granted, because the 10 percent standard of *Cardoza-Fonseca* does not require an applicant's claim to be conclusive.

Another seemingly sympathetic officer, Gerald, explains why he has not approved the claim by an Algerian applicant:

> I think that the woman's telling the truth, and I think Algeria's a dangerous place, but she didn't establish a well-founded fear of future persecution to me. She had lived there for a significant length of time since her last trouble. There was *confusion over dates,* which I couldn't get past. And basically I didn't think that she established a well-founded fear. That combined with a lack of past persecution made me refer the case [to the immigration court]. (Emphasis added)

First of all, past persecution is not necessary to establish a well-founded fear of future persecution. And should "confusion over dates" be a disqualification, especially as Gerald felt that the applicant was "telling the truth"? In my view, some confusion over dates does not negate a 10 percent chance that the person will be persecuted—especially when the person may have experienced trauma and may be suffering from post-traumatic stress disorder.

The BIA deserves much of the blame for leading the way with un-realistic credibility demands. After its *Mogharrabi* decision, the BIA denied the asylum claim for a twenty-nine-year-old Bangladesh applicant in *Matter of A-S-* due to "credibility" problems in three parts of his testimony.[14] The applicant testified that one forced intrusion in his home took place on July 12, 1993, but his application stated that the incident occurred on March 12, 1991. He also testified that he was beaten and rendered unconscious in July 1993, while his application stated that this incident took place in January 1992. He then testified about a third incident where he was physically assaulted, but the application did not mention that incident. The BIA also noted that the immigration judge found that the applicant testified in a "very halting" and "hesitant" manner. The BIA's nitpicking over discrepancies in testimony and licensing subjective observations of "halting" or "hesitant" manner are of course problematic. A halting delivery in a court proceeding can be caused by factors unrelated to fabrication. And it isn't uncommon to have difficulty remembering dates or details—especially related to traumatic events. Even the chair of the BIA observed in a dissenting opinion:

> The majority concludes, as reasonable adjudicators perhaps could, that the [applicant] is likely an imposter who has fabricated his claim, or the material portions of it. I, on the other hand, take him for what he appears to me to be: a persecuted individual with a less than perfect memory who was not properly prepared to testify at his asylum hearing.[15]

Unfortunately, Congress made matters even tougher on the credibility front for asylum seekers. When we see a reference to the REAL ID Act of 2005, most of us think about the secure driver's licenses that we need to obtain to board an airplane. But the REAL ID Act also added provisions related to asylum-seeker credibility. First, asylum seekers are no longer presumed to be credible at the beginning of the hearing. Second, "any" inconsistencies can be used to find that applicant not credible—even those that don't go "to the heart of" the claim.[16] Third, the law encourages judges to consider applicants' "demeanor [or] responsiveness" in their decision. Fourth, applicants must provide documents to corroborate their claims. If documents are not available, the applicant must explain why they are unavailable or cannot be obtained. So the REAL ID Act struck a profound blow against giving asylum seekers the benefit of the doubt.

Examples of asylum denials based on credibility are easy to find. In one case, an applicant testified that a threat had occurred in February 2016, but a report submitted indicated that the threat had occurred in January 2016.[17] The immigration judge described the applicant's demeanor as evasive and unresponsive. A 2021 case involved purported inconsistencies between notes taken during an interview at the border and testimony given at a removal hearing.[18] The border interview was done by an asylum officer over the phone. In that interview, the applicant talked about being arrested, detained, and threatened for his opposition to the Cuban government. At the subsequent deportation hearing, the immigration judge denied the application on the grounds that the applicant was not credible. The judge said that during the border phone interview, the applicant told the asylum officer about four incidents, but at the deportation hearing, the applicant said there were eight incidents. During the phone interview, the applicant said "a" person stabbed him during an incident. At the hearing, the applicant testified that one person had stabbed him during an attack carried out by four individuals. To me, some of these so-called "discrepancies" aren't discrepancies at all, and others could have been easily explained if we had taken the time with the applicant to figure out what happened and why the storyline appeared to change. I know the latter is possible, because that happens with our clinic clients all the time, and it takes hours and hours over several meetings to really get things straight.

This denial of a rape survivor's asylum claim in another case is particularly disturbing. The events leading to Mirabel Munyuh's plea for asylum began in July 2018 when Cameroonian police officers forced their way into Munyuh's home, ransacked her belongings, and took her into custody. She was accused of being a member of a separatist group and was severely beaten before being taken to a detention center. Hours later, Munyuh said she was loaded with other detainees from her cell onto a truck headed to another prison in Yaoundé, the capital of Cameroon. At some point along the way—the actual time and distance being in dispute—the truck broke down. The officers then dragged the women into the bush to sexually assault them, Munyuh said.

After she was raped by two different officers, Munyuh said she managed to escape into the surrounding wilderness under the cover of darkness and then ran as fast as she could. Traveling by foot until daybreak, Munyuh eventually reached the town of Bafia, where she was able to call her husband to rescue her. She was taken to a hospital in Yaoundé, where doctors noted bruising on her head, chest, back, and feet, as well as lacerations on her genitals supporting a conclusion of forceful vaginal penetration. She decided not to stay at the hospital, however, because she was worried the police would recapture her.

Cameroonian police continued to search for her, forcing Munyuh to flee by bus to Ghana before flying to Ecuador and eventually to the United States. Lacking valid entry documents, she was detained near San Diego. Shortly after, a US asylum officer determined that Munyuh had a credible fear of returning to Cameroon, and her family back home managed to send her supporting documentation for her asylum application, including a medical report and an arrest warrant.

At her removal hearing, Munyuh told her story, but on cross-examination, the government pointed out some discrepancies related to when the truck broke down and how far she walked to find help after she was raped. Her attorney argued that after a horrific day of beatings and sexual assault, it was to be expected that she had not focused on the actual distance traveled.

In the end, Munyuh said she wasn't sure how far a kilometer is and said the truck had been going for about four or five hours before it broke down. But the immigration judge questioned her again on the discrepancies in her testimony and declaration. The judge also reportedly questioned her on the injuries she had sustained that day, asking her why she hadn't testified earlier to experiencing vaginal bleeding. Finally, the judge noted that Munyuh had not shown "any emotion particularly" during her testimony about the rape. Asked why,

Munyuh did not directly answer but explained: "It's not because I don't . . . I don't feel that I was being raped. I do feel it, Your Honor."[19]

The immigration judge then contrasted Munyuh's affect at the hearing with her emotions during the credible-fear interview, in which she had cried. Asked why she had been able to express those emotions during the asylum officer interview but not the hearing, Munyuh simply replied, "I don't know, Your Honor."

Based on those discrepancies, the immigration judge determined that Munyuh was not credible and therefore had not proven persecution or torture. The judge denied asylum. Fortunately, a federal court of appeals revived Munyuh's claim, ruling that the immigration judge had cherry-picked discrepancies in the woman's testimony to justify deporting her and "displayed a dubious understanding of how rape survivors ought to act." The court criticized the immigration judge for not weighing the credibility of Munyuh's entire account before rejecting her asylum, while questioning her reported lack of emotion while testifying.

In its opinion, the court said Munyuh had given a reasonable explanation for the discrepancy in travel time, finding that the trauma of being beaten and raped had impaired her focus at the time on peripheral matters and her memory of the events. Munyuh's basic account was not inherently incredible or inconsistent and was strongly supported by corroborating evidence; after all, Munyuh didn't have an odometer during the trip, the court wryly noted.

As fortunate as this federal court's review was, this type of intervention is not common. The behavior of the immigration judge and the government attorney in Munyuh's case is an excellent example of exactly how the asylum process should not be handled. The hostile, adversarial environment they created is the opposite atmosphere that should be fashioned in a country that has international obligations to protect those fleeing persecution.

The constant focus on credibility in the US asylum system is misplaced. By focusing on credibility with a fine-tooth comb, immigration judges and asylum officers are asking applicants: "Prove to me that you are telling the truth before I will grant your asylum claim."

While this may seem like a reasonable thing to ask, we might want to stop and think about that approach in the asylum context. Demanding precise testimony in order to find an applicant credible is the equivalent of demanding proof that something is more likely than not to be true—the standard rejected in *Cardoza-Fonseca*. The Supreme Court made clear in *Cardoza-Fonseca* that a preponderance of evidence is not necessary; only the existence of a reasonable possibility is necessary, and a 10 percent chance of persecution is sufficient.

Post-Traumatic Stress Disorder

The most glaring problem with focusing so intensely on credibility is the total lack of concern over the impact that post-traumatic stress disorder (PTSD) has on refugees. The BIA and REAL ID approach to credibility manifests little understanding of how the trauma of persecution and threat of persecution can result in seemingly inconsistent accounts of events, dates, and experiences. Any immigration practitioner knows, and immigration judges and asylum officers should as well, that hours and hours over several meetings are often necessary to bring out in full detail the experiences that our asylum applicants have endured. And memory of those experiences is severely affected by the trauma endured. For that reason, attorneys who are competent in representing asylum seekers understand the need to be trauma-informed practitioners.[20]

It does not take many discussions with most asylum seekers to realize that they have suffered trauma. For the clients with whom my law school clinic staff and students have worked over the last several years, it's clear that our clients' experiences with gang, cartel, and domestic violence have left them with various degrees of PTSD. They forget things. Sometimes they cry; sometimes they are stoic. Some talk a lot; some don't talk much. Dates are hard to remember for many. Most have seen or experienced horrendous events—including rape, kidnapping, and the murder of relatives. Even given the many hours that staff attorneys and students spend to learn the entire story, some aspects may still be left out. Truthfully, the experience of interviewing is so stressful that I worry about the secondary trauma that staff and students may be experiencing.

Carol Suzuki, who runs a law school clinic at the University of New Mexico, has done extensive research on the effects of PTSD on storytelling. She found that asylum clients may be especially reluctant to divulge experiences of torture and trauma due to their vulnerable noncitizen status. Additionally, PTSD sufferers often endure other mental disorders, including depression and drug and alcohol dependence.

The results of a study on Kosovan and Bosnian refugees indicate that the refugee participants had discrepancies in their firsthand accounts.[21] The discrepancies were more likely to involve those details that were peripheral to the experiences than those that made up the central narrative of the event. Although a subject was more likely to have clear recall of the central elements of an experience when the experience had a high level of emotional impact on the subject rather than a neutral impact, the subject became less accurate in the recall of peripheral details of the experience. There was no significant difference regarding whether the experience recalled was a traumatic event or a nontraumatic event. Refugee participants with high levels of traumatic stress were more likely to have a greater number of discrepancies the longer the time between interviews. Therefore, discrepancies in recall over time do not necessarily indicate lying. Also, subjects who were depressed and who suffered from PTSD had difficulty recalling central details. Furthermore, the results indicated that the level of detail conveyed in the subjects' response was dictated in part by how the question was worded.

Other studies also show that memories of the details of a traumatic event are not recalled consistently over time. A study of Gulf War veterans, for instance, found that even details that seem immutable, generally objective, and highly traumatic—such as whether a soldier saw other soldiers killed or wounded—often shift or change after two years have passed.[22] In this study, fifty-nine veterans of Operation Desert Storm completed a questionnaire regarding potential traumatic stressors faced by Desert Storm personnel. These subjects were also evaluated for PTSD. The study concluded that subjects with PTSD are more likely to have difficulty remembering details of traumatic events and that their stories are more likely to become inconsistent over time. There were inconsistencies in the recall of events that were generally objective and highly traumatic in nature. This study found a positive correlation between high levels of PTSD in subjects and inconsistency in memory of traumatic events.

Traumatic memory is stored differently than nontraumatic memory. Unlike explicit memory, traumatic events are stored as implicit memory, which are sensory, emotional, reflexive, or conditioned responses. A person who experiences a traumatic event processes the event in terms of the senses of sight, sound, touch, taste, and smell. During the traumatic event, the brain becomes overwhelmed with all of the information it absorbs and stores the information as fragments. These fragments become associated with other, similar memories of possibly unrelated events. Retrieval of the memory of the traumatic event may also retrieve fragments of these unrelated events. In other words, a person who has suffered repeated, and similar traumatic events, such as numerous jailings and beatings, may blend the different occurrences together and not remember details from a particular event.[23]

Recall the BIA's denial of the Bangladeshi applicant in *Matter of A-S-* and its criticism of discrepancies in dates and the applicant's halting manner of speech. These studies blow a huge hole in the BIA's reasoning.

I assisted in an asylum case involving the sexual assault of a woman in front of her daughter, where the woman's testimony was taken via a teleconferencing line because she was detained at an ICE facility three hundred miles from the immigration court. The government attorney was critical of the halting manner in which the applicant testified, so we supplemented the record with an assessment by a specialist in dealing with trauma victims. The specialist's expert affidavit discussed how the client's trauma and PTSD affected her testimony:

Each individual survivor has a complex array of conscious and unconscious coping strategies and defenses to manage the unspeakable experiences, unbearable memories and overwhelming emotions that plague them. This broad range of affective and cognitive presentations is normal, well documented in the trauma research literature, and very familiar to clinicians working with this population. Having blunted or incongruent affect does not in any way indicate that a person has not experienced trauma, is not suffering from post-traumatic symptoms, or is being untruthful in their account. To the contrary, these varying and at times incongruent responses are typical reactions to trauma, and characteristic for highly traumatized populations.

[Indeed, it] is likely that she was in a post-traumatic state after having experienced a sexual assault in the presence of her daughter, and being forced to flee and leave her young child behind . . . Many survivors have difficulty relaying such details, especially when highly anxious and under pressure such as during a court hearing.[24]

Given what we know about the effects of PTSD, the exacting demand by the BIA and the REAL ID Act for consistency and the failure to presume credibility are clearly misplaced in the asylum arena.

Perhaps it is human nature for adjudicators to want to be convinced that what is being alleged is truthful or is actually going to happen. But that is not what the court demanded in *Cardoza-Fonseca*. The 10 percent standard is a deferential benefit-of-the-doubt standard. That means that the benefit of the doubt should be given to the applicant when it comes to what appear to be discrepancies in testimony as well.

PROBLEMS WITH THE CURRENT ASYLUM FRAMEWORK

Beyond the use of a credibility approach to skirt the deferential purpose of asylum, the interpretation of asylum law itself is problematic.

Since the headline-grabbing surge of unaccompanied children in 2014, the focus on the US southern border has taken on a new dimension. For decades, the focus was on the purported entry of undocumented Mexican migrants, even though undocumented Mexican migration has dropped to its lowest levels in nearly fifty years.[25] But in 2014, more than sixty thousand unaccompanied minors—mostly from Honduras, Guatemala, and El Salvador—reached the southern border mostly fleeing gang violence. Simultaneously, another sixty thousand Central American family units (primarily women and children) also approached the border seeking protection from both domestic and gang violence. Instead of welcoming Central American refugees, the Obama administration responded hostilely by opening children and family detention centers, instituting "rocket dockets" (expedited removal proceedings), and generally opposing asylum. I started the deportation defense clinic at the University of San Francisco because of the surge in numbers and the Obama administration's deportation approach. We have represented hundreds of clients, and the vast majority are asylum seekers from Central America and Mexico fleeing gang, cartel, and domestic violence.

When you think of asylum, you might not think of protection from gangs or a former husband as the type of claim for which asylum is designed. But in fact, those types of claims fall well within the law of asylum of the United States. Yet, the Obama administration opposed most gang and domestic violence claims, and I was disappointed that a government attorney appealed the grant of asylum to my client Maria, who was run down by a car driven by a gang member who was upset that she refused to be his girlfriend. Taking that approach to a different level, the Trump administration did its best to end protections for all gang and domestic violence claims.

Donald Trump's first attorney general, Jeff Sessions, eventually got on the wrong side of his boss when Sessions recused himself from the Russia investigation that was headed by special counsel Robert Mueller. But Sessions acquitted himself quite well with Trump when it came to the president's anti-immigrant agenda. Sessions was the driving force behind the mean-spirited policy of separating parents from their children at the border in 2017 and 2018.[26] His hardline policies on asylum led to the Migrant Protection Protocols soon after he was fired by Trump, requiring asylum seekers to remain in Mexico in squalid, unsafe shelters while their asylum claims were pending. Substantively, he clamped down on gang and domestic violence claims. As the attorney general, with authority over the BIA and all immigration courts, he issued a directive decision overturning board precedent, announcing: "Generally, claims by aliens pertaining to domestic violence or gang violence perpetrated by nongovernmental actors will not qualify for asylum. . . . The mere fact that a country may have problems effectively policing certain crimes—such as domestic violence or gang violence—or that certain populations are more likely to be victims of crime, cannot itself establish an asylum claim."[27]

Sessions's decision was appalling. The legal community was stunned; it took inspired litigation and creative arguments to avert total catastrophe for some applicants. But thousands of asylum seekers from Central America were denied asylum under Sessions's policy, mostly because they were unrepresented. Joe Biden's attorney general, Merrick Garland, canceled Sessions's handiwork, but even then, claims based on threats of domestic or gang violence are never a sure thing.

"A PARTICULAR SOCIAL GROUP"

In establishing an asylum provision in our immigration laws in 1980, Congress borrowed language from the international 1967 Protocol and 1951 Convention on Refugees. In order to qualify, the applicant must establish past persecution or a well-founded fear of future persecution on account of one of five bases: race, religion, nationality, political opinion, or membership in a particular social group.

When it comes to asylum claims for women and children fleeing gang or domestic violence, the asylum categories of race, religion, and nationality are not good fits. Claiming a fear of persecution in those circumstances because of political views is a viable argument. But you have to make the case that opposing a machismo culture is a political opinion because that culture of female subordination pervades the social and political culture of the country.[28] So the vast majority of gang and domestic violence applicants claim that the persecution is on account of membership in a particular social group.

The following domestic violence cases are examples of successful particular social group claims.

In *Matter of A-R-C-G-* (2014), the BIA recognized the particular social group comprising "married women in Guatemala who are unable to leave their relationship." The facts were typical of these cases:

> It is undisputed that the respondent, who married at age 17, suffered repugnant abuse by her husband. This abuse included weekly beatings after the respondent had their first child. On one occasion, the respondent's husband broke her nose. Another time, he threw paint thinner on her, which burned her breast. He raped her.
>
> The respondent contacted the police several times but was told that they would not interfere in a marital relationship. On one occasion, the police came to her home after her husband hit her on the head, but he was not arrested. Subsequently, he threatened the respondent with death if she called the police again. The respondent repeatedly tried to leave the relationship by staying with her father, but her husband found her and threatened to kill her if she did not return to him. Once she went to Guatemala City for about 3 months, but he followed her and convinced her to come home with promises that he would discontinue the abuse. The abuse continued when she returned. The respondent left Guatemala . . . and she believes her husband will harm her if she returns.[29]

The immigration judge denied the asylum claim because the abuse resulted from "criminal acts, not persecution." However, the BIA disagreed. Within the domestic violence context, the BIA recognized that country conditions, law enforcement statistics, and "other reliable and credible sources of information," like expert witnesses, can support the recognition of a particular social group claim. Credit the Obama administration here: before the BIA, the government conceded that the applicant's mistreatment was due to being a married woman in Guatemala who was unable to leave her relationship.

A similar particular social group claim was made by Sontos Maudilia Diaz-Reynoso, who claimed that she belonged to a targeted group: indigenous women in Guatemala who are unable to leave their relationship. She was born in a small, rural town in the Guatemalan highlands and is a member of the indigenous group known as Mam.

Diaz-Reynoso moved in with a man named Arnoldo Vasquez-Juarez, who is also Mam. Although they did not legally marry, Diaz-Reynoso and Vasquez-Juarez had a common-law marriage, and Diaz-Reynoso refers to Vasquez-Juarez as her husband.

Vasquez-Juarez subjected Diaz-Reynoso to physical and sexual abuse, including forcing her to work in the coffee fields without pay and raping her. When Diaz-Reynoso did not comply with his demands, Vasquez-Juarez hit her on her head and elsewhere on her body, sometimes with a belt. Diaz-Reynoso testified that she was attacked weekly, and that the resulting bruises sometimes lasted for eight to ten days. After four years of living with Vasquez-Juarez, Diaz-Reynoso fled and entered the United States without documentation. She was apprehended and, after roughly a month in detention, returned to Guatemala. Diaz-Reynoso moved back in with her family.

As soon as Diaz-Reynoso returned, Vasquez-Juarez came to find her. Vasquez-Juarez told Diaz-Reynoso that if she did not return to live with him, he would kill her, kill her daughter, or harm her mother. Diaz-Reynoso returned to live with Vasquez-Juarez for about a year. The abuse got worse during that time. Diaz-Reynoso then escaped and with her daughter went to live with a friend in another town for roughly a year. She was in hiding during this period and did not leave her friend's house. After that, Diaz-Reynoso returned to her family home in the hope that Vasquez-Juarez had forgotten about her, but Vasquez-Juarez found Diaz-Reynoso and ordered her to come back with him. At the urging of her mother, Diaz-Reynoso again fled to the United States. The BIA denied Diaz-Reynoso's claim because her proposed particular social group was not recognized, but the court of appeals disagreed and sent the case back for reconsideration.

Can domestic violence in a particular country be so bad that all women in the country constitute a particular social group for asylum purposes? Yes. Lesly Yajayra Perdomo left Guatemala at age fifteen to join her mother in the United States. When deportation proceedings were started against her, she applied for asylum because she feared persecution as a member of a particular social group defined by her attorney as consisting of women between the ages of fourteen and forty. Lesly testified that her fear was based on the high incidence of murder of women in Guatemala and her own status as a Guatemalan woman. Her attorney provided the immigration judge with several reports by the Guatemala Human Rights Commission documenting the torture and killing of women, the brutality of the killings, the non-responsiveness of the Guatemalan government to such atrocities, the countrywide prevalence of such murders, and the absence of explanations. Her attorney argued that Guatemalan women were murdered at a high rate with impunity.

Although the immigration judge was sympathetic to Lesly's plight, she refused to find that Guatemalan women between the ages of fourteen and forty form a particular social group that would entitle Lesly to relief.[30] The BIA agreed that the proposed particular social group was too broadly defined. But the federal Ninth Circuit Court of Appeals felt that rejecting a proposed group simply because the group represents too large a portion of a population is improper. The court sent the case back to the BIA for reexamination.

This wide-ranging approach to gender asylum claims is similar to that of a different federal court, which held that "young Albanian women living alone and thus vulnerable to being trafficked" could constitute a particular social group,[31] and even to a BIA decision that tribal women not yet subjected to female genital mutilation or women who faced honor killings because of social or religious norms can qualify.[32]

In gang-violence asylum cases, some social group claims have succeeded. Nelson Benitez Ramos grew up in El Salvador. At fourteen, he joined the Mara Salvatrucha (MS-13), a violent street gang, and remained a member for about nine years, when he came to the United States. Shortly afterward, having become a born-again Christian, he decided that if he returned to El Salvador he could not rejoin the gang without violating his Christian scruples and felt that the gang would kill him for his refusal to rejoin and the police would be helpless to protect him. He had gang tattoos on his face and body, but even if he had them removed, the gang would still recognize him. The BIA ruled against Ramos on the ground that "tattooed, former Salvadoran gang members" does not constitute a particular social group. But the federal Seventh Circuit Court of Appeals disagreed and ruled that former gang members could constitute a particular social group.[33]

Similarly, the Ninth Circuit Court of Appeals has recognized the particular social group of "people testifying against or otherwise opposing gang members."[34] In that case, a young girl witnessed the murder of her father by four members of the M-18 street gang in El Salvador. She testified against the defendants at trial, but after one of the men got out of prison, she and her sister were threatened and fled to the United States.

But there are numerous examples of courts refusing to recognize a particular social group in gang or domestic violence cases.

For example, in 2021, the Ninth Circuit Court of Appeals refused to recognize asylum claims for Salvadoran women who refuse to be the girlfriends of MS-13 gang members and for Salvadoran women who refuse to be victims of the violent sexual predation of gang members.[35] The BIA refused to recognize prosecutorial witnesses against gangs as a particular social group, unless the cooperation was public in nature, such as testifying in public court proceedings. That was despite evidence that the gang knew the person had provided information to the police.[36] And the Ninth Circuit Court of Appeals also ruled against an asylum applicant who was the victim of domestic violence, because the applicant did not establish that Guatemalan authorities would not or could not protect her.[37] The court cited reports that Guatemala is trying to prevent violence against women through laws that criminalize rape and domestic violence and through programs and shelters that help victims of abuse. That case illustrates another challenge faced by applicants who are claiming persecution by nongovernmental entities like gangs or domestic partners. Besides needing to define a social group that the court accepts, applicants also have to prove that the government is unable or unwilling to control the persecutor.

The persecution of family members is commonly related to gang and domestic violence. Gangs often target relatives of an individual who has somehow crossed the gang. A domestic abuser often lashes out at the entire family. For those reasons, "family" is successfully presented by immigration lawyers as the prototypical particular social group in those circumstances—although once again the claim must be supplemented with evidence that authorities are unable or unwilling to control the persecutor.

Presenting the family as a social group in these circumstances makes sense, because as one federal court has recognized, family is the "quintessential" particular social group in asylum law.[38] But President Trump's second attorney general, William Barr, did not like that pathway for asylum. He targeted asylum based on family-group membership and departed from longstanding precedent by offering this guidance to immigration judges: in "the ordinary case, a nuclear family will not, without more, constitute a 'particular social group' because most nuclear families are not inherently socially distinct."[39] Fortunately, Joe Biden's attorney general reversed that order as well, but difficulty in making a family-based social group claim is not limited to responding to the guidance of William Barr or various narrow-minded immigration judges.[40] The asylum case of Rudina Demiraj and her son, Rediol, shows that federal appellate judges also are quite capable of coming up with puzzling reasoning to refuse protection to relatives.[41]

Federal prosecutors had arranged to have Rudina's husband, Edmond Demiraj, testify against Bill Bedini, an Albanian wanted in the United States for human smuggling. But Demiraj never actually took the stand because Bedini fled to Albania. After Demiraj was deported to Albania, Bedini kidnapped, beat, and shot Demiraj because of his cooperation with US prosecutors. Demiraj recovered and local police in Albania took his statement but did nothing further. Bedini threatened Demiraj again, so he fled back to the United States, whereupon he was granted withholding of removal. During the same time period, two of Demiraj's nieces were kidnapped by Bedini and his associates and trafficked to Italy. After escaping, the nieces fled to the United States and were granted asylum. Rudina and Rediol Demiraj were in the United States, so they too applied for asylum, fearing Bedini's wrath.

Knowing what we now know about asylum requirements, the logical claim for their asylum case was that Rudina and Rediol had a well-founded fear of persecution at the hands of Bedini because of their membership in a particular social group: Mr. Demiraj's family. After all, it would seem pretty easy to make the case that there was at least a 10 percent chance that something bad would happen to them in Albania at the hands of Bedini. There was also clear evidence that the Albanian government either was unwilling or unable to control Bedini.

The immigration judge, BIA, and federal court of appeals all agreed that the core question was whether Rudina reasonably feared persecution "on account of" her family membership. They also seemed to agree that the Demiraj family was a social group. But here's where the case gets bizarre. The court of appeals did not doubt that Rudina and her son would be hurt by Bedini, but in the judges' twisted reasoning, the harm would be inflicted not because of their relationship to Demiraj but because they were important to him:

> The crucial finding here is that the record discloses no evidence that Mrs. Demiraj would be targeted for her membership in the Demiraj family *as such*. Rather, the evidence strongly suggests that Mrs. Demiraj, her son, and Mr. Demiraj's nieces were targeted because they are people who are important to Mr. Demiraj—that is, because hurting them would hurt Mr. Demiraj. No one suggests that distant members of the Demiraj family have been systematically targeted as would be the case if, for example, a persecutor sought to terminate a line of dynastic succession. Nor does the record suggest that the fact of Mr. and Mrs. Demiraj's marriage and formal inclusion in the Demiraj family matters to Bedini; that is, Mrs. Demiraj would not be any safer in Albania if she divorced Mr. Demiraj and renounced membership in the family, nor would she be any safer if she were Mr. Demiraj's girlfriend of many years rather than his wife. The record here discloses a quintessentially personal motivation, not one based on a prohibited reason under the [law].[42]

Thus, the court of appeals denied asylum and ordered Rudina and her son deported. The illogic of the court of appeals judges is obvious. Yes, Bedini would hurt Rudina and her son because they are "important" to Demiraj. But they are important to Demiraj because they are his family.

A dissenting judge on the court of appeals criticized the majority opinion. First, he clarified the record on what happened to Demiraj's nieces. Bedini and his men kidnapped the two nieces in Albania and took them to Italy, where the captors attempted to force the nieces—ages nineteen and twenty-one—into prostitution. Upon being given clothes to wear as streetwalkers, the girls began to cry and protest that they were not prostitutes.[43] Bedini became angry and beat the girls, saying that "this was payback to your uncle Edmond [Demiraj] for when I was in the United States." The captors then tied up the nieces for days with no food, water, or access to a toilet. Eventually, the nieces, who "both had pain all over, felt sick and nauseated," and had urinated on themselves, consented to work as prostitutes. They were told to clean themselves up and to put on makeup. They were taken to the streets, where Bedini gave them condoms and told them how to use them for sex. Not long afterward, the nieces, through sheer luck and thanks to a kind taxi driver, managed to escape from their captors and contact their family. Although the court's majority opinion characterized all of this as involving merely personal revenge, there was no evidence that Bedini had any grudge against Mrs. Demiraj, her son, or any other Demiraj family members as individuals—rather, his only interest in them was because of their membership in the family of Demiraj.

Fortunately, other federal courts do not look at families-as-a-particular-social-group so narrowly. And the deportation of Rudina and Rediol to Albania was stopped through successful political efforts behind the scenes. But the lesson from Rudina's case is clear: the outcome of asylum cases is highly uncertain, hinging on how fair-minded the decision maker might be.

Head-Scratching Asylum Outcomes

Anyone familiar with asylum law can easily recount judicial decisions that defy logic.

Being forced to clean and cook for kidnappers is still material support. In *Matter of A-C-M-*, the BIA denied asylum to a Salvadoran woman who had been kidnapped by guerrillas in El Salvador in 1990.[44] The BIA did not dispute the fact that the applicant had experienced "horrific harm." In addition to being kidnapped and required to perform cooking and cleaning for the guerrillas under threat of death, the applicant was forced to witness her husband, a sergeant in the Salvadoran army, dig his own grave before being killed. It may not be surprising to learn that someone who has engaged in "terrorist activity" is barred from asylum or that terrorist activity includes providing "material support" to a terrorist organization. What might come as a surprise, however, is that the BIA refuses to recognize an exception when the support is provided under duress or when the amount of support is small. Despite what happened to the applicant in this case, the BIA denied asylum:

> There is no legislative history to support taking a quantitative approach and separating out what amount of support is necessary to make it "material." If an alien affords material support to a terrorist organization, he or she is subject to the bar, regardless of how limited that support is in amount. . . .
>
> Thus, we conclude that an alien provides "material support" to a terrorist organization, regardless of whether it was intended to aid the organization, if the act has a logical and reasonably foreseeable tendency to promote, sustain, or maintain the organization, even if only to a de minimis degree.

In other words, even though she was kidnapped, forced to witness her husband's killing, and coerced to do cleaning and cooking, her coerced work aided the cause of the guerrillas, making her actions material. I believe we can do better.

Attempted rape is not past persecution. Asylum rules provide that if the applicant has suffered past persecution, the person is presumed to have a well-founded fear of future persecution.[45] That makes sense of course. For our clients, that means that we offer evidence such as past beatings or imprisonment for political reasons to establish past persecution. Even credible death threats can constitute past persecution. The problem is that the same facts in the hands of different immigration judges may or may not be deemed to constitute past persecution. Physical violence, torture, unlawful detention, and even substantial economic harm are usually deemed persecution. But the infliction of mental, emotional, or psychological harm may not meet the standard depending on the judge. That leads to Chanpreet Kaur's case—another puzzling example of how different judges look at the same facts differently.

Chanpreet Kaur was from the state of Punjab, in India. As a result of her political activities, a group of men from the Indian National Congress Party, one of India's major political parties, accosted her while she was alone at her parents' store, dragged her into the public street, started ripping off her clothes, and attempted to gang-rape her.[46] As a result of this assault, she suffered scrapes and facial bruising that required medical attention, as well as experiencing emotional trauma. This was not an isolated incident. Just months before this attack, agents of the Congress Party threatened Kaur while she was walking on the street. And just months after the attack, when Kaur left Punjab for Cyprus, Congress Party agents threatened her by phone "that they wanted to kill her" and bring her "dead body back to India." Congress Party agents subsequently tracked down Kaur's father, asked him about her whereabouts, and beat him. The police later came to her parents' house, asked about her location, and beat both her father and mother when they told the police she was in the United States.

Incredibly, the BIA concluded that none of this was sufficient to constitute past persecution. The BIA reasoned that the attempted gang rape "did not rise to the level of persecution" because Kaur lacked evidence of "treatment for psychological harm" or other "ongoing issues" stemming from this assault. Fortunately, for Kaur, two judges on the federal circuit court of appeals agreed that attempted rape constitutes past persecution, noting that sexual assault is more than just a violation of bodily autonomy; its psychological effects are severe.[47] It's shocking that it took an appeal to prevail because the BIA ruled that attempted gang rape was not past persecution.

The expectation that the victim track down and bring perpetrators to the police. Stanley Afriyie, a citizen of Ghana, was persecuted by Muslims because he proselytized as a Baptist preacher in predominantly Muslim areas of Ghana.[48] On one occasion, Muslim villagers became hostile, chasing and attacking Afriyie and his fellow Baptist group members with sticks. Afriyie was beaten unconscious and hospitalized.

After recovering, Afriyie and his group ventured into a different Muslim village and began preaching. Muslim villagers warned him to stop. That evening, Afriyie and his group were attacked and fled. Afriyie asked the police for protection, but the police had only one gun for the entire station, and Afriyie was told that he would have to pay the police for protection. The police also told the victims to get the culprits on their own and bring them to the police station.

Within a month, three of Afriyie's group members were murdered. One victim's family reported the murder to the police, who stated that they had no evidence to solve the crime. Afriyie went into hiding. Visitors went to Afriyie's village and set afire his sister's house, where he had previously been staying. Afriyie's sister and nephew were killed in the blaze. The fire and deaths were reported to the police, but there was no resolution to the case. Afriyie fled Ghana and eventually made it to the United States, where he applied for asylum.

In order to win asylum based on persecution of nongovernmental actors, the applicant must show that the government is unable or unwilling to control the perpetrators. Even though the police station had only one gun and police were demanding money before they would act, and though Afriyie's sister and nephew were killed by arsonists, and that at least two murders had been reported to the police with no apparent progress in solving them, the BIA ruled that Afriyie had not met the burden of showing that the police were unable or unwilling to control the perpetrators. Fortunately, a federal court of appeals reversed the BIA's decision.

Blatant Racism

Let's face it: most of the problems with decision-making over asylum cases are tinged with racism. We witnessed the blatant racism against Haitians, discussed in chapter 1. But think also of factors that go into assessing credibility, such as inconsistencies in storytelling and "halting" mannerisms, that are affected by implicit bias against noncitizens from outside the US. The REAL ID Act requirements of corroboration and no presumption of credibility were enacted after years of asylum applications dominated by applicants from Latin America and

Haiti. Particular social group analysis has evolved in the context of refugees from Guatemala, El Salvador, Honduras, and Mexico. The refugee standards adopted in the 1980 Refugee Act came from 1951 and 1967 international agreements formed from a post–World War II era that did not contemplate the many types of refugees reaching the United States today (e.g., those fleeing gang, cartel, and domestic violence, much less climate migrants) and from other parts of the globe.

Donald Trump's efforts to close the US southern border even before the COVID-19 pandemic were blatantly racist. He tried to challenge agreements over the detention of children leading to families seeking asylum being detained indefinitely. He infamously separated children from their parents at the border. He instituted a misleadingly named "Migrant Protection Protocol," which required non-Mexican asylum seekers to remain in Mexico while their applications were pending. New regulations added a third-country transit bar, which made an applicant ineligible for asylum unless they first applied for asylum in any third country through which they traveled. And when the pandemic started, he barred all asylum seekers from entering under an esoteric federal health-law provision known as Title 42.

But Trump is hardly the only president whose administration discriminated against Central American asylum applicants.

The United States' reluctance to treat Central American migration as a mixed refugee flow rather than as illegal immigration was evident when Guatemala, El Salvador, and Nicaragua were each in the midst of civil turmoil in the 1980s. The repression and violence compelled thousands of migrants from those countries to seek refuge in the United States. Cold war politics affected the treatment that these refugees received here. After the left-leaning Sandinistas (led by Daniel Ortega) took control in Nicaragua, the United States supported rebels (known as the *contras*) who were trying to regain power.[49] The Reagan administration officials commonly referred to these rebels as *freedom fighters*.[50] Nicaraguans who fled their country during that period were given asylum at a higher rate than refugees from other Central American countries, and deportation was not enforced against Nicaraguans who were denied asylum or who simply wanted to remain in the United States.[51] On the other hand, the

United States supported the right-wing governments of Guatemala and El Salvador.[52] The rebels in those countries were labeled guerrillas who engaged in "terrorist" tactics.[53] Refugees fleeing the civil strife in Guatemala and El Salvador were quickly labeled "economic migrants" by the US and were generally denied asylum and deported.[54] While it's easy to attribute these discrepancies in treatment of refugees to geopolitics, there's no denying the systemic racism that has been embedded in US relations with those countries.[55]

The Reagan administration sought to discourage asylum seekers from Guatemala and El Salvador and routinely denied asylum except in the most extreme cases. Of the thousands of Guatemalans and Salvadorans who applied for asylum, only about 2 percent of their applications were approved due to the discriminatory practice.[56] That discrimination is highlighted in two federal court cases: *Orantes-Hernandez v. Smith* and *American Baptist Churches v. Thornburgh*.[57] In *Orantes-Hernandez*, the federal court found that the Salvadorans apprehended chose to forgo asylum and depart voluntarily because of the coercive practices and procedures employed by immigration and Border Patrol agents, with officers regularly misrepresenting the meaning of asylum. In *American Baptist Churches*, a different federal court unearthed discriminatory treatment of asylum seekers from El Salvador and Guatemala, resulting in denial rates of 97 percent and 99 percent, respectively. Simultaneously, unaccompanied minors were detained and held as bait to lure their parents into INS hands, resulting in the *Reno v. Flores* case and the Flores settlement agreement, discussed in chapter 2.

The asylum office was set up in response to the bias against Salvadoran and Guatemalan asylum claims exposed in the *American Baptist Churches* case. And certainly, the procedure is less adversarial: An asylum officer interviews the applicant. There is no government attorney appearing in opposition, and the officer can grant but not deny asylum. If the officer is not inclined to grant, then the case is referred to an immigration judge in deportation proceedings.

The problem is that the asylum office procedure is not available to the typical adult or family who arrives at the border seeking asylum. Those folks are placed in adversarial deportation immigration court proceedings. Even for those who do get to apply to the asylum office first, such as unaccompanied minors or asylum seekers who enter the country on tourist or student visas, the process can be very hostile and often last several hours. And as in immigration court hearings, there is no attorney provided for the applicant.

In May 2022, the Biden administration instituted a new procedure to allow all asylum seekers at the border to go through the asylum office first. The new procedure is intended to expedite asylum decisions. But without guaranteed legal representation for applicants, the program has not helped.

Changes in the approach to asylum must minimize the ability to exercise racial bias against groups of applicants.

Political Pressure

Political pressure led to Obama's expansion of detention, rocket dockets, and the criminal prosecution of adults for illegal entry at the border. Similar pressures resulted in Trump's multiple restrictions to deter migrants. While Joe Biden tried to end most of Trump's policies upon taking office, it took him more than a year to end Title 42, only to be stopped by lawsuits filed by Arizona, Louisiana, and Texas.

Ignoring the root causes of migration, "Republicans smell blood" when it comes to surges of migrants at the US southern border as a political issue.[58] They blamed Biden for the surge because of his more welcoming approach. Giving in to political pressures, Biden instituted a version of Obama's rocket dockets. His administration placed the most recent arrivals on an immigration court "Dedicated Docket" in an effort to streamline the yearslong asylum backlog. Officials vowed to not sacrifice fairness for speed, but judges were ordered to decide cases within three hundred days. It was clear from the beginning of this revised practice, however, that speeding up the process would hurt applicants' chances for success, in large part, of course, because there was no assurance they would get adequate legal help.

An analysis of the Los Angeles Immigration Court's Dedicated Dockets confirmed that the Biden administration failed to live up to its promises of fairness. The Los Angeles court is one of the busiest

146 BILL ONG HING

in the country.[59] Asylum applicants placed on the dedicated docket were granted asylum at a rate of less than 1 percent—a figure that's reminiscent of the Reagan era. Of 449 cases handled on the dedicated docket from mid-2021 to early 2022, 99.1 percent resulted in deportation orders. LA judges issued 72.4 percent of those orders in absentia, meaning the applicants did not show up. Half of those in absentia removal orders involved children, most of whom were under age seven.

More than 70 percent of the families on LA's dedicated docket were unrepresented, as opposed to approximately 33 percent of those on LA's non-accelerated docket. The fast turnaround makes it difficult for people to find lawyers, even in a city with many immigration legal-services programs. Court papers are confusing for many facing removal. One asylum seeker, William, and his six-year-old son were both unrepresented and ordered removed for failing to show up in court. They waited seven hours in the lobby of the court building on the day of their hearing. William mistakenly believed that his court notice had described the location for a mandatory check-in with ICE, which had provided him with the notice, rather than at a court hearing upstairs.

The Biden administration boasted that the dedicated dockets were rolled out in cities with an established pro bono network. The problem was that in Los Angeles, New York, San Francisco, and other cities, the organizations are at capacity. They take on all the cases they can, but that's not enough to meet the need.

CONCLUSION: TURN ASYLUM ON ITS HEAD AND PRESUME ELIGIBILITY

The US asylum system needs to be abolished. Because of restrictive legal analyses, political pressures, and racism, applicants who face a reasonable possibility of persecution are being barred. In its place, we need a system that guarantees the following perspective: The decision maker may not be certain the applicant will be persecuted, but certainty or even suspecting there's a good chance they will be persecuted isn't required. If the decision maker believes there is even a 10 percent chance persecution might occur, it is their duty to approve the application. Asylum should be granted, even when there is a 90 percent chance that the person will not be persecuted.

In our legal papers to the Supreme Court in the case of Luz Cardoza-Fonseca, Dana Marks, Susan Lydon, Kip Steinberg, and I urged the court to recognize that the legislative history of the Refugee Act of 1980 required increased "flexibility" in approaching asylum.[60] Importantly, in reaching its "10 percent chance" of persecution standard, the court relied on information that we provided from the UN High Commissioner on Refugees and from international law scholars. The High Commissioner has a handbook on refugees that adds important insight to the question of how much should be demanded of asylum applicants. Consider this passage:

> After the applicant has made a genuine effort to substantiate his story there may still be a lack of evidence for some of his statements. [It] is hardly possible for a refugee to "prove" every part of his case and, indeed, if this were a requirement the majority of refugees would not be recognized. It is therefore frequently necessary to *give the applicant the benefit of the doubt.*[61]

Given the risks of an erroneous decision in an asylum case, providing the applicant with the benefit of the doubt makes sense. After all, if you are going to make a mistake in an asylum case, you should prefer granting asylum to someone who is not going to be persecuted over denying asylum to someone who gets persecuted.

After the *Cardoza-Fonseca* decision, the BIA had to acknowledge the lower burden of proof for asylum. But it came up with its own interpretation: "[A]n applicant for asylum has established a well-founded fear if . . . a reasonable person in his circumstances would fear persecution."[62]

The BIA's "reasonable person" standard may have appeal, but it does not instruct immigration judges to give the benefit of the doubt to an applicant and falls well short of the 10 percent chance of persecution standard. I surmise that the BIA came up with the "reasonable person" language because, in its decision, the Supreme Court wrote that a "reasonable possibility of persecution" should be sufficient.[63] Again, words matter. The court tells us in *Cardoza-Fonseca* that a 10 percent chance of persecution constitutes a reasonable possibility of persecution. However, a reasonable person may not like the 10 percent odds of an occurrence, but there's still a reasonable possibility of the occurrence. That's why the reasonable-person standard doesn't make sense in the asylum context, given the Supreme Court's lesson that a 10 percent chance of persecution constitutes a reasonable possibility of persecution and is sufficient for asylum.

One way to come up with a better approach is by analogizing to the criminal law context. In a criminal case, the judge instructs the jury that they should only vote to convict the defendant if guilt has been established by the prosecutor "beyond a reasonable doubt." The idea is that if the jury thinks that the defendant probably committed the crime, but there's still a reasonable doubt that the person did it, then the juror should vote to acquit. There is good reason for that approach in the criminal law area where the person's liberty is at stake. We should err on the side of freedom rather than imprisonment.

In the asylum arena, I would make the same argument. We should err on the side of granting asylum. If we are going to make a mistake, we should grant asylum to someone who might not actually get persecuted, rather than deport someone who will get persecuted. That's what giving the "benefit of the doubt" means. That approach provides the right frame of mind to the 10-percent-chance-of-persecution standard.

Erring on the side of granting asylum means giving the benefit of the doubt across the board. This means that the benefit of the doubt should be given to applicants when it comes to the applicant's credibility—even when there are inconsistencies. It means giving the benefit of the doubt when the judge is not sure if a particular social group will be targeted or if it's not clear whether the authorities are unable or unwilling to protect that applicant. But I am skeptical that all immigration judges and federal courts will take that route without a substantive or procedural change to asylum adjudication by Congress. As I argue in chapter 6, a new court system needs to be institutionalized in a form free of political influence and with better tools. The new system would stop the detention of asylum applicants, provide applicants with free counsel and mental health services, and train decision makers on a humanitarian and trauma-informed approach to adjudication.

As part of the new asylum adjudication system, another policy modeled after criminal procedure should be included. In criminal law, the concept of "innocent until proven guilty" or "presumed innocent" is fundamental. Similarly, in the asylum arena, we should presume eligibility once the application is filed, and the applicant should be granted asylum, unless the government can prove beyond a reasonable doubt that the applicant will not be persecuted. The life-and-death stakes in asylum cases could not be higher and demand this presumption.

CHAPTER 6

DYSFUNCTIONAL IMMIGRATION COURTS

M ORE THAN A CENTURY AGO, the Supreme Court stated the
obvious: deportation not only deprives the person of liberty
but can result "in loss of both property and life, or of all that
makes life worth living."[1] Yet, as Dana Marks, the former president
of the National Immigration Judges Association, puts it, immigration judges are "doing death penalty cases in a traffic court setting."[2]
She ought to know. Dana was appointed to the immigration court
in 1987, not long after she and I co-counseled the Supreme Court's
precedent-setting asylum case, *INS v. Cardoza-Fonseca*. She retired
after serving as an immigration judge for thirty-five years.

Dana's comments raise two challenges for immigration judges:
the lack of resources and the lack of authority to do much. But Dana
and other immigration judges have complained about a more serious problem: the lack of judicial independence. In other words, their
decisions are subject to the political whims of whoever runs the Department of Justice, which is related to who sits in the White House.
Other immigration attorneys and I can attest to another problem with
immigration judges related to the political influence over the immigration court: some individuals appointed to the court lack a sense
of compassion and fairness. In fact some immigration judges are simply mean-spirited, running roughshod over those facing deportation
without legal representation. For all those reasons, the current immigration court system needs to be abolished and remade.

JEFF SESSIONS AND WILLIAM BARR:
DO THINGS OUR WAY OR FEEL FREE TO LEAVE

Removal proceedings are conducted by about five hundred immigration judges in sixty immigration courts across the country that are

part of the Department of Justice's Executive Office for Immigration Review (EOIR). A decision of an immigration judge can be appealed to the Board of Immigration Appeals (BIA), which is also part of the EOIR. The problem is that the EOIR is housed in the Department of Justice, which is run by the attorney general of the United States and is where political influence comes into play.

Immigration judges and members of the BIA are appointed by the attorney general, who is selected by the president. The attorney general can also remove judges or remove cases from their dockets, which does not happen in other courts. The BIA writes precedent decisions that guide immigration judges on how to approach different legal cases like asylum, whether certain crimes are deportable offenses, and whether certain types of hardship suffered by noncitizens or their families are enough to earn cancellation of removal. But as the boss of the BIA and the immigration judges, the attorney general can also override BIA decisions. That kind of power was made clear under the Trump administration, when his attorneys general—first Jeff Sessions, then William Barr—eroded immigration judges' authority time and again.

During the Sessions-Barr reign over the Department of Justice, they directed immigration judges to deny entire categories of asylum cases related to domestic violence and families, ordered judges to strictly limit or deny continuances to unrepresented noncitizens who were trying to find lawyers, and demanded that each judge complete a minimum of seven hundred cases per year, no matter how complex or difficult the cases. These actions simply are not indicators of a fair and impartial court system.

Faced with a choice between following orders and delivering impartial justice, immigration judges quit in 2019 at double the rate of previous years. Immigration judge Lisa Dornell, who served in that position for twenty-four years, left in April 2019, observing that immigration courts had become "a toxic environment."[3] Judge Ilyce Shugall quit around the same time, saying that the administration "was doing everything in its power to completely destroy the immigration court system, the board of immigration appeal and the immigration system in general."[4]

HEY, KID: BEHAVE OR I'LL SIC MY DOG ON YOU

Besides imposing their own political, legal, and social views on sitting immigration judges, the corollary problem is that some of the individuals picked by attorneys general to be immigration judges lack fundamental humanity, and it's difficult to understand how their temperament and background were deemed suitable for the complex nature of the job.

One Trump-era appointee was Nicholas Ford. He was a criminal court judge in Cook County, Illinois, before being named to the immigration court bench in 2019 by Attorney General William Barr. During his time as a criminal court judge, he was criticized for jailing a pregnant woman without bail for a nonviolent crime and for ignoring a complaint by a defendant who had been tortured into a false confession by two police officers.[5] One of Ford's cases was reversed by an appeals court for challenging a psychiatrist's testimony in a manner that demonstrated that Ford was biased and acted like a prosecutor rather than as a neutral judge. In fact, Ford had an inordinate number of rulings overturned by appellate courts. He retired as a criminal court judge in Illinois, but Barr rewarded Ford by appointing him to the immigration court in San Francisco. It didn't take long for Ford's partiality to emerge once again. In November 2020, a coalition led by the San Francisco Bay Area chapter of the National Lawyers Guild called for his removal, alleging that Ford acted in an "aggressive, unprofessional and demeaning" manner toward immigrants. Attorneys appearing before Ford complained that he was biased and hostile:

> Judge Ford has demonstrated that he is unfit to hear immigration cases due to discriminatory statements and behavior, particularly on the grounds of race, class, gender, and sexuality. We have become aware of his bigoted and unconstitutional actions through our own observations and reports of his treating individuals with immigration hearings, practitioners, and witnesses in an unprofessional and hostile manner as well as engaging in unlawful manifestations of bias or prejudicial conduct.

Judge Ford has a sordid history of complicity in racially motivated torture schemes (1), disrespect of transgender respondents
(2), and overall disregard for the actual experiences of immigrant
communities (3). Given this track record, we believe Judge Ford is
unable to fairly adjudicate immigration cases, especially those involving torture, persecution, and abuse and cases of Africans and
Afro-descendants.[6]

Exposed, Ford abruptly quit the immigration court.[7]

Then there's V. Stuart Couch, who was elevated to the BIA during
the Trump administration. Initially appointed to the immigration court
by Attorney General Eric Holder during the Obama era, Judge Couch
developed an asylum denial rate of 94.1 percent while serving as an
immigration judge.[8] Infamously, three years before being elevated to
the BIA, he threatened to sic a dog on a fidgety two-year-old in his
immigration courtroom. According to a paralegal who was present:

> The child was calm, but was making some small babbling noises
> while the judge was doing the roll call. . . . The judge showed signs
> of frustration and proceeded to use an extremely strong tone of
> voice with (the boy) while forcefully pointing his finger at the child.
> On multiple occasions, he demanded that the child sit down and
> be quiet. When the babbling continued, the judge continued with
> an even higher level of forceful language and yelled: "I have a very
> big dog in my office, and if you don't be quiet, he will come out
> and bite you!"
>
> The child continued to squirm a bit in the chair, and the judge
> proceeded to yell "(the child's name)! Want me to go get the dog?
> If you don't stop talking, I will bring the dog out. Do you want
> him to bite you?" The judge was yelling at the child directly. The
> judge would continue questioning the child until he would answer
> the judge's questions with a "si" or a "no."[9]

According to the complaint, Judge Couch, a Marine Corps veteran, threatened other children in previous hearings as well.

And there's Jack H. Weil, an assistant chief immigration judge, who, in 2016, helped coordinate training for other immigration judges and court staff. The ACLU sued the Department of Justice for not providing attorneys to children in deportation proceedings, a case the ACLU ultimately lost. Speaking as an expert witness on behalf of the government in a deposition, Weil asserted that children did not need attorneys because, he said, migrant children as young as three are capable of representing themselves in deportation hearings. Incredibly, Weil insisted:

> I've taught immigration law literally to 3-year-olds and 4-year-olds. It takes a lot of time. It takes a lot of patience. They get it. It's not the most efficient, but it can be done. I have trained 3-year-olds and 4-year-olds in immigration law.[10]

The belligerent disposition and poor judgment of these individuals demonstrate a serious problem with the current selection system for immigration judges.

ZOE LOFGREN'S ANSWER WON'T WORK FOR JUANA AND YELENA

For years, Dana Marks and others have argued that Congress should make the immigration courts independent of the executive branch. In response, in February 2022, Rep. Zoe Lofgren (D-Calif.), then chair of the House Subcommittee on Immigration and Citizenship, unveiled sweeping legislation to overhaul the immigration court system by moving the courts outside the executive branch and making them an independent entity. Her ideas go a long way toward addressing the independence issue, but the issue of how to address immigration judge incompetence is not being examined.

Under Lofgren's bill, immigration courts would be restructured as an independent legislative court to review agency decisions, such as the US Tax Court, the US Court of Appeals for Veterans Claims, and the US Bankruptcy Courts.[11] In these courts, judges operate under a set of laws and serve for specified years in office. For example, tax court judges are appointed for fifteen-year terms by the president.

Politics would still play a role, because under Lofgren's system, presidents would be able to appoint judges to the immigration appeals court for renewable fifteen-year terms, subject to Senate confirmation. The twenty-one-judge appellate court would manage the hires of lower court judges. Lofgren's goal is to prevent presidents and attorneys general from using the courts to shape their immigration policies on a day-to-day basis. Once appointed, the executive branch could not overrule a decision of the new immigration courts as they can today. In short, it would be an important step in bringing legitimacy and fairness to immigration decisions.

The bill would allow the immigration court system to establish its own budget and empower its judges to control their own cases and compel agency action that is withheld or delayed. Lofgren's bill would also allow immigration judges to impose civil fines for contempt of court and allow the court system to appoint temporary judges and establish temporary court facilities.

However, the reforms need to go further and, for example, provide judges with flexible approaches to achieve justice, as well as to apply humanitarian principles. In chapter 3, I discuss approaches that should be available for immigration judges to apply principles of proportionality in cases involving the deportation of lawful permanent residents who have committed crimes. But think also about Antonio Sanchez's case, discussed in chapter 4, in which prosecutorial discretion was reviewed and the ability for agency officials to do the right thing was exercised, albeit, inconsistently. Empowering immigration judges with the ability to terminate proceedings where deportation would simply be unjust should also be part of the package. I faced the need for that kind of judicial authority in the 1970s, when Juana Zoraida Lopez-Telles walked into my legal aid office with an order to show up for a deportation hearing.

Juana and Imelda

Juana and her daughter, Imelda, were from Managua, Nicaragua, where they were living when the area suffered a devastating earthquake shortly before Christmas in 1972. Thousands were killed, another twenty thousand were injured, and three hundred thousand lost their homes. Juana was among those whose home was destroyed, and many of her relatives were killed. Shortly, after the earthquake, US embassy officials, out of an act of kindness, issued visitors' visas to many survivors—including Juana and Imelda.

Soon after arriving in San Francisco in early 1973, Juana found domestic work through friends. A couple of years later, she walked into the federal immigration building, went to the public information counter, and asked whether there was a way she could become a lawful permanent resident. Unfortunately, lacking close relatives or a special job skill, Juana was told no, and she was sent upstairs to the investigations unit where she was charged with overstaying her tourist visa. She was instructed to show up at a deportation hearing in a few weeks.

I was able to delay Juana's hearing for a few months in order to try to work on a strategy. I sought deferred action (the version of prosecutorial discretion available at the time) from the local immigration agency, but district director David Ilchert told me that if he granted my request, "then every victim of an earthquake who made it to the United States would qualify." Ilchert's response gave me a different idea on how to handle Juana's case.

At the time, an immigration law refugee-like provision for "conditional entries" included "persons uprooted by catastrophic natural calamity as defined by the President who are unable to return to their usual place of abode."[12] When the December 1972 earthquake struck Nicaragua, Richard Nixon was the president, but by the time Juana was placed in deportation proceedings, Nixon had resigned in disgrace. I wrote to him at his home in San Clemente, California, asking if he was aware of his authority to define the earthquake as a "catastrophic natural calamity" and, if so, whether he would have considered taking that action. I was hoping the former president would respond with something that I could take back to Ilchert or submit in court for Juana. But Nixon never responded.

I then contacted several members of Congress to see if they were willing to help. I was hoping that someone would introduce what's known as a "private bill" on behalf of Juana and Imelda to grant them lawful status.[13] Disappointingly, no one was willing to help.

By the time the deportation hearing took place, there was little left to do but ask the immigration judge to grant Juana permission to leave voluntarily rather than be deported. But as I prepared for the hearing, a local San Francisco municipal court judge was making headlines for using her discretionary authority to dismiss criminal charges against women arrested for prostitution. After becoming a judge in 1974, Ollie Marie-Victoire dismissed more than a hundred prostitution charges against women as a matter of equity because the district attorney was not prosecuting the men who solicited them.[14] It seemed to me that if Judge Marie-Victoire had the inherent authority to dismiss cases as a matter of fairness, then why couldn't an immigration judge do the same?

With little else to defend her at her deportation hearing, Juana testified about the devastating earthquake, the deaths of relatives, the loss of her home, the turmoil she witnessed, and the sympathetic gesture of the US embassy official who granted her visitor's visa. I then asked the immigration judge to dismiss the deportation case as a humanitarian act, arguing that he had the inherent authority to do so as a judge. He declined, disagreeing that he had the authority. I appealed the case and ended up before the federal Ninth Circuit Court of Appeals, which agreed with the judge:

> Nowhere [in the law] is there any mention of the power of an immigration judge to award the type of discretionary relief that was sought here. . . . There is no hint in [any decisions] that the immigration judge can terminate proceedings on equitable or humanitarian grounds alone. Rather, these decisions plainly hold that the immigration judge is without discretionary authority to terminate deportation proceedings so long as enforcement officials of the INS choose to initiate proceedings against a deportable alien and prosecute those proceedings to a conclusion. The immigration judge is not empowered to review the wisdom of the INS in instituting the proceedings. His powers are sharply limited, usually

to the determination of whether grounds for deportation charges are sustained by the requisite evidence or whether there has been abuse by the INS in its exercise of particular discretionary powers.[15]

It was a sad day for Juana and Imelda, who left a few weeks later and returned to Managua. Juana sent me a gift that I still have. She thanked and reassured me that friends had taken them in and that she and Imelda were doing okay.

I still think that Juana and Imelda should have been allowed to stay in the US because of the circumstances. But given the limitations that we confronted, until a special immigration category is established, the only solution for cases like Juana's is to give authority to immigration judges to do the right thing. That authority should be part of the overhaul proposed by Representative Lofgren. Until then, a regulatory change can be made by the attorney general. The regulations once permitted the district director and other officials to terminate deportation proceedings as "improvidently begun."[16] Immigration judges should be granted that type of power.

In fact, immigration judges need many more tools at their disposal to achieve more just results.

Yelena Gorev

You would think that given what's at stake in deportation hearings, for example, life and death in asylum cases or the possibility of family separation in many other cases, that immigration judges would have a variety of tools at their disposal to achieve justice. You would be wrong, because, as in Juana's case, the system is not set up to render an objectively just outcome. The system is limited by whatever authority the immigration laws provide to the immigration judge. In contrast, judges in areas such as criminal law, family law, and juvenile law have a range of tools: resources for mental health evaluations, counseling services, diversion options, and probation departments. Another particularly strong tool that judges in every other system have and generally use is the ability to convince the parties to negotiate a settlement agreement that makes sense to both sides.

Additional tools or at least more flexibility for the immigration court could have made a world of difference in the case of Yelena Gorev (not her real name). She was an abused, adopted teen mother who had abused her own child, and she was blocked from the opportunity to obtain rehabilitation services and be reunited with her child because she was deported.[17]

Yelena was born in Russia in 1978 with multiple health problems, including heart defects. Both her hands and feet were small and partially deformed. Her parents abandoned Yelena immediately after birth. She spent the first several years of her life in hospitals, rehabilitation facilities, and a boarding school for disabled children without contact with her parents. She underwent several surgical procedures to correct her birth defects, but the abnormalities of her hands and feet were never fully corrected.

When she was about seven years old, after she was released from the hospital, Yelena's maternal grandmother took responsibility for her. At the time, Yelena was unaware that she had a family. A year or so later, her father began to visit, and about three years later, he decided to bring Yelena back into the family. By all indications, her father brought Yelena home to live with family because that made the family eligible for a better apartment in Russia.

The atmosphere in the home was hostile, chaotic, and filled with conflict. Yelena's mother was opposed to her return and was openly hostile and critical of Yelena. Yelena was constantly beaten by both parents, who continually told her that she was "inadequate and worthless." The psychological evaluation reported a "history of neglect, physical and verbal abuse as a child and one attempted molestation between the age of 8 and 10."

The tense home life led to the disintegration of the family. Her parents divorced when Yelena was twelve. Her father departed, and Yelena was left with her mother, who did not want her. So when Yelena turned fourteen, her grandmother, who had legal custody, signed papers giving Yelena up for adoption. Howard and Mary Carter (pseudonyms), who were sixty-eight and sixty-three years old, respectively, at the time, adopted Yelena and arranged for her to live with them in Sonoma, California, in 1993.

Yelena had difficulty adapting to her new family. Her dislike of being touched or held persisted into her late teens. She had difficulty addressing her new parents as "mom" and "dad."

Concerned with the conflict, Howard and Mary had Yelena evaluated by a psychologist. The psychologist prescribed medication, and they threatened to send Yelena back to Russia if she did not take the medication. Yelena did not appreciate the psychological treatment and argued with Howard and Mary; they often called the police after the altercations. When the police arrived after one call, in 1999, Yelena was so upset that she kicked Howard in the leg in front of the police officer. Yelena was taken into custody, but charges were later dismissed. After another call to the police, in 2000, Yelena threatened to kill herself, and she was held in a mental health facility for three days.

Yelena eventually moved out of the Carter home. Howard passed away, and she lost contact with Mary. Yelena rented a room from a young man with whom she later became emotionally involved. She soon noticed that he mistreated his six-year-old son. On one occasion, the child was complaining about stomach pain, and the father refused to do anything. Yelena called an ambulance. In 2002, after an argument, Yelena kicked the landlord. He called the police, and she was arrested and pled guilty to a misdemeanor battery.

Yelena held a variety of jobs in Sonoma County and attended junior college. She became pregnant and gave birth to a baby boy, Ricky, on October 17, 2005. Although Yelena tried to get the father involved, he never took part in Ricky's life. She had no one to rely on for financial help or other assistance in the child's upbringing. A probation officer later noted that Yelena lacked "a support system for parenting and when she needs a break, she has been unable to secure a reliable babysitter." When her son was a year and a half old, Yelena got a job at a wireless phone company in an attempt to get off welfare assistance.

On June 26, 2007, when Ricky was just under two years old, he spilled some water and grabbed a roll of paper towels to clean up the mess. Ricky scattered paper towels all over the floor. Yelena grabbed Ricky, took him to the bedroom, threw him on the bed, and slapped him on his head or legs, leaving a bruise on his face.

Yelena then took Ricky to a daycare center, explaining to an employee that she had become frustrated with him at home and had struck him with her bare hands. She left the child at the daycare and went to her job. Daycare staff called authorities.

As a result of this incident, Ricky was removed from Yelena's care, and she was charged with child abuse. Yelena pled guilty and was sentenced to 120 days in jail and four years' probation. Ultimately, she was only required to serve about a month in jail. A probation officer who interviewed Yelena in custody observed that she was very remorseful and forthcoming throughout the interview, noting that she "has struggled with shame and guilt while in custody, and has spent much time in introspection." When she was first taken into custody, Yelena was very upset and she cried a lot. The mental health staff in the county jail determined that she was likely suffering from depression, perhaps due to a chemical imbalance in her brain, and she was prescribed Zoloft.

While she was in jail, Yelena was placed on a "no mix" status because ICE was notified of her conviction. She was unable to participate in counseling and other resources offered to other inmates. In spite of those restrictions, she participated in anger-management correspondence courses and realized that she needed to take responsibility for her actions. She was committed to doing whatever was required to reunite with her son. At a court appearance, she testified, "My baby is first in my life now. I know I need to get help myself in order to take care of my baby." The child protective services investigator observed that the child was "healthy, had suffered no long-term injury, and appeared to be slightly advanced for his chronological age."

Ricky was placed into foster care and the juvenile court took over. In early October 2007, the court ordered that family reunification services be offered to Yelena. As in most cases—even those involving child abuse—the court's goal was to reunify Yelena with her child. Yelena was ordered to participate in a number of different services, including counseling and domestic violence programs. The problem was that, by then, Yelena had been turned over to ICE detention, unable to comply with the juvenile court's order. ICE refused her request to take her to the family reunification services offered by the juvenile court.

If Yelena had been a US citizen, after her month in jail, she would have been free to take part in the reunification services offered by the county. However, she was a lawful permanent resident alien who now had committed a deportable offense. So ICE officials kept her in custody pending removal proceedings.

Yelena was frustrated. She wanted to abide by the juvenile court's mandate because she wanted to resolve her personal problems and regain custody of her son. If she had been able to comply with re-unification services, the posture of the deportation case would have been far different.

Before her hearing, Yelena wrote to the immigration judge:

> I love my baby very much. . . . Because of my own stupidity, I turned my baby's world upside down instead of following through with my goal to give him a life I was deprived of. I recognize that I've been on the path of self-destruction for too long. Now I'm ready to get off that path and I'm determined to take the necessary steps toward my recovery, so that I am then able to look after my baby's well-being.[18]

During the hearing, the immigration judge heard evidence of Yele-na's background as a child, her interactions with the criminal justice system, and statements from psychologists and the probation depart-ment. Unlike the cases of Lundy Khoy and Kim Ho Ma, discussed in chapter 3, her conviction was not classified as an aggravated felony. So Yelena could apply for cancellation of removal. The judge's task was to determine whether Yelena deserved a second chance and, re-latedly, whether she was likely to recidivate.

And at the end of the hearing, Yelena pleaded with the judge, who permitted her to read this statement to the court:

> My son is my only family. Having him, I feel truly blessed for the first time in my life. He is a big, beautiful, healthy baby with a good-natured disposition. I am devastated to have inflicted so much pain on my own son. I thought I could take on parenting all by myself, and I made a very bad choice not to accept help with it.

I was wrong. There is nothing I want more than to make it up to him. . . . I want to do whatever it takes to become the best parent I can be to my son. I know it's not going to be easy for me, but I'm up for the challenge. . . . My parents turned their backs on theirs. I want to learn to embrace mine.[19]

However, the judge felt that Yelena's past behavior was too much to overcome.

No one could really predict whether Yelena could be rehabilitated at this point, but the judge felt that he had to make a decision at this point. The evidence was in. The record was closed. He felt that he either had to take a chance and grant Yelena relief and let her stay in the United States, or order her deported. He weighed the evidence of her harsh childhood, abusive relationships, efforts at recovery, and psychological challenges against her history of violence against her child, her stepfather, and her ex-boyfriend. He concluded that "the negative factors far outweigh the positive [and Yelena had] not shown that it is in the best interests of the community that she remain in the United States."[20]

A central part of the immigration judge's decision was this conclusion: "The difficulty is that no person can eliminate situations of stress from their lives, and this pattern of behavior gives this court grave concern that [Yelena] may act in a violent or dangerous way in the future. . . . [T]here is a real concern that she is a danger to others." The judge essentially proclaimed that because of her bad behavior in the past, Yelena had little chance of ever changing her behavior. He made no mention of Yelena's health condition, or of the possibility that appropriate medication could make a difference, or of her expression of willingness to reform.

What's most troubling about the judge's decision is that his deportation order functionally became a family law decision to sever the parent-child relationship as well. The denial of Yelena's cancellation application prevented her from following the reunification conditions of the state court, thereby making termination of the relationship a fait accompli. The sad irony is that had we been able to hit a pause button on the removal proceedings and released Yelena to follow the reunification plan (parenting classes, anger management, mental health medication), and if she had been able to regain custody of her son or at least make clear progress in her parenting skills, the outcome of the deportation case might have been different once the hearing resumed. The judge's decision blocked these possibilities, as he simultaneously acted as a family law judge without using family law tools.

Unlike the immigration judge, the state superior court judge was acting in one of her areas of expertise in conjunction with the probation department in establishing a reunification plan. In making their determination, the probation officer and state court judge made their choices, taking into account Yelena's criminal history and concluding that offering reunification services was appropriate. This is important because terminating parental rights is a grave matter, and the state's main concern is the best interest of the child. Significantly, reunification services are not to be provided if parents are suffering from a mental disability that renders them incapable of utilizing those services. But here, the immigration judge's action overrode the expertise of the state court judge, instead making his own decision—without the benefit of experience or special expertise—to determine that it was in the best interests of Yelena's child to be taken from Yelena permanently.

No one can know for sure what would have occurred if Yelena had been granted relief in her removal hearing. However, I have discussed the facts and circumstances of her case with several family law experts. They all agreed that in child abuse cases like this, the prospects for rehabilitation and transformation are very good, especially when mental health is a factor that can be controlled through medication. They tell me with great confidence that Yelena could have reformed and regained custody of her son within two years had she not been removed.

COMPARING TWO OTHER DETENTION CASES

I was teaching at the University of California, Davis, when I learned about Yelena's case. The immigration clinic I directed at UC Davis was not able to accept her case because our caseload was maxed out. Certainly, no one can say for sure that the outcome would have been different if Yelena had different representation. And while no two cases are precisely the same, and outcomes can vary irrespective of the amount of time spent on case preparation, two other detention cases that the clinic handled provide some evidence that representation does matter.

Fento's Case

The Mendesha family was from Ethiopia.[21] All of the Mendesha family children had been orphaned due to the Ethiopian government's persecution of their family. During the war, all ten children had been separated and fled in different directions. Two children, Mina and Gitau, lived for years in a refugee camp in Kenya without family. After years of searching, the children found their older brother and sister in Oakland, California. That brother, Fento, raised the children like he was their father once they were reunited in the United States. The children eventually were granted political asylum.

Fento went on to college at UC Davis with a full scholarship. He was one of the first Black students from his high school to receive such an honor and received awards for his academic excellence. Unfortunately, in his last year at UC Davis, Fento began to develop a serious mental illness and never graduated. He began to self-medicate while in school and had minor contacts with the criminal justice system due to his drug use. As a result, ICE arrested Fento and sent him to a detention facility in Eloy, Arizona, where he faced deportation.

In his eight months in Arizona, Fento received no mental health treatment and had completely decompensated. The UC Davis immigration clinic agreed to take his case. A student flew to Arizona and spoke to the medical staff who confirmed that Fento was not receiving any treatment, but the medical staff refused to release the files to the clinic.

A second student then drafted a request to move the case from Eloy to San Francisco so Fento could have family visits and the immigration clinic could monitor his treatment more closely. The immigration judge denied the request. The judge wanted solid proof that Fento was not receiving any treatment at all in Eloy and that

California's detention system would provide better treatment. Despite repeated requests for the medical files, the Eloy prison would not budge. A third student prepared a Freedom of Information Act request for the records, but the request was ignored. Then she filed a request for Fento's medical records under the Health Insurance Portability and Accountability Act (HIPAA) that was granted. Finally, solid evidence was unearthed that Fento had never received any treatment in Eloy; in fact, he had never even spoken to a psychiatrist throughout his stay, despite repeated requests for treatment. The immigration judge finally granted the request to move the case to San Francisco.

Fento was transferred to California and detained in the Santa Clara County Jail. Law students then coordinated with the county mental health staff to ensure a proper treatment plan.

At that point, the immigration clinic faced the next major legal issue: how could an individual deemed mentally incompetent be adequately represented in immigration proceedings when he does not have sufficient ability to consult with his lawyer with a reasonable degree of rational understanding? The students consulted with the Mental Health Advocacy Institute in Los Angeles, where an attorney was working on challenges that face mentally ill ICE detainees. The attorney helped write a motion for the appointment of a guardian ad litem on behalf of Fento. The term "guardian ad litem" describes a guardian appointed by a court to represent a child or an adult who is not mentally competent for legal proceedings. Though guardian ad litems are uncharted territory for most immigration courts, the immigration judge granted the motion, and Fento's sister was appointed.

The students secured five expert witnesses in the case. One provided expert testimony on Fento's mental illness. Two doctors in Ethiopia were found who work at the only psychiatric hospital in all of that country and who described psychiatric treatment conditions there. An Australian doctor, who had extensively studied the Ethiopian mental health care system, provided testimony regarding its deficiencies and the problems Fento would confront if he were deported back to Ethiopia.

The clinic students authored a sixty-page trial brief on asylum law, the effects of persecution on the children, and whether Fento merited a favorable grant of cancellation of removal, the relief that was also sought in Yelena's case. One student prepared Fento's sisters' testimony and researched issues of eligibility. A second student prepared the testimony of Fento and that of three expert witnesses. A third student prepared the testimony of the guardian ad litem and a volunteer psychologist. The same student was also prepared to state Fento's claim to severe past persecution.

A week prior to the hearing, Fento suffered adverse effects from the medication and had serious seizures due to a sodium imbalance in his brain. A clinic student closely monitored his treatment, visiting him in the hospital and speaking with the medical staff regarding his past psychiatric history. For most prisoners or detainees, medical history is not provided to the new medical staff each time the prisoner is transferred. The student knew the hearing was fast approaching and wanted Fento to heal so he would be physically able to attend his hearing.

At the final hearing, Fento's family and the immigration clinic team were there to support him. One student conducted the direct examination of the sister who had been appointed guardian. The sister provided lengthy, powerful and emotional testimony regarding her brother's condition, the family's dramatic history of exile and persecution, and the likely hardship to Fento and their family if he were deported.

After the guardian's testimony, the government trial attorney determined that he did not need to hear more evidence, essentially conceding Fento's claim for relief. The immigration judge granted the cancellation of Fento's removal.

JC's Case

JC, a native and citizen of Mexico, entered the United States when he was nineteen years old in order to be with his family. He became a lawful permanent resident, and for the first several years, JC helped support his family by working to earn money. He also assisted his family by acting as an interpreter and taking on family responsibilities, such as interacting with teachers and parent groups at his younger siblings' schools.

When he was twenty-five, JC was accepted as a student at a seminary in another state. For the first year, he worked hard and received good grades. In his second year, he began having emotional, behavioral, and functional difficulties. A priest at the seminary took him to a hospital emergency room, where doctors diagnosed him with schizophrenia. The seminary sent JC home, telling his family that he was ill but not disclosing his diagnosis. JC's condition deteriorated, and six months later, the county's mental health department diagnosed him with psychotic disorder and approved him for treatment. He saw a psychologist once, but unfortunately, the county where he resided was having budget and staffing problems, and JC's case was lost in the backlog of mental health cases.

Three months later, JC wandered away from home while in a psychotic state and lost contact with reality. He thought that a woman was telling him that he owned some property and a house nearby, so he went to the house, opened the screen door, and jiggled the knob of the front door. The residents told him to go away and he went to the road, but then returned to the property and started to pick walnuts from their tree to eat. The residents called the police, and JC was charged with first-degree burglary. JC was jailed, but due to court continuances and disagreements about his clinical condition, he spent six months in jail before he was found incompetent to stand trial and sent to a penal psychiatric facility. There, for the first time, JC received medication for his schizophrenia. It took a year for JC to recover enough to be found competent to stand trial.

JC was appointed a public defender. When reviewing JC's records, the public defender carelessly failed to notice that he was reviewing a different person's criminal record sheet. The other person—who had a different name—had a number of serious prior convictions. The public defender then recommended that JC plead no contest to the burglary charge with a sentence of 365 days. The public defender was not aware that, under federal immigration law, a conviction with a sentence of 365 days is considered an aggravated felony, automatically making the defendant deportable, as discussed in the cases of Lundy Khoy and Kim Ho Ma in chapter 3. Since JC had already spent nearly two years in custody, he had credit for serving far more than

365 days' time (including credit for good behavior), and the judge finally released him with three years' probation.

Of course, JC's troubles were far from over. Four days after his release, ICE detained him and started removal proceedings. At that point, his family contacted the UC Davis immigration clinic. Law students reviewed the records and discovered that JC had grounds to withdraw his criminal plea and negotiate a fairer plea bargain; they helped JC file a motion to do so.

JC was being held in a county jail under contract with ICE, as the challenge to his conviction proceeded. Every time he appeared in court, he had to be transferred from the custody of one system to another and then back again. At the time, JC's mental health remained quite fragile. Each time he was transferred, his medical records were supposed to go with him. Each time he returned to a facility, the transferred records were supposed to be used to guide his treatment until his other records could be obtained. Unfortunately, JC's records were frequently not transferred, were sent at a later time, or were otherwise misplaced. Every time this happened, JC missed a few days of his medication. After several months in detention, JC was moved, without notice to anyone, to a detention facility several hundred miles away from his family and his legal team. At this new facility, JC received no medication for weeks. When his family finally located him and the law students were able to visit, he was catatonic and completely unable to communicate or function. Despite persistent efforts of the law students, JC was not immediately treated or returned to his original detention center, and he ended up spending thirteen days on suicide watch.

While this was taking place, ICE also began refusing to transport JC to state court to contest the conviction upon which his immigration detention was based. This happened at least five times. By the time the clinic was able to get a court order for JC to be released on bond, JC had spent an additional year in jail as an immigration detainee. During his detention, attorneys and law students spent well over four hundred hours on his case, attempting to get JC medical treatment, transportation to court, and the release on bond to which he was entitled in the first place.

The immigration clinic was ultimately able to convince the state court to withdraw JC's plea and allow him to reach a plea deal that did not jeopardize his immigration status. With the aggravated felony conviction removed, the deportation case was terminated.

Despite the disastrous mistakes and misunderstandings in JC's criminal case, he was at least provided with certain protections while in criminal custody that he did not have while in immigration detention. JC had a public defender (albeit of questionable competence) provided at all stages of his criminal proceedings. He was also provided with a translator at every criminal hearing. His medical condition was assessed by a psychiatrist before his criminal hearing, and a hearing was held to decide whether or not he was competent to stand trial. When found to be mentally incompetent, he was not expected to proceed to trial. He received continuous medical care, even after he left the psychiatric facility, which enabled him to maintain daily functioning and remain competent enough to understand and participate in his own legal proceedings. These protections ensured that JC received meaningful due process of law in the criminal justice system.

In marked contrast, the time that JC spent in the immigration system unnecessarily compromised his right to due process. Although JC's schizophrenia was well documented, he was refused medication to the point that he became acutely suicidal. JC was not informed that he was eligible for release on bond. He was transferred between facilities a number of times, and most transfers resulted in a break in his medication regime. At one point JC was suddenly transferred to a facility hundreds of miles away from his family and legal team, and he could only access them with great difficulty. Immigration authorities refused to transfer JC to criminal court so he could participate in his hearings there—hearings in which he was contesting the very conviction that was the basis for his immigration detention. JC was indefinitely detained until the immigration clinic obtained a writ of habeas corpus for him.

Further, JC was not guaranteed an attorney at any point during his immigration proceedings. In fact, even though noncitizens have a right to legal representation, the noncitizen must pay for their attorney, find a pro bono attorney, or represent themselves.

If JC had not had representation, the immigration judge would have had the heavy burden of having to decide at the beginning of the hearing, on the spot, whether or not JC was mentally competent. If the immigration judge suspected mental incompetence, he could have referred JC to a list of nonprofit organizations that provide free or low-cost representation. However, this does not mean that an attorney from one of these organizations would have been available. Sometimes immigration judges will reschedule a hearing over and over, in the hope that the noncitizen will get help but also consequently prolonging their detention. That is essentially what happened in Yelena's case, until the judge convinced a private attorney who was in court for a different matter to take her case pro bono.

What Does This Tell Us About Yelena's Case?

Yelena's case introduced us to the options and tools available to juvenile and family law courts. In criminal courts, probation departments often work with defendants on taking parenting classes, attending substance abuse support groups, and seeing therapists. Over the years, the criminal justice system has come to include drug courts, mental health courts, community service options, and diversion programs. Why have these options evolved? Because criminal and juvenile courts realize that incarceration is not the answer for every defendant. They understand that, in certain cases, a different option is worth trying for the sake of the defendant as well as the community.

Like criminal courts, immigration courts also need more tools. The problem with the immigration court system is that the immigration judge essentially only has two options for a respondent: deportation or a grant of the full right to stay lawfully. Thus, if an immigration judge has some doubt about the respondent's rehabilitation or is not inclined to give the respondent the benefit of that doubt, the easy choice for a court may be deportation. Allowing a "criminal" alien to remain in the United States involves a risk of recidivism that an immigration judge may not want to take. If relief is granted, the immigration judge loses immediate control or influence over the life of the noncitizen. In contrast, drug courts, mental health courts, diversion programs, and community courts are constructed in a manner that involves regular reporting to probation departments, community partners, or directly to the court. Ironically, in Yelena's case, if relief had been granted, the immigration judge actually had a surrogate who would have taken control of Yelena: the Superior Court of Sonoma County, which had a family reunification and behavior monitoring plan ready for her.

What the experiences of Yelena, JC, and Fento teach us is that immigration judges need special options, at least when a respondent is suffering from mental illness. Current procedures provide the judge with no professional assistance in determining the nature and extent of the mental illness, a process for appointing guardians ad litem, in providing for the appointment of counsel to represent respondents, and in establishing the discretion to release the person from detention and/or to order appropriate medical care for the respondent. When the mental illness is directly related to the ground of removal, as in Yelena's case, the immigration judge needs the discretion to cancel the proceedings—with or without prejudice—or to hold the matter in abeyance while the noncitizen is able to access appropriate care. Currently, only detained noncitizens with severe mental disabilities and who cannot understand their deportation hearings may be provided an attorney at government expense, but no other tools or avenues for counseling, care, or treatment are provided.

While I strongly disagree with the judge's reasoning in Yelena's case, his position had objective support, and some could agree that his decision was reasonable. However, I would have taken a different approach. I have a strong belief in the ability of criminal offenders to rehabilitate. I have represented criminal clients who have rehabilitated themselves, and I have met countless other ex-offenders who are now rehabilitated. These include former gang members, attempted murderers, drug offenders, sex workers, violent criminals, and even batterers. If Yelena could not be rehabilitated, I am confident that county officials would not have returned Ricky to her. But she was deported, so we never found out if she could rehabilitate.

Yelena was represented by counsel. The immigration judge gave her a continuance to speak with an attorney, and the judge eventually convinced a private firm to represent her pro bono. Yelena's pro bono counsel chose to represent her, but the firm was operating under the constraints of Yelena's confinement, some 125 miles away. These choices pertaining to representation—by the judge, by pro bono counsel, and by the immigration clinic—reflect a hit-or-miss system that results in variations in the availability and quality of representation of people in ICE detention. Because those facing deportation have no right to counsel at government expense and they often can't afford private counsel, detainees often go without representation. Even though the private bar, legal services programs, and law schools have banded together to help, these efforts are not sufficient. The New York City Know Your Rights Clinic reports that despite its best efforts and the diligence of its volunteers, they are only able to help ten detainees a week. This is particularly troubling because almost 40 percent of the detainees have possible meritorious claims for relief.

Would the judge have ruled differently in Yelena's case if more tools were available? Perhaps. Her attorney told me later that he had a sense that the judge was concerned that with little family support, mentally challenged clients would be left on the street to fend for themselves. Would the judge have made a different decision if Yelena was out of custody? Out of custody, pro bono counsel would have been able to prepare more thoroughly, work with Yelena to gather more evidence, and build a stronger case for cancellation.

Outcomes are often a matter of chance or circumstance. It may be said that the results of Yelena's case could have been quite different without changes in the law if the personalities were different. For example, a different immigration judge might have seen things differently. A different ICE attorney may have been more sympathetic and taken a more humanistic approach to the facts in the case. UC Davis immigration clinic representation of Yelena may have yielded a different result had there been an opening in the caseload for her. While all that may be true, when the stakes are so high, do we really want to leave results to such speculative chance? Such matters should not be left to simple chance or circumstance; processes should be institutionalized in order to better assure high standards of fairness and consistency. This is just one set of lessons that need to be incorporated into immigration reform proposals like those offered by Representative Lofgren.

One could argue that these problems could have been avoided if Yelena had made her own choice to not abuse her child; that certainly was the tone of the judge's decision and the ICE attorney's questioning and argument during the proceeding. However, it would behoove us to know more about the effect of mental illness on Yelena's behavior before we attribute her behavior to an exercise of free choice. The shame of our current detention and removal system is that tools are not provided to the immigration court to adequately address the challenges posed by noncitizens suffering from mental illness—especially those in detention. Yelena was a victim of that failure.

Immigration Judge Dana Marks's sarcastic characterization of immigration courts as "doing death penalty cases in a traffic court setting" has a truthful, catchy ring. But if you've been to traffic court, you realize a sad truth: traffic court judges actually have more leeway to come up with creative solutions to adjust penalties to achieve a just result than immigration judges do.

WHERE'S MY LAWYER?

If there's one thing the JC and Fento cases illustrate, it's this: good representation makes a difference. Given the complexities of immigration law and what we know is at stake in deportation cases, noncitizens facing removal must look for a good lawyer for help. Under current law, a person in deportation proceedings has a right to an attorney, but only if they can pay a private attorney or find one who will take the case for free. Otherwise, you're out of luck, because unlike criminal cases, the government will not provide you with a free public defender. It turns out that only about a third of those facing deportation are able to afford counsel.[22]

How much does having an attorney matter in deportation cases? A great deal. If you have an attorney, you are seven times more likely to win your case.[23] If you are in ICE detention, your situation is extremely challenging. For those in detention without an attorney, only one out of seven avoid removal; those with attorneys prevail almost half the time. Only 15 percent of unaccompanied minors facing deportation without representation are permitted to remain in the country.

As a law professor and immigration lawyer for fifty years, I can say that, with some exceptions, attorneys are not needed for most family immigration and citizenship through naturalization cases. But lawyers are essential when it comes to deportation matters. The US immigration legal system is often referred to by federal judges as a "labyrinth" and "byzantine." The Supreme Court recognized those complexities and the importance of lawyers being well-informed about immigration law in *Padilla v. Kentucky*, a 2010 case that imposed a duty on criminal defense attorneys to inform clients of the risk of deportation.

The reasons that legal representation makes a difference in deportation cases are obvious. First, of course, it helps to know how the process works in the immigration court and the legal requirements for applying for such things as asylum or cancellation of removal relief. From there, the list of what attorneys can do for clients is long. An attorney might be able to help someone arrested by ICE prove their US citizenship because sometimes a person is a US citizen and simply doesn't realize it. If a client is arrested as the result of egregious misconduct by ICE agents, an attorney may be able to make a motion to suppress the evidence against the person. An attorney will research whether the government's allegations are accurate; for example, maybe the crime is not an aggravated felony. The attorney will gather letters of support, expert testimony, country conditions, psychological evaluations, and other evidence to support a cancellation or asylum claim. The attorney will prepare the client to testify credibly and consistently, and to face cross-examination by the government's attorney (the government is always represented in deportation cases even if the respondent is not) and questioning from the judge. Clients suffering from PTSD—most asylum applicants—need to be evaluated and counseled more carefully than others. For clients who are unaccompanied minors fleeing gang or cartel violence, the attorney may need to go into state court for a special immigrant juvenile status order to protect the child from deportation. Similarly, for clients facing deportation because of criminal charges, the attorney may need to go back into state criminal court to challenge the viability of the guilty plea that resulted in the criminal conviction that led to deportation charges.

The Catholic Immigration Legal Network operates a program for detained noncitizens who are in desperate need of removal representation. Unfortunately, the program is unable to meet the needs for most of those individuals. Through that program, my students and I regularly volunteer to represent some of the detained noncitizens on appeal after they were forced to represent themselves at the immigration court. To put it mildly, noncitizens who are forced to represent themselves are at a huge disadvantage. My students and I frequently review trial transcripts that reveal clear misunderstandings on the part of the noncitizens and unsympathetic immigration judges who do little to clear things up.

My students also regularly monitor the local immigration court by observing what goes on at preliminary hearings, where dozens of individuals and families—often unrepresented—must appear for the first time. One of my students who observed several preliminary hearing sessions, referred to as "master calendar" hearings, told me that on many occasions, the judges are incredibly disrespectful. In one instance, the judge said that one allegation against the noncitizen was that she entered without a passport. The person tried to explain that she had a passport from her home country, clearly not understanding what the judge was speaking about. The judge kept interrupting her, saying that he did not need explanations—only yes or no answers.

Norma Jacinto's case is a good example of an immigration judge being unhelpful to an unrepresented family facing deportation. Norma and her son Ronald were from Guatemala. They applied for asylum because the Guatemalan military was persecuting Norma and her family, including her common-law husband, who was a former member of the military. They were denied asylum by the immigration judge, but fortunately, they were able to find an attorney to appeal their case, and a federal court of appeals ordered a new trial. At the initial hearing concerning Ronald, the immigration judge discussed his right to an attorney with Norma.

Q. At this hearing he has a right to an attorney at his own expense, at his family's expense. You are now being handed a Form I–618 and also a copy of the local legal aid list which contains the names of organizations and attorneys who may be able to help him for little or no fee. Do you understand all that I've said so far, Ms. Jacinto Carrillo?

A. Yes.

Q. All right. Do you wish the Court to give you additional time to get an attorney to speak for you, rather[,] for your son, in these proceedings, or do you wish to speak for him?

A. Yes.

Q. Which one?

A. The problem is—

Q. Which one? I don't want to hear about the problems, I just want to know whether you want to speak for him or whether you want time to get an attorney to speak for him?

A. I want to speak for him.

Q. All right. At this hearing, your son has certain rights, one, to present evidence in his own behalf; two, to examine and object to evidence presented against him; and three, to question any witnesses brought into hearing. Do you understand the rights that your son enjoys?

A. Yes.[24]

The court of appeals focused on the likely misunderstanding that is revealed in Norma's answer "The problem is—." A reasonable interpretation of this exchange is that Norma was given a choice: either she could get an attorney to speak for her son or she could speak for her son, but not both. The court of appeals pointed out that, in fact, that is not the rule. She could have obtained an attorney and she also could have spoken for her son as a witness (and as an adviser to the attorney). This was never clearly explained to her. In other words, from the standpoint of a witness unfamiliar with removal proceed-ings, the immigration judge gave her the choice of either being silent or getting somebody else to speak for her son.

The ambiguity over self-representation or having an attorney con-tinued during the latter part of this initial hearing. The immigration judge told Norma that she was scheduled for a hearing the same day as her son, and the following exchange occurred:

Q. Do you remember everything that I told you regarding your son's right to an attorney?

A. Yes.

Q. The same thing applies for you. Do you understand?

A. Yes.

Q. And you've already been given a . . . legal aid list and we'll give you another one right now. Do you want time to get an attorney to speak for you or do you want to speak for yourself?

A. I'd like to speak for myself.

Q. All right. As I advised you a moment ago [about] the rights that your son [has to present] evidence [on] his own behalf, [t]he same rights apply to you. Do you recall?

A. Yes.

The confusion was apparent to the court of appeals. Norma may well have believed that she was being given a choice between speak-ing for herself at the proceedings or having an attorney. The immi-gration judge never adequately explained to her that she could have an attorney and also speak for herself, by being a witness, or that if she took the part of the attorney herself, she could still present her own testimony in narrative form, in addition to acting as an advocate.

More confusion surfaced when the immigration judge asked if Norma intended to introduce documentary evidence in support of her application. The transcript shows that Norma did not understand what evidence was requested:

Q. All right. Very well. At these hearings you also have the right to present any documentary evidence in support of your claim for asylum. Do you have any documents that you wish to submit at this time in support of your case?

A. Documents for, yes, I think I have some right here.

Norma produced no documentary evidence at this time but offered to present evidence later in the hearing. Then when Norma offered to show some photographs, the judge stated that it was not necessary for him to view them. He thus denied her the opportunity to present evidence that could have been relevant to her application, particularly since he later concluded that she was not credible.

The court of appeals found that Norma was severely disadvantaged by the way the judge conducted the hearing. The hearing began with the immigration judge asking preliminary questions. Rather than permitting Norma to present her own testimony, the immigration judge then turned questioning over to the government attorney. The questioning of Norma then alternated between the immigration judge and the government attorney. At no point was she given the chance to present her case in her own way.

The immigration judge's initial questioning concerned Norma's family background, but it completely omitted any questions that would have determined whether she possessed the experience that would enable her to comprehend the proceedings. Some questions were posed like a cross-examination without giving Norma an opportunity to fully explain or elaborate on her testimony. Here is an example:

Q. Government attorney: Let's start from the beginning. You stated that [your common-law husband] Mr. Lopez had problems in Guatemala, by the Guatemalan army, is that correct?

A. Yes, he worked there. I'll explain. He—

Q. Ma'am, I'm going to ask you some questions, try to answer these (indiscernible) in an organized way. Okay. When did Mr. Lopez, if you know, become a member of the Guatemalan army?

The questions focused on a number of matters to which Norma appeared to not fully respond. During questioning by the government attorney, the immigration judge would interrupt frequently and ask questions, and then turn the questioning back to the government attorney. Some of the questions related to the credibility of Norma's statements. For example, the following exchange occurred between the government attorney and Norma:

Q. Ma'am, if they came to your house so often, and you were so afraid, why did you stay there for two years?
A. In the house?

Q. Why didn't you leave Guatemala earlier?
A. It's that we, they started, like I said, they started to bother us because he told them if they continued [to] bother him he was going to say everything he knew because he knew all the bad things that they did. That's when they started to persecute him to kill him.

Q. See, but, ma'am, please answer my question. If you were so afraid of these people and they were bothering you so often, why did you wait two years to leave Guatemala?
A. I did not wait that long. They threatened him, but they did not bother me, just at the end that they would come and bother me.

At the end of the question, the immigration judge did not give Norma any opportunity to explain her answers, but turned to the government attorney and inquired, "Anything further, counsel?"

At that point, the government attorney said that he wanted to ask about voluntary departure. However, at no time did the immigration judge explain that Norma could testify further with respect to the asylum claim, explain or add to her previous answers, or offer additional evidence to support her asylum claim.

After the government attorney completed questions on voluntary departure, the court called Norma's only witness, Francisco Javier Lopez, her common-law husband. Lopez made some statements that one might deem to be harmful to Norma's cause. For instance, he stated that initially Norma wanted to return to Guatemala until recently when he convinced her that it would be dangerous for her to return and that the family should stay together.

After the immigration judge and the government attorney finished questioning Lopez, the immigration judge asked Norma:

> Q. To the Respondent, do you have any questions that you would like for the witness to answer?
>
> A. No.

The immigration judge did not explain to Norma that she could use this opportunity to clarify any matters, dispel any conclusions, highlight certain facts, or present additional evidence supporting her right to remain in the country. For instance, Norma never asked Lopez to further clarify his statement that he knew of several instances of killings of Guatemalan citizens by the Guatemalan army. Norma failed to amplify this matter, and there is no indication that she recognized the importance of showing a political motivation for the adverse action taken against her and Lopez while in Guatemala that served as the reason to leave the country. After all, how could she know what to do? She was not a lawyer and did not know what was required to qualify for asylum.

Fortunately, the court of appeals ruled that Norma did not receive a fair hearing, so she was granted a new hearing. It was fortunate that Norma had attorneys to represent her at the court of appeals, but thousands of others in Norma's situation cannot obtain representation for appeals, and they get deported. Despite Norma's treatment at the hearing, the court did not order that she be provided with an attorney by the government for her new hearing.

People who appear at their preliminary master calendar hearings without an attorney are asked by the immigration judge if they want an attorney. If they say yes, the judge will usually grant at least one or two continuances to give the noncitizens a chance to find one.

If you're poor, it's not easy to find free legal assistance. When I started practicing immigration law as a young legal services attorney in 1974, I was thoroughly impressed by the fact that private immigration lawyers took on cases pro bono regularly. They regarded helping low-income clients for free as a duty of the legal profession. Big corporate firms got into the act in the 1980s, taking on thousands of Central American asylum cases pro bono across the country. But even then, the vast majority of noncitizens facing deportation and asylum seekers could not find free help. The same is true today, even in urban areas where immigration legal services programs abound. For example, as one of more than twenty legal services programs in the San Francisco Bay Area funded to represent noncitizens facing deportation, the University of San Francisco immigration clinic that I help run has about five hundred open and active cases, with a waiting list of more than a few hundred. Some of the other area agencies have even larger waitlists. The challenge to find free legal help is that much greater in rural areas, such as where ICE detention centers are generally located.

Many great organizations in the San Francisco Bay Area provide free immigration legal services to low-income noncitizens because counties, the state of California, and private funders recognize the need. In fact, cities and states around the country recognize the importance of providing immigration attorneys to people facing removal. The New York Immigrant Family Unity Project, a program funded by the New York City Council, was the nation's first public defender system for immigrants facing deportation. NYIFUP pioneered representation for detained indigent immigrants in deportation proceedings in New York City who were unrepresented at their initial hearing. In northern California, San Francisco, San Mateo, Alameda, Sonoma, and Santa Clara counties provide funding for individuals facing removal—including many who are not detained. The state of California regularly provides funding for immigration services, including special funding for representing unaccompanied minors. Chicago also created a fund for immigrant legal services in response to the Trump administration's aggressive immigration enforcement tactics. These efforts are encouraging, but thousands of noncitizens facing removal continue to go unrepresented by this patchwork system. And during the Obama administration, with the exception of some funding for representing minors, the federal government did little to help provide representation.

The Sixth Amendment provides a right to government-appointed counsel to criminal defendants, but that right does not apply in deportation cases where the noncitizen is classified as a respondent in civil proceedings. Federal courts have been unreceptive to the argument that the federal government should provide free counsel to those facing removal as a matter of due process. The only exception is one federal court that ordered the government to provide counsel to immigrant detainees who are incapable of understanding the deportation charges due to severe mental disabilities.[25] But that's it. Non-detained individuals who are mentally incompetent are not covered by the ruling. Even children facing deportation are not provided free attorneys, and they are regularly forced to represent themselves in court. So if you cannot afford a private attorney, you have to hope a law school clinic, a legal services attorney, or a pro bono attorney can take your case—otherwise, you are on your own.

The Supreme Court has never ruled on the question of whether due process or fundamental fairness requires the government to provide a public defender for noncitizens facing deportation. Before 1963, states were not required to provide counsel to every criminal defendant under the Sixth Amendment. However, in *Gideon v. Wainwright* (1963), the Supreme Court reinterpreted the Constitution to mandate that every defendant in criminal court be provided an attorney. There was too much at stake, namely personal liberty, to rule otherwise— even for Gideon, who was charged with breaking and entering with intent to commit petty larceny. In the court's view, the assistance of counsel is a safeguard necessary to ensure the fundamental human rights of life and liberty. In a concurring opinion, one of the justices emphasized that it would be difficult to make the "value judgment" that "deprival of liberty [is] less onerous than deprival of life."[26]

We are at a *Gideon v. Wainwright* moment in immigration law today. There is too much at stake in deportation hearings to allow the outcome to be determined by whether the person facing removal is wealthy enough to afford counsel or lucky enough to obtain competent counsel pro bono or through an opening in a legal services program. The racial implications are clear. Almost 97 percent of deportations are of individuals of Latin American descent.[27] Providing universal representation is a strategy to "counter the systems that perpetuate racial inequities once [Black and Brown] immigrants are pulled into the deportation machinery."[28] However, these individuals largely go unrepresented. Unfortunately, I rather doubt that, given its conservative makeup, today's Supreme Court would adopt a *Gideon v. Wainwright* approach to deportation cases.

That means that it's up to Congress to make universal representation for noncitizens facing removal part of the law. The vast majority of those in deportation proceedings are either facing the prospects of separation from loved ones here or extreme violence in places such as Honduras, Guatemala, and El Salvador. For them, getting an attorney to help is a matter of life and death. Counsel should be provided at government expense.

Great Britain provides a model for representation in asylum cases. Legal help is currently available to all eligible asylum seekers from the outset of their claim. Normally, asylum seekers are entitled to around eight hours of legal help before an asylum interview but are then entitled to full legal support for appeals. The goal is to improve the quality of asylum decisions through better representation. The hope also is to change the culture in the asylum determination process on the part of the decision maker.[29]

CONCLUSION: DISRUPT THE IMMIGRATION COURT SYSTEM

The immigration court system has to be overhauled. Representative Lofgren's proposal is right: the court needs to be made independent of the Department of Justice. But immigration judges also must be provided with resources and tools to ensure that results are proportional to any immigration violations.

More needs to be done to disrupt the current immigration court system. A change in culture is required if we are to minimize the risks of seeing mean-spirited judges like Nicholas Ford and V. Stuart

Couch on the bench. In short, the function of the immigration court should be redefined: Maintaining family unity should be a goal. Second chances should be standard. Understanding the effects of PTSD on testimony is a must. Providing the benefit of the doubt in asylum cases is required. Immigration judges should be encouraged to be flexible to achieve a just result and should be authorized to take a humanitarian approach to their cases, including the power to terminate proceedings in the interest of justice.

To keep everyone honest, the person facing removal must have an attorney. Given the complexities of immigration law, the potential bias of immigration judges, and the fact that deportation can result in family separation and the loss of all that makes life worth living, the right to legal representation should be guaranteed to every person facing removal.

Besides the absolute right to counsel, another principle from criminal law should be incorporated. While defendants can always appeal convictions in trial, prosecutors are generally prohibited from appealing acquittals. The same rule should apply in deportation cases: if the immigration judge rules in favor of the noncitizen, the government should not be able to appeal the decision. That would be consistent with a humanitarian approach to removal.

ON DISRUPTION

T HE REVEREND DEBORAH LEE was working at the Pacific School
of Religion in Berkeley, California, around 2004 when I was
invited to give a talk there. She was very interested in the
Clinton administration's role in Operation Gatekeeper, which was
resulting in migrants dying at the border, as well as in the post-9/11
national security lens that was evolving and in immigration raids.[1]
Focused and committed, she didn't simply have an intellectual interest in this; she wanted to know who was actively working to oppose
these enforcement efforts and how she could get involved.

Fast-forward about fifteen years to July 2018. The sheriff of Con-
tra Costa County announced that he would end his contract with ICE
to house about two hundred noncitizens—men and women—in the
West County Detention Facility in Richmond, California. Deb, now
executive director of the Interfaith Movement for Human Integrity,
would never claim that the sheriff's decision was due to her efforts
alone, but her fingerprints were all over the crusade to end ICE detention in her Bay Area backyard.

When Deb first heard that the county was contracting with ICE,
in 2011, the stories were familiar: the conditions were bad, families
were unnecessarily being separated, access to counsel was constrained,
and communications were limited. Deb started a protest, holding a
vigil outside the facility demanding that the sheriff end his arrange-
ment with ICE. The vigil became a monthly event that began with fifteen people every first Saturday of the month. Steadily, the numbers
grew to fifty, then sixty, then one hundred. When Donald Trump was
elected, the protestors grew to over two hundred each month. The

group convinced politicians, including Sen. Dianne Feinstein and Rep. Nancy Pelosi (D-Calif.), to write letters condemning the deplorable conditions. The vigils attracted leaders and people of all faiths, professions, immigration statuses, ages, and races. The vigils were neither quiet nor polite—in fact, Deb told me, "We make a lot of noise, because we want those inside to know that there are folks outside who care."

Leading the effort to shut down the West County Detention Facility is just one of many anti-ICE disruptions that have been part of Deb's life. She is often in the news for blocking ICE buses in downtown intersections, getting arrested, and leading protests outside immigration courthouses. One week Deb will be in Honduras leading a delegation to learn about the root causes of migration, and the next week she'll be on a pilgrimage of activists visiting seven immigration detention centers around California. She and the Interfaith Movement for Human Integrity were a constant presence in Sacramento pushing the state legislature and then governor Jerry Brown to enact a state sanctuary law. Deb is the perfect example of someone at the forefront of fighting to abolish ICE and to disrupt its actions.

In the foregoing chapters I have made my case for abolition by focusing on specific areas. I've argued in favor of stopping the deportation of longtime residents like Lundy Khoy and Kim Ho Ma, who already paid the price for their crimes. I've noted that deporting a person without documents, like Antonio Sanchez, who had steady work, a supportive family, and strong community ties, makes no sense, and that he and millions of others in his shoes should be granted legalization. I've advocated that the current approach to asylum should be turned on its head, and that applicants like Rudina Demiraj and Chanpreet Kaur should be granted asylum, unless the government can prove beyond a reasonable doubt that they will not be persecuted. I've explained why the current immigration court system needs to be dismantled and replaced with a new system of humanitarian adjudication that can deal flexibly and humanely with cases like those of Yelena Gorev and Juana Lopez-Telles. And finally, I've explained that immigration detention should be discarded because it is not only cruel but totally unnecessary.

Until these institutions are abolished, we should take a page from Deborah Lee's life and do everything we can to disrupt the system. Here are my recommendations.

PUBLIC DISRUPTION

Public Oversight Disruption

Until we dismantle the Department of Homeland Security, the system that provides the foundation for the racist and abusive treatment of immigrants in detention, deportation, and asylum, let's disrupt DHS by requiring oversight of the agency through an ethical lens. The oversight should be grounded in a sense of morality, fairness, and human dignity. Like all federal agencies, DHS is subject to congressional oversight, but an independent public entity is needed to review and report on the enforcement actions of the DHS branches ICE and the Border Patrol so that the agency's actions are transparent and free from political manipulation. My accounts of racism, human rights abuse, and due process violations demonstrate that congressional oversight and agency internal affairs reviews have failed. Abusive ICE and Border Patrol enforcement go unchecked except for the occasional courthouse challenges by organizations like the ACLU, creative lawyering in individual cases, random *Flores* inspection reports as in the case of Clint, Texas, or persistent organizing efforts like those led by Deborah Lee.

Civilian review boards of police departments are fairly common today. Their functions vary from city to city, but the idea is to provide civilian oversight of the police and an avenue for public complaints. Cities such as Berkeley, Detroit, Chicago, and San Francisco have developed and maintained citizen oversight agencies since the 1970s and 1980s. In 1993, New York also reconstituted an all-civilian complaint review board (CCRB). The CCRB is now the largest civilian review board in the United States and presides over thousands of complaints annually. Today, about 130 citizen oversight agencies operate across the country and, although their effectiveness is open to dispute, they have an important impact on the oversight of police misconduct and accountability.

A massive ICE operation targeting Swift & Company meatpacking plants in 2006 led to the establishment of a short-lived review body that is a good example of the potential public review of immigration enforcement. Early on the morning of December 12, ICE conducted a military-style raid on six Swift sites across the nation's heartland.[2] Hundreds of agents in riot gear, armed with assault weapons, descended upon plants in Cactus, Texas; Greeley, Colorado; Grand Island, Nebraska; Worthington, Minnesota; Marshalltown, Iowa; and Hyrum, Utah. ICE rounded up nearly thirteen thousand workers that day—the vast majority were US citizens—forcibly detaining them for hours.

United Food and Commercial Workers Union (UFCW) president Joe Hansen was shocked at the raid. He reached out to me and a group of former elected officials, labor leaders, academics, civil rights leaders, and immigration experts to investigate what happened and to give voice to the victims of the raids. We spent more than a year holding regional hearings, interviewing witnesses, and soliciting input from a wide range of workers, elected officials, policy experts, psychologists, and community leaders. We then released a comprehensive report documenting the devastation and destruction that immigration raids had on families, workplaces, and communities across the country. The report, *Raids on Workers: Destroying Our Rights*, offered a critical analysis of one of the central components of the George W. Bush administration's immigration strategy and provided a detailed account of how heavy-handed enforcement tactics led to the systemic abuse of workers' rights and a willful disregard for the rule of law.[3]

Joe issued this statement:

> What we have uncovered is that during the Bush Administration ICE agents repeatedly trampled on innocent workers' constitutional rights. These were not isolated incidents, but systemic problems that occurred in almost every region of the country. No government agency is above the law, and no worker should have to face the mistreatment and misconduct that these hardworking men and women were subjected to under the Bush Administration.

The ICE abuse and misconduct was apparent. The testimony we heard revealed several disturbing patterns: US citizens and legal permanent residents detained for hours unable to leave even after establishing their status; a lack of coordination by ICE with state and local labor and child welfare agencies; violations of the Fourth Amendment; the use of massive amounts of taxpayer resources and personnel to administer civil warrants; repeated incidents of racial profiling and harassment; the human toll of immigration enforcement, including family separation and children left without proper care; and the lasting economic and psychological devastation of communities and families in the aftermath of workplace and community raids.

Among its many recommendations, the report urged vigorous oversight of ICE's activities and the enhancement of legal protections against abuse. The report had an immediate impact. As the Obama administration came into office, in 2009, new DHS secretary Janet Napolitano announced that Bush-style ICE raids were not part of her enforcement strategy. However, by 2013, ICE restarted strikingly similar operations under the auspices of targeted enforcement raids. And the Obama administration instituted other enforcement abuses, such as the detention of children and families, a year later. Then the Trump administration reinstituted armed ICE workplace raids again. If the oversight recommended by the UFCW had been in place, these abuses might have been stopped or at least restrained.

IMMIGRANT DISRUPTIONS
May Day 2006 March Against the Sensenbrenner Bill

Noncitizens and their immigrant rights allies have engaged in countless examples of disruptive actions to challenge detention, deportation, and the failure of Congress to enact comprehensive immigration reform. Hunger strikes by ICE detainees, advocacy for sanctuary ordinances, and coalition work with Black Lives Matter have become part of the daily struggle for abolition.[4] One of the most spectacular disruptions took place on May Day (May 1), 2006, when thousands of noncitizens took off from work to protest the passage of the Border Protection, Antiterrorism, and Illegal Immigration Control Act of 2005, often known as the Sensenbrenner bill after its chief sponsor, Rep. James Sensenbrenner (R-Wisc.). The legislation would have made being undocumented a felony subject to imprisonment as well as deportation.[5] Anyone providing humanitarian assistance to noncitizens without documents also would have been subject to criminal prosecution.

For weeks that spring, television and newspapers featured dramatic images of masses of humanity marching peacefully in cities from New York and Chicago to Los Angeles and San Francisco. In San Jose, California, thousands of noncitizens and their supporters marched on Interstate 101, shutting down the freeway. The protests worked, and the Sensenbrenner bill never got past the US Senate.

DREAMers

One of the most effective public disruptions of ICE was conducted by DREAMers, who convinced President Obama to institute the Deferred Action for Childhood Arrivals (DACA) program.[6]

During his campaign for the presidency, in 2008, Barack Obama pledged to push for comprehensive immigration reform within the first year of his administration. However, the president spent most of his first year dealing with the financial crisis, and his primary legislative efforts were focused on health-care reform. When the Affordable Care Act was signed, in 2010, the president and Democratic congressional leaders, who controlled both houses of Congress at the time, tried unsuccessfully to pass a comprehensive immigration bill.

With the chance of comprehensive reform fading in 2010, DREAMers urged congressional leaders, at the very least, to pass the DREAM Act. Earlier that year, four DREAMers—Gaby Pacheco, Carlos Roa, Felipe Matos, and Juan Rodriguez—walked 1,500 miles on the "Trail of Dreams" from Miami to Washington, DC, to put a spotlight on the proposed law. The House of Representatives passed the bill on December 8, 2010, by a vote of 216–198. However, a few days later, the Senate only came up with fifty-five votes—five short of the sixty needed to bypass a filibuster. The DREAM Act died. Gaby later told me how she "watched and cried" from the Senate balcony as the legislation failed to pass.[7]

Disappointed, DREAMers and immigrant rights advocates continued their determined campaign of protests. For example, on June 27, 2011, six DREAMers were arrested in Atlanta for blocking an intersection in front of the state capitol. Nataly Ibarra, a sixteen-year-old high school student, stated: "It's time to stand up and let the world know that we need to fight for what we believe in."[8] A month later, about twenty DREAMers interrupted a speech by President Obama at a conference in Washington, DC. Felipe Matos explained: "We stood up while President Obama gave another of his predictable speeches on immigration because we are outraged at his trying to promote his election among Latinos while continuing to deport us at a time when there is no legislative solution to the immigration crisis."[9] The protestors wore shirts that read "Obama Deports DREAMers." During the 2012 presidential campaign, two dozen DREAMers staged a sit-in at Obama campaign headquarters in Denver in early June. They demanded an executive order ending the deportation of DREAMers.

The DREAMer disruptions worked. On June 15, 2012, President Obama announced that he would exercise prosecutorial discretion and not deport DREAMers who had entered the United States prior to the age of sixteen. They also would be granted work permits for two years with an opportunity to renew. It was an amazing triumph that would benefit hundreds of thousands of individuals.

While President Obama's action on behalf of DREAMers was consistent with the immigration agency's traditional prosecutorial discretion to grant deferred action to sympathetic, deportable immigrants, the scope was unprecedented. Republican critics argued that he went beyond the scope of his authority. And the president himself, only a year earlier, denied that he could "just suspend deportations [of DREAMers] through executive order."[10] By the time Donald Trump took over the White House and attempted to end the DACA program, about eight hundred thousand DREAMers had benefited from work permits and protections from deportation.

DREAMers came close to helping to obtain executive protection for others without documentation. Serious bipartisan immigration legislation was not considered again until after the 2012 presidential election. With the Obama reelection, many in the pre-Trump Republican Party sensed that if they were ever to retake the White House, Latinx votes would be necessary, and passing comprehensive immigration reform was a prerequisite.

With much fanfare and relative swiftness, on June 27, 2013, the Senate passed a comprehensive bill that included legalization for millions of undocumented immigrants. The bipartisan Senate bill was attacked by the right as providing amnesty for lawbreakers and by the left for being too strict on enforcement and providing an unreasonably long path to citizenship. But the Republican-controlled House never permitted an up-or-down vote on the legislation, ignoring any concern over appeasing Latinx voters. Thus, efforts at comprehensive immigration reform failed again, as they had in 2010.

While congressional efforts over immigration reform ebbed and flowed in 2013 and 2014, the ICE enforcement machine did not ease up. Although the DACA program for DREAMers was in full swing, Obama's ICE deportations continued at a record pace. Families continued to be separated as immigrant workers and the parents of citizens and DACA recipients were removed. Enforcement was so intense that President Obama was dubbed the "deporter-in-chief" by immigrants, their allies, and even the news media.[11] That image was exacerbated by the fact that Congress inserted into the Department of Homeland Security's 2009 spending bill, signed by Obama, a requirement that ICE keep a minimum of 33,400 undocumented immigrants locked up at all times.[12]

Human Rights Watch reported that close to 47 percent of those deported under the Obama administration were separated from their US-citizen children; the vast majority had no serious criminal history.[13] Immigrant rights advocates argued that the Obama administration was only paying lip service to a different strategy and that the detention of criminal and noncriminal immigrants under the Bush and Obama administrations were essentially the same.

With no realistic hope for comprehensive reform, critics of the continuing deportations demanded that the president act administratively to defer the deportation of anyone who would have been granted protection under the 2013 Senate bill. In one well-publicized exchange, a DACA recipient I knew well, Ju Hong, interrupted the president's speech in San Francisco's Chinatown, exclaiming: "[O]ur families are separated. . . . Mr. President, please use your executive order to halt deportations for all 11.5 [million] undocumented immigrants in this country right now."[14] Ju had been invited on stage at a community event to stand behind Obama during his speech. Startled, the president turned and responded: "[I]f in fact I could solve all these problems without passing laws in Congress, then I would do so. But we're also a nation of laws. That's part of our tradition. And so, the easy way out is to try to yell and pretend like I can do something by violating our laws." When Ju called me the next day to confirm that he had not gone too far in his challenge of the president, I assured him: "Are you kidding? You made us all proud!"[15]

In spite of President Obama's remarks suggesting that he could not act administratively—just as he had previously denied that he could act specifically on protecting DREAMERs—on November 20, 2014, the president took executive action to block the deportation of four million to five million more undocumented immigrants, primarily the parents of US-citizen children. On cue, Republicans claimed that Obama had acted unconstitutionally, and a legal challenge was filed by Texas that stopped the new program from going into effect. But at least until February 2015, when a federal judge halted Obama's new efforts, the disruption of DREAMers reduced the power of the immigration enforcement machine.

Corporate Disruption on Behalf of Noncitizens

About nine months after he took over the White House, President Trump fulfilled a campaign promise and announced that he was terminating DACA. As expected, the response from DREAMers and their supporters was swift and angry. But one voice opposing the president caught me pleasantly off-guard. When asked whether the company would lay off their employees who are DREAMers if they lost their work permits as a result of Trump's actions, Airbnb spokesman Nick Papas stated, "No. We are 100% committed to protecting DREAMers."[16] I was surprised because that meant that Airbnb was willing to be publicly vulnerable and risk civil or criminal penalties for employing unauthorized workers. That was an amazing pledge of civil disobedience.

Beyond the disruptions by noncitizens and their conventional social justice supporters like community-based organizations and legal services programs, corporate America has a big opportunity to disrupt ICE enforcement. Texas and several other states have challenged the authority of Presidents Obama and Biden to establish and extend the DACA program, and the Supreme Court will soon be deciding its fate. I suspect the court will rule that Obama was without power to grant work permits to DREAMers, and DACA recipients will lose the right to work. As the Airbnb statement demonstrates, that's where the opportunity for businesses to help in the abolition movement comes in. Corporate America should ignore federal hiring restrictions and continue to employ noncitizens without employment permission. In other words, businesses should engage in civil disobedience and defy employer sanctions on behalf of DREAMers, whom they have long praised.

Federal law lays out the penalties for hiring undocumented workers. Since 1986, employers who "knowingly" hire unauthorized workers are subject to civil fines.[17] However, penalties get worse for employers who engage in a "pattern or practice" of hiring or recruiting unauthorized workers. At that point, the employer faces criminal charges. For a first-time civil violation, the employer is usually just ordered to "cease and desist" the employment. A fine in the range of $250 to $10,000 also is possible, depending on a business's possible prior violations. Businesses that engage in a "pattern or practice" of violating the employer sanctions law are subject to criminal penalties of six months in prison on top of a $3,000 fine for each unauthorized worker hired.

Trump's DACA termination announcement was in September 2017, but the litigation challenging his actions took nearly three years to get to the Supreme Court. In June 2020, the court decided that although Trump had the authority to end DACA, he had not followed procedures to do so properly. So DACA was saved on a technicality. Trump could have followed the process outlined by the court, but by then, in the midst of his reelection battle with Joe Biden, Trump made the political calculation to stop trying to end DACA. My challenge to big business to defy employer sanctions arises from the strong statements employers expressed and the advocacy efforts they engaged in on behalf of DREAMers during that period.

In response to Trump's initial efforts to cancel DACA, corporate America was united in its criticism. Facebook CEO Mark Zuckerberg commented that the end of DACA would be "a sad day for our country."[18] He continued, "The decision to end DACA is not just wrong. It is particularly cruel to offer young people the American Dream, encourage them to come out of the shadows and trust our government, and then punish them for it." Google CEO Sundar Pichai agreed that "Congress needs to act now to [help DREAMers]." The US Chamber of Commerce and over eight hundred American businesses, including General Motors, Target, and Walmart, signed onto a letter in support of the DREAMers.[19]

The support for DREAMers by the corporate world is not surprising given that three-fourths of major US companies employ DACA recipients. Apple and Microsoft promised to provide legal counsel to any of its DACA employees facing removal, and they have collaborated on court challenges to preserve DACA. But the Airbnb position was by far the most bold.

When you think of civil disobedience, Gandhi, Martin Luther King Jr., Henry David Thoreau, and the Tiananmen Square protesters might come to mind—but not corporations. However, people do not abandon their conscience just because they are in a business setting; they can choose to violate state and federal regulations as a matter of moral principle as well. Moral judgments in the corporate context are made by shareholders, executives, board members, and employees. The key questions for corporations are (1) when is civil disobedience appropriate, and (2) whether different considerations apply to businesses than to individuals considering acts of civil disobedience.[20]

Of course, we should be concerned if the business chooses to violate regulations simply for economic reasons. For example, in the employer sanctions context, if an employer hires unauthorized workers simply to save money, that act would hardly constitute civil

disobedience for moral reasons. However, if the employer hires unauthorized workers at standard wages because they are trying to feed
their families or because they have resided in the United States for
many years, then the act could be considered "conscientious evasion,"
which should be respected as a form of civil disobedience.[21]

Passionate advocacy on behalf of DREAMers and DACA recipients requires employers to disrupt employer sanctions laws. Hiring undocumented workers presents corporations with an important choice
of whether to protect their workers or cooperate with the government.
The workers are human beings who are victims of failed immigration
policies, and the racism institutionalized in the employer sanctions
laws needs to be considered since the vast majority of unauthorized
workers are people of color. More than 70 percent are from Mexico
and Central America, while 13 percent are from Asia.

Rules and regulations are supposed to be followed, and without
consistent adherence to regulations, confidence in businesses would
be eroded. However, civil disobedience in some business contexts is
in order, and, simply put, unjust laws should not be obeyed.[22] The
business leaders rave about their DREAMer workers, so those leaders should help by disrupting immigration enforcement and defy employer sanctions.[23]

ATTORNEY DISRUPTIONS

Jacqueline Brown

I started one of the first law school immigration clinics in the country
at Golden Gate University in 1979, began another one at Stanford
University in 1985, and oversaw the clinical program at the University of California, Davis, beginning in 1999. Throughout that period,
civil wars in Central America, NAFTA-driven migration from Mexico, the militarization of the southern border, and increasing immigration detention kept the need for those programs strong. When I
began teaching at the University of San Francisco in 2010, I did not
intend to start yet another law school clinic, but renewed violence in
Central America changed that.

Sometime in 2011, Jacqueline Brown approached me with the idea of an unaccompanied-minor representation clinic. In her private practice, Jacqueline regularly volunteered through the Bar Association of San Francisco to represent noncitizens at the immigration court. She reminded me about the ever-increasing flow of unaccompanied minors fleeing Honduras, Guatemala, and El Salvador, and she was passionate about helping them. She convinced me of the need for representation and what a great training opportunity this could be for law students. Knowing what it takes to run a clinic, I could not start a new one on my own. But the law school would not spring for the funds necessary to bring Jacqueline on board. However, she had made a lasting impression.

A record-setting surge of unaccompanied minors in 2014 changed everything. More than sixty thousand reached the US southern border that year, with a comparable figure the next year. Community agencies and legal services programs convinced both San Francisco and the State of California to fund legal representation, so I was finally able to hire Jacqueline to join the unaccompanied-minor representation clinic.

I now saw firsthand what a talented attorney Jacqueline is—a brilliant lawyer and an expert on a range of immigration topics but especially in the areas of asylum and Special Immigrant Juvenile Status. After graduating from law school, she clerked for the San Francisco immigration court for two years and practiced immigration law after that, while collaborating with several prominent legal services programs. She also traveled as a volunteer to represent women and children detained at notorious ICE detention facilities in New Mexico and Texas, and she eventually took our students to volunteer there.

Recognized for her impactful work by organizations including the American Immigration Lawyers Association, Jacqueline epitomizes the smart, tireless, nose-to-the-grindstone lawyer that you want on your side. She works with clients, staff attorneys, students, and paralegals to come up with the most creative, winning approaches to our cases involving families or unaccompanied minors who have fled violence in Central America and Mexico.

Jacqueline engages in the day-to-day battle in the immigration court and asylum system—systems whose institutionalized racist laws and procedures make the odds of prevailing small. She disrupts that system ably over and over again, achieving great success with our clients, prevailing even when facing a government attorney who is a total bulldog and objects to everything, wearing down applicants. She prevails even before a hard-nosed immigration judge who seldom grants asylum without evidence of past persecution. And I realize those of us who work with her are blessed to be able to learn from her methods of disruption. The problem is Jacqueline is only one great lawyer. The system needs the heroic actions of a million more Jacquelines to work with all noncitizens who need representation in the rigged system if we are ever to achieve anything close to a level playing field. We need the resources and the energy of clinic students like those who represented Fento and JC (see chapter 6). We need the expertise and political connections to obtain pardons like those for Eddy Zheng (see chapter 3). We need teams of creative and well-connected lawyers like Jay Stansell and others who helped Lundy Khoy. Because we can't be assured of enough advocates of Jacqueline's caliber, the current system needs to be abolished.

Julie Su

I've been intrigued by the term "disruptive" as it has come to be used in the business world. The term is used to describe innovations that improve a product or service in ways that the market does not expect, typically first by designing for a different set of consumers in a new market and later by lowering prices in the existing market.

In much the same way, DREAMer actions targeted the immigration enforcement regime causing President Obama to disrupt the conventional way of looking at prosecutorial discretion. Their actions emboldened him to develop the DACA program, disrupting the conventional rules of enforcement and forcing ICE officers to defer action against a large class of removable individuals for policy reasons. When John F. Kennedy won the White House in 1960, he attempted to disrupt the system of immigrant visa distribution that favored western Europeans by proposing a first-come, first-served system open to everyone. Although his entire program was not achieved, after his assassination, Congress did disrupt the status quo by replacing the old system with one that at least opened the door to Asian immigrants and eventually more from Africa.[24]

One of my favorite attorney disruption examples is about a young legal aid workers' rights attorney who knew little about immigration law and procedure. But she could think out of the box and ended up disrupting the system's approach to trafficking victims.[25] In 1995, Julie Su learned about seventy-one Thai garment workers who were enslaved in a two-story apartment complex with seven units in El Monte, California. They were forced to work eighteen-hour days, some for as long as seven years. Armed guards were present around the clock. Because the workers were not permitted to leave, their captors brought in groceries and other daily necessities and sold them to the workers at four or five times the actual price.

When state and local officials busted into the complex, the operators were arrested, but so were the workers. Because they had been trafficked into the country without proper immigration documents, the workers were turned over to immigration officials, who threw them into a federal penitentiary where they found themselves again behind barbed wire. When they were transported to a downtown Los Angeles immigration holding facility, they were shackled and held for several days. Julie and other supporters set up a makeshift office in the basement waiting room of INS detention and demanded that the workers be released. She and her colleagues filed paperwork that was ignored initially, so they protested and banged on windows of the detention facility. Julie broke the basement pay phones because she slammed them back onto the receivers in frustration each time she received an unsatisfactory response about the release of the workers. At the end of nine long days and nights, the workers were released pending their deportation hearings.

In the process of representing the women, Julie filed civil lawsuits against their captors, collaborated with Latina workers who had worked at the garment company, got local media coverage, and filed claims with the California Labor Commissioner.[26] All the while, she gave voice to the workers, making sure that they could tell their story of modern-day slavery in their own words. Eventually, the women were granted "S" visas, available to witnesses and informants to law enforcement agencies in criminal cases. Julie's innovative advocacy in persuading the government to grant the workers "S" visas contributed to the creation of "T" and "U" visas in subsequent legislation for victims of trafficking and serious crime. This is an impressive disruption of immigration enforcement, especially for someone who was not an immigration lawyer. (President Biden nominated her to be secretary of labor on February 28, 2023.)

Explicit Racial Strategies

Jacqueline Brown's example illustrates the role immigration lawyers play in the systemically racist immigration courtroom, where they have the opportunity to disrupt the status quo on a daily basis. Julie Su's disruption against seemingly insurmountable odds exemplifies how sheer determination and collaboration with allies can educate and convince policy makers to adopt new creative approaches to racial injustice. Impact litigators like ACLU lawyers Cecilia Wang and Lee Gelernt aren't afraid to disrupt by going outside the immigration court system and filing lawsuits in federal courts to challenge racist and constitutionally defective immigration laws, such as Trump's family separation policy.[27] In addition to filing the *Flores* case, Peter Schey has sued the federal government for deporting US citizens and challenged Texas's attempt to deprive undocumented children of public school education.[28]

During the 2020 presidential primary season, Julián Castro, the former US secretary of housing and urban development, stood out to me because he was the first Democratic candidate to announce a comprehensive immigration plan. His progressive plan called for the repeal of illegal entry, the federal criminal offense of crossing the border without authorization. Not only did Castro know that the provision was used by the Trump administration as one reason to systematically separate children from their parents at the border, but he also knew the racist origins of the law that was aimed at Mexican migrants.[29] He famously challenged all the other Democratic candidates to support his proposal on the debate stage.[30]

Consistent with Castro's argument, a group of defense attorneys has worked on a racial defense to the criminal charge of illegal entry on behalf of several defendants. Significantly, they enlisted the help of historians like Kelly Lytle Hernández, who has testified in federal court on the racist intent behind the law. Although the claim has been dismissed by some federal judges, in August 2021, federal district judge Miranda Du in Nevada agreed that the illegal entry law had been passed with racial malice and was being applied in a discriminatory manner. She dismissed the illegal entry charges against Gustavo Carrillo-Lopez as an unconstitutional violation of the equal protection clause.[31] This creative, disruptive legal strategy exposing the racism of the law worked for Carrillo-Lopez.

I also think that lawyers operating within the immigration courtroom should consider disruptive strategies to directly expose the racism that our clients are forced to face. In the appendix to this epilogue, I offer alternative defenses and motions based on the systemic racism that our clients have suffered from US immigration laws and enforcement policies, as well as from US imperialism in Central America. Raising matters of racial justice should be practiced not just in the realm of advocacy for immigration policy change but also in the immigration courtroom. When victims of racism are before an immigration judge, their representatives should introduce the evidence of racism as relevant to whatever relief we are seeking on behalf of our client. This has worked in some motions to exclude evidence obtained as a result of racial profiling.[32]

Immigration judges may resist our efforts to introduce evidence of racism, and if our evidence is ruled irrelevant by the judge, we should state our objection on the record and explain our theory. At the federal appellate level, we can then re-raise the racism argument. And if the appellate review also bears no fruit, then we should appeal to administrative and legislative policy makers for change. At the very least, the evidence of racism must be displayed for all to see the very nature of the system in which we practice. That is part of the argument needed to abolish ICE.

If the events following the 2020 murder of George Floyd have taught us anything, it's that everyone should be committed to seeking justice when victims of racism due to official misconduct, policies, or law are identified. Excluding evidence of that racism silences the victim. In the immigration enforcement world, we would do well to remember a wise admonition of the Board of Immigration Appeals years ago: "Immigration enforcement obligations do not consist only of initiating and conducting prompt proceedings that lead to removals at any cost. Rather, . . . the government wins when justice is done."[33]

CONCLUSION

Speaking before an audience at Washington State University many years ago after a debate with Peter Brimelow, a leading activist in the white nationalist and anti-immigration movement, I was challenged by a member of the campus Republican student group. He was upset at my criticism of the attempted criminal prosecution of Shanti Sellz and Daniel Strauss in 2005. Sellz and Strauss were college students who volunteered with No More Deaths, a human rights organization that provided food and water to migrants facing the searing summer heat of the Sonoran Desert in southern Arizona. They were arrested and charged with transporting undocumented immigrants *within* the United States after they drove two migrants who were dying of exposure to the hospital.[34]

"How can you defend their actions? They knew the crossers were illegal," demanded the young man in the audience. I responded with a question: "What would you have them do—allow the individuals they came across to simply die?" His answer was a quick and emphatic "yes." Stunned, my reaction was esoteric—about how the US attorney should have exercised prosecutorial discretion not to file charges because the actions of Sellz and Strauss were acts of compassion rather than defiance of the law.

Back at my hotel later that evening, I thought back on the exchange. In retrospect, perhaps I should have asked the young man, "Really, let them die? Are those the values you've learned growing up in your community? Is that what your family and friends have taught you?" Since that time, I have realized that the young man's reply was not just about whether his parents or neighbors should have done a better job helping him develop a more compassionate moral compass. That task belongs to all of us. We have the duty to remind him and others that there is more to life and more to being a member of a global society than enforcing immigration laws that separate families in the name of maintaining borders.

The Martha's Vineyard community in Massachusetts responded to that duty with the unexpected arrival of nearly fifty Venezuelan migrants in September 2022. The flights for the asylum seekers from Texas were arranged by Florida governor Ron DeSantis as a political stunt to draw attention to the number of migrants arriving at the Texas border. Texas governor Greg Abbott engaged in a similar game plan by busing migrants to New York and in front of Vice President Kamala Harris's home in Washington. But the Martha's Vineyard community responded to the theatrics with compassion, not anger. Disrupting DeSantis's intent to embarrass the community, residents provided food, shelter, cash, and friendship.

The nation's racist immigration policies have led to increased ICE raids, stepped-up border enforcement, and the expansion of ICE detention. The results are family separation, abusive detention facilities, the denial of asylum to those who have suffered persecution, and the removal of individuals who are part of the American fabric. This is simply untenable. If we are at all committed to an anti-racist agenda, the system that supports those results must be dismantled. Until then, we should commit ourselves to its constant disruption.

Short of the total abolition of immigration laws, many allies advocate for major reforms to the visa system, deportation procedures, asylum requirements, border enforcement, and even detention. Admittedly, I find myself falling into the trap of coming up with suggestions for a modification here or a change there to make things fairer. My friends who would bristle at my characterization of our reform advocacy as a "trap" would argue that the hard task of step-by-step reform is necessitated by a realistic perspective that abolition is impossible. The conventional wisdom is that big change—much less abolition—is not happening. They would remind us that even the bi-partisan DREAM Act never passed.

But I urge all who will listen to ignore the conventional wisdom. For change to happen, we must believe that change is possible, and that's where our advocacy should be focused. The barriers to the goal of abolition are daunting. But one thing I know for sure is that without radical change, racist immigration policies will be perpetuated. Without abolition, people who should not be deported will be removed. Families will be separated. And children will be detained in cages. Bend the ears and rattle the cages of policy makers at every opportunity. Be an ally: stand with immigrant communities at the workplace, in their neighborhoods, and in the streets. Be creative and look for allies in the name of disruption. Be on the right side of history on these matters of fundamental human rights. Believe that abolition and transformation are possible.

HISTORICAL OVERVIEW

The Racism of US Immigration
Laws and Enforcement

AS THE BLACK migrant experience demonstrates, even a cursory view of recent immigration enforcement efforts demonstrates the clear intersectionality between racial justice and immigrant rights. However, a deeper dive into this historical framework of immigration laws and enforcement reveals a system that has institutionalized racism. This review makes it even more apparent that the battle for immigrant and refugee rights is an essential part of the battle for racial justice, which makes the Abolish ICE movement all the more important.

Forces of racism have become embodied in US immigration laws, and the enforcement of immigration laws is accepted as common practice despite the racial impact. We might condemn particular laws or enforcement policies because they abuse human dignity or people's civil rights, but we may overlook the embedded racism because we are unaware of the dominant racial framework. Understanding the evolution of US immigration laws and enforcement provides us with better awareness of the institutional racism that controls those policies.

As a preface to this discussion, the concept of immigration must include the forced immigration system of chattel slavery and the policy of chattel slavery as a relevant historical antecedent to today's immigration law. Forced African labor migration set the stage for prejudicial enforcement and exclusionary reforms targeting Mexicans and Chinese.[1]

Mexican Immigration

When policy makers and the public have heard about "caravans" of Central Americans traveling to the United States in recent years, the focus often turns to the so-called illegal immigration problem and the purported lack of control at the US southern border. Historically, this "problem" became synonymous with Mexican migration, and anti-immigrant activists began to refer to Mexican immigrants as the enemy. Anti-immigrant activists view themselves as the voice for law and order, not as proponents of racism. But the history of labor recruitment and border enforcement illustrates how the institutionalization of anti-Mexican immigration policies created a structure that allows these voices to claim racial and ethnic neutrality, and for many Americans to accept that claim.

Years before the North American Free Trade Agreement (NAFTA) and terms like "globalization" or "transnationalism" came into vogue, Mexico and America enjoyed largely interconnected economies and societies. The southwest border of the United States was transformed in 1848, when the United States and Mexico entered the Treaty of Guadalupe Hidalgo. The United States acquired the land presently known as California, New Mexico, Nevada, Utah, and Arizona. Mexico was forced to recognize the Rio Grande as the southern boundary of Texas and lost almost 55 percent of its former territory.[2] All Mexicans then living in the acquired territory were given the option of becoming US citizens or relocating within the new Mexican border. In the years immediately following the execution of the treaty, most of the people living on those lands continued to treat the territories as part of Mexico and did not relocate. Mexicans and Americans paid little attention to the newly created international border, which was unmarked and wholly unreal to most.

Law professor Gerald López contends that the United States promoted Mexican immigration as part of a larger pattern of labor recruitment that began to emerge in the US in the late nineteenth century.[3] From 1910 to 1920, the United States actively recruited and admitted approximately two hundred thousand Mexicans to fill labor shortages caused by the curtailment of cheap European labor migration. After World War I, economic necessity forced the US to recognize the value of Mexican labor. Almost five hundred thousand Mexicans came to the US for work during the 1920s.

In 1942, the United States and Mexico instituted the Bracero Program, which provided Mexican workers as temporary labor in US agriculture. The program served US economic interests in a manner similar to slavery in the 1800s. Braceros were tied to American private employers by contracts guaranteed by the federal government. The law controlled transportation, wages, and working and living conditions. The program was renewed consecutively for over twenty years, covering five presidential administrations. Braceros accounted for a quarter of the agricultural labor force in California, Arizona, New Mexico, and Texas, allowing the United States to dominate the global agriculture industry.

During this time, undocumented Mexican migration remained significant, even while the program was in effect. López asserts that US policy makers "must have been aware that recruitment activities designed to promote the Bracero Program would encourage poor Mexicans to believe the United States was a land of opportunity, thereby encouraging those who could not be admitted legally to enter" without inspection. News accounts note that when the number of undocumented workers reached a politically intolerable level, the public and political response was fierce. In 1954, the Immigration and Naturalization Service (INS) launched Operation Wetback, which resulted in the deportation of over one million undocumented Mexicans.

After the Bracero Program ended, in 1964, employers' reliance on undocumented Mexican workers increased. Although Congress passed legislation to make it illegal to hire unauthorized workers in 1986, direct and indirect recruitment of undocumented labor has persisted. Contractors for farm labor in the United States traveled to Mexico to convince potential farmworkers to cross the border for work. Major US agricultural companies created well-organized networks of contractors and contractor agents to further their interests by recruiting undocumented labor, willing to risk the potential penalties should they be caught using such labor or aiding illegal immigration.

The Immigration and Nationality Act of 1965 imposed a quota on the number of visas for immigrants from Western Hemisphere countries for the first time. While the rest of the world enjoyed an expansion of legal immigration after 1965, Mexico and other Western Hemisphere countries suddenly faced numerical restrictions. The United States allotted a total of 120,000 immigrant visas for Western Hemisphere countries each year, and while the first-come, first-served basis for immigration sounded fair, applicants were forced to adhere to strict labor certification requirements and demonstrate they would not be displacing US workers. Some waivers were available for certain applicants; for example, parents of citizen children could avoid labor certification requirements. By 1975, the new requirements created a severe backlog of approximately three years and a waiting list with nearly three hundred thousand names.

Congress further attempted to curtail Mexican migration in 1976 as Mexican immigration became the focus of more debate. That year a new law created a twenty-thousand-visas per country numerical limitation on Mexico and other Western Hemisphere countries. As a result, Mexico's usual annual visa usage rate, about forty thousand, was effectively cut in half, and thousands were stranded on the waiting list of the old system. Though the INS budget increased during the 1970s and 1980s, the Supreme Court gave more flexibility to INS enforcement strategies in a series of cases that deferred to government action. These cases, which involved Mexican nationals, illustrate the court's role in institutionalizing racism in the United States. As the case law evolved, the policy rationale from the court was couched in terms of procedure and focused on the race-neutral term "illegal aliens," rather than referring to the defendants as Mexicans coming to the United States seeking a better life.

In 1973, the Supreme Court ruled on a Border Patrol practice of "roving" near the United States-Mexico border to search vehicles without a warrant or probable cause. In *Almeida-Sanchez v. United States*, the court held that the search of an automobile by the Border Patrol without a warrant or probable cause violated the Fourth Amendment. Immigration officials unsuccessfully argued that the proximity of the border was the "functional equivalent" of the border. But within two years, the court—influenced by government claims of a crisis at the border—opened the door to stops by roving patrols near the border under certain circumstances. In *United States v. Brignoni-Ponce* (1975), two Border Patrol officers were observing northbound traffic from a patrol car parked at the side of Interstate 5, north of San Diego. They pursued Brignoni-Ponce's car and stopped it because the three occupants appeared to the officers to be of Mexican descent. The court paid lip service to condemning racial profiling but allowed the stop because trained officers are assumed to be able to recognize the characteristic appearance of persons who live in Mexico, relying on such factors as the mode of dress and haircut.

A year later, the court carved out a major exception to the Fourth Amendment's protection against search and seizure to further accommodate the Border Patrol. The case, *United States v. Martinez-Fuerte* (1976), involved the legality of a fixed checkpoint located at another point on Interstate 5, near San Clemente, California. Officers would randomly stop cars at these checkpoints, sixty-six miles north of the border, when "Mexicans" were in the car. The court gave its blessings to those actions, finding that traffic-checking programs in the interior are necessary because "the flow of illegal aliens cannot be controlled effectively at the border."[4] Fixed checkpoints, many miles from the border, were now deemed constitutional, even with nothing more than racial appearance as evidence of noncitizen status. As Justice William Brennan warned in dissent: "Every American citizen of Mexican ancestry and every Mexican alien lawfully in this country must know after today's decision that he travels the fixed checkpoint highways at [his] risk."

Less than a decade later, in 1984, the Supreme Court also made it clear that the Fourth Amendment's protection against illegal search and seizure did not apply to noncitizens fighting deportation, even if INS officials acted illegally. In *INS v. Lopez-Mendoza*, INS agents arrested Adan Lopez-Mendoza at his place of employment, a transmission repair shop.[5] The agents had no warrant to search the premises or to arrest any of its occupants. The proprietor of the shop refused to allow the agents to interview his employees during working hours.

Nevertheless, while one agent engaged the proprietor in conversation, another entered the shop and approached Lopez-Mendoza. After questioning Lopez-Mendoza, who admitted he was not a legal resident, the INS agent arrested him. Though the arrest was illegal, the Supreme Court refused to exclude Lopez-Mendoza's admission at the deportation hearing that he was not a legal resident. The court concluded, "There comes a point at which courts, consistent with their duty to administer the law, cannot continue to create barriers to law enforcement in the pursuit of a supervisory role that is properly the duty of the Executive and Legislative Branches." Applying the exclusionary rule would simply be too inconvenient for immigration enforcement officials—even when the Fourth Amendment is violated.

The Immigration Reform and Control Act of 1986

IRCA allowed three million immigrants to obtain lawful citizenship in the United States, but employer sanctions (making it unlawful to hire unauthorized workers) were the driving force behind the legislation—not legalization. Public concern over the number of undocumented workers (predominantly Mexican) in the United States grew in the 1970s and early 1980s. Nobody knew exactly how many undocumented workers were present in the United States, but the highest estimates ranged from eight million to twelve million. The public viewed Border Patrol and INS efforts as ineffectual at best. Employer sanctions were the most popular proposals to combat the perceived lack of control at the southern border, and Mexican workers were the scapegoat.

The Asian Exclusion Era

The discovery of gold, a rice shortage, and the recruitment of Asian labor led to significant Asian migration to the United States in the nineteenth century, which in turn triggered a backlash against those immigrants. Examining the impetus and development of exclusion laws directed first at Chinese and eventually at all Asian immigrants reveals a sordid tale of racism and xenophobia.

Early in American history, Chinese people were officially welcomed in the United States. American companies recruited Chinese workers to fill labor needs in the railroad construction, laundry, and domestic service industries. In 1852, the governor of California recommended using land grants to induce Chinese immigration and settlement. After the Civil War, Southern plantation owners considered substituting Chinese labor for Black labor, worried that newly freed slaves would be difficult to manage.[6] Southern plantation owners traveled to California with this in mind during the 1870s, and Chinese workers were imported to states including Louisiana and Mississippi to compete with Black workers. By 1882, about three hundred thousand Chinese had entered the United States and worked on the West Coast.

In the late 1860s, Chinese immigration became a focal point in the politics of California and Oregon. White workers felt threatened by the perceived competition from Chinese immigrants, while employers favored Chinese workers as inexpensive laborers and subservient domestics. Employment of Chinese people by the Central Pacific Railroad was at its peak. Anti-"coolie" (a derogatory term for a Chinese laborer) clubs, organized against Chinese immigrant labor, increased in numbers and size, causing a sharp increase in the frequency of mob attacks against Chinese people. Most of the resentment toward Chinese immigrants stemmed from a perceived need to preserve the white race and Western culture.

Sinophobic sentiment also prevailed in the US Congress. First, Chinese immigrants were judged unworthy of citizenship in the Naturalization Act of 1870, which amended the Nationality Act of 1790, extending the right of naturalization to aliens of African descent, but Chinese people were intentionally denied the same right because Chinese people had "undesirable qualities."[7] In 1875, Congress passed legislation prohibiting the importation of Chinese women for immoral purposes, after hearing claims from law enforcement that the importation of Chinese prostitutes was occurring. Referred to as the Page Law, overzealous enforcement of the statute effectively barred Chinese women from entering the United States, exacerbating an already imbalanced sex ratio among the Chinese population in America.

The exclusion of Chinese women under the Page Law marked the beginning of direct federal regulation of immigration to the United States. Twenty-five anti-Chinese petitions were presented during the 1881 congressional session by several civic and religious groups, including the Methodist Church and the New York Union League Corps, and from states including Alabama, Ohio, West Virginia, and Wisconsin. California was the epicenter for demands of exclusion.

Congress responded by enacting the Chinese Exclusion Act on May 6, 1882, excluding Chinese laborers for ten years. Chinese women were defined as laborers, so Chinese immigrants already in the United States could not bring wives and families previously left behind. The ban on laborers' spouses reinforced the bar on immigration for Chinese women, which began under the Page Law, preventing family formation for Chinese immigrants.

In 1904, the Chinese exclusion laws were extended indefinitely, cementing thirty-five years of laws that limited or otherwise excluded Chinese immigration. Congress would not reconsider any barrier to Chinese immigration until the United States and China became allies in World War II, and Congress would not substantially alter any other laws aimed at keeping Chinese people marginalized until 1965.

Uncoincidentally, an appreciable number of Japanese immigrants entered the United States at the height of the Chinese exclusion movement. Agricultural labor demands, particularly in Hawaii and California, resulted in increased efforts to recruit Japanese workers after the exclusion of Chinese workers. As with the initial wave of Chinese immigrants, American employers were happy to acquire Japanese laborers, and those workers felt, at first, warmly received. So many Japanese immigrants came to Hawaii alone that the Japanese became the largest group of foreigners on the islands. In San Francisco in 1869, the new immigrants were described in newspapers as "gentlemen of refinement and culture . . . [who] have brought their wives, children, and . . . new industries among us."[8]

But by the turn of the century, American sentiments toward Japanese laborers became unfavorable as they began migrating increasingly to the western United States. After Hawaii's annexation, in 1898, Japanese immigrants used that state as a stepping-stone to immigrate to the continental United States, where most immigrant laborers engaged in agricultural work. Economic competition with white farmworkers soon erupted. With the backing of statewide organized labor, California nativists, motivated by racial prejudice toward Asians, formed the Japanese and Korean Exclusion League (later renamed the Asiatic Exclusion League). Exclusion once again became a major political issue—this time the target was the Japanese.

After the 1906 San Francisco earthquake, fierce anti-Japanese rioting caused numerous incidents of physical violence and injuries. Authorities ordered Japanese students in San Francisco to attend segregated schools, which irritated the Japanese government and became a major stumbling block in negotiations over US restrictions on Japanese immigrant laborers. Eventually, the US and Japanese governments reached a solution to concerns over Japanese immigration, but not in conventional legislative fashion. Japan's emergence as a major world power (having defeated China in 1895 and Russia in 1905 wars) meant the United States could not restrict Japanese immigration in the heavy-handed, self-serving fashion in which it had curtailed Chinese immigration. The United States did not want to jeopardize its access to Japan's markets, and overzealous immigration restrictions on Japanese people would have offended the burgeoning world power. As a result, President Theodore Roosevelt negotiated informal agreements with Japan in 1907 and 1908 that minimized any potential disharmony between the two nations, while the United States retained the initiative to control immigration.

Under the terms of the so-called Gentlemen's Agreement, the Japanese government denied travel documents to laborers who wished to go to the United States. In exchange for this severe limitation, the US government permitted Japanese wives and children to reunite with their husbands and fathers in the United States and promised that it would pressure the San Francisco school board into rescinding its previous segregation order. However, citizenship through naturalization to Japanese migrants was foreclosed in spite of the agreement.

US history also demonstrates racial prejudice toward Filipinos and nationals of other Asian nations. After the United States' victory in the Spanish-American War of 1898, President William

McKinley reported that the people of the Philippines were "unfit for self-government" and "there was nothing left for [the United States] to do but to take them all, and to educate the Filipinos, and uplift and civilize and Christianize them."[9] Naturally, the Filipinos did not take kindly to more colonial rule, and the United States' takeover was met with violent resistance.

Ironically, because the Philippines became a US colony, Filipinos automatically became noncitizen nationals of the United States rather than being classified as aliens. They enjoyed the ability to travel to and from the United States without hindrance from immigration laws, as well as relaxed requirements for obtaining full citizenship. When appreciable numbers of Filipinos came to the continental United States after World War I (when Chinese and Japanese workers could no longer be recruited), xenophobic sentiment grew, and the public directed exclusionary efforts at them.

Other Asians began to enter the United States at the beginning of the twentieth century, only in smaller numbers, such as educated Asian Indians. Some of the newly arriving Asian Indians agitated the Asiatic Exclusion League, a movement originally focused on Japanese and Korean immigration. The commissioner of state labor statistics in California stated: "Hindu is the most undesirable immigrant in the state. His lack of personal cleanliness, his low morals and his blind adherence to theories and teachings, so entirely repugnant to American principles, make him unfit for association with American people."[10] Eventually, Asian Indians were prevented from immigrating through the congressional enactment of the Asiatic Barred Zone in 1917.

Limitations on Japanese immigrants led to an intense recruitment of Filipino laborers because of their open travel status as noncitizen nationals. By the late 1920s, Filipino workers were blamed as one reason for high unemployment during the Great Depression, so demands for their exclusion followed. However, dealing with anti-Filipino agitation was not as simple for legislators to respond to as with to earlier anti-Chinese, anti-Asian Indian, and even anti-Japanese campaigns. As US nationals, Filipino workers could travel in and out of the country without constraint. Until the Philippines was granted independence, Congress could not exclude Filipinos.

The Tydings-McDuffie Act, passed in 1934, paved the way for exclusion. When their nation became independent on July 4, 1946, Filipinos lost their status as US nationals. Any Filipinos remaining in the United States were deported unless they formally immigrated and attained citizenship. Between 1934 and 1946, the Philippines was given an annual quota of only fifty visas. Tydings-McDuffie was the formal cap on this era of exclusion.

The refusal to extend Asians the right to naturalize, the laws against the Chinese, the Gentlemen's Agreement with Japan, the 1917 and 1924 (national origins quotas) immigration laws, and Tydings-McDuffie were the legacy of xenophobia that explicitly codified racial exclusion.

THE 1965 FRAMEWORK FOR IMMIGRATION

In 1952, Congress overhauled the immigration laws but failed to address concerns over the national origins quota system of the 1920s favoring western Europeans and continuing the blatant form of racial and ethnic discrimination that epitomized the system. Although the new law repealed the Asian exclusion laws, in their place a new "Asia-Pacific Triangle" was established with a trivial two-thousand-visa annual quota. Since the Immigration and Nationality Act changed little in the immigration selection system, the question over which immigrants to admit to the United States remained hotly contested.

Entering office in January 1961, President Kennedy submitted a comprehensive program that provided the impetus for ultimate reform. Kennedy called on Congress to repeal the discriminatory national origins quota system and to end racial exclusion from the Asia-Pacific Triangle. The president's hopes for abolishing the quota system were only partially realized when the 1965 amendments were enacted. The racial quotas and the Asia-Pacific Triangle geographic restrictions were both repealed, but his egalitarian vision of visas on a first-come, first-served basis gave way to a narrower and more historically parochial framework that provided few obvious advantages for prospective Asian immigrants. The new law provided twenty thousand immigrant visas annually for every country in the Eastern

Hemisphere. The United States granted such allotments regardless of the population of a country, so China had the same quota as, for example, Tunisia. Of the 170,000 visas designated for the Eastern Hemisphere, 75 percent were earmarked for "preference" relatives of citizens and lawful permanent residents in the United States, and an unlimited number of visas remained available to immediate relatives (parents of adults, minor unmarried children, and spouses) of US citizens. The per country limitation of twenty thousand visas eventually led to severe backlogs in high-visa-demand countries—most notably Mexico and Asian countries. So neutral-sounding visa allotments of twenty thousand per country actually resulted in racial disparities, because Asian and Latin countries had more visa demands—something quite foreseeable.

AFFIRMATIVE ACTION FOR WESTERN EUROPEANS: THE "DIVERSITY" VISA PROGRAM

Despite growing visa demands and backlogs for immigrants from Mexico and Asian countries since the 1970s, legislation to address those challenges has never been enacted. Instead, in 1986, Congress added a provision to the Immigration Reform and Control Act in response to increasing immigration numbers from Asia and the Philippines, to help thirty-six other countries that had been "adversely affected" by the 1965 changes. A country was considered "adversely affected" if the United States issued fewer visas to its nationals after 1965 than before. As a result, the "adversely affected countries" included Great Britain, Germany, and France, but no countries from Africa, which had sent few immigrants prior to 1965. This "diversity" initiative for immigration was, in reality, an affirmative action program for natives of countries whose race already constituted a majority of the United States.

The 1986 law granted five thousand extra visas to the "adversely affected countries" per year in 1987 and 1988, but the number increased to fifteen thousand per year in 1989 and 1990. The program required applicants to meet only health and moral qualifications of the immigration laws.

The difficulty for Irish nationals to fit into regular immigration categories was another impetus for the "diversity" program. In the 1980s, many Irish nationals traveled to the United States on temporary visas in search of opportunity amid the ailing Irish economy. Many overstayed their visas, and the Irish government estimated that fifty thousand Irish nationals resided in the United States without documentation in 1989.

In 1988, Congress allocated twenty thousand extra visas for two more years to further increase immigration diversity. An "OP-1" visa lottery was created for nationals of countries that were "underrepresented," or a foreign state that used less than 25 percent of its twenty thousand available preference visas in 1988. All but thirteen countries in the world were eligible, and the ineligible countries included Mexico, the Philippines, China, South Korea, and India.

Legislation in the 1990s extended the diversity visa concept even further. By October 1, 1994, the United States offered fifty-five thousand diversity visas annually in a lottery-type program to natives of countries where immigration fell under fifty thousand over the preceding five years—clearly excluding Mexico, China, South Korea, the Philippines, and India. In this scheme, applicants needed a high school education, or, within five years of application, they needed to attain at least two years of work experience in an occupation that required such training or experience. That left out most Africans who wanted to immigrate.

DISRUPTIVE RACIAL JUSTICE COURTROOM STRATEGIES

MURGIA MOTIONS

In the criminal law context, defendants can raise racial justice issues in their defense under certain circumstances. For example, in California, a *Murgia* motion, based on a state decision *Murgia v. Municipal Court* (1975), can be made requesting dismissal of a case on the grounds that the prosecution is being conducted in an arbitrary or discriminatory manner. In the *Murgia* case, six defendants who were members of the United Farm Workers were prosecuted for activities related to picketing and organizing activities. The California Supreme Court said no one has a right to commit a crime such as driving without a license or malicious mischief. But under equal protection principles, law enforcement authorities have to enforce the criminal statutes evenhandedly. So discriminatory enforcement may be invoked as a defense in a criminal action.

Could evidence of selective prosecution or racial profiling by DHS officials be useful in representing noncitizens in removal proceedings? It's worth a try in an effort to disrupt. In *INS v. Lopez-Mendoza* (1984), the Supreme Court refused to extend the Fourth Amendment exclusionary rule in criminal settings to the immigration court setting as a general matter.[1] Under the exclusionary rule, evidence obtained by the government in violation of the Fourth Amendment cannot be introduced against the criminal defendant. But although the court did not extend the general rule to the immigration court setting, the court said the application of the exclusionary rule might be appropriate if Fourth Amendment violations by immigration agents are "widespread" or "egregious." In other words, a different approach is in order when "notions of fundamental fairness" are "transgress[ed]." That's an invitation to disruption. In my view, the racist enforcement of immigration laws provides a basis for a *Murgia*-type motion to terminate removal proceedings that are fundamentally unfair. Given the racism imbedded in US immigration laws and ICE enforcement, a motion to terminate is appropriate because the discrimination is egregious and widespread.

NECESSITY DEFENSE

At the University of San Francisco law school's immigration clinic, the vast majority of the clients are from the northern triangle of Central America—Honduras, Guatemala, and El Salvador—with many from Mexico as well. More than 90 percent of our clients are asylum seekers. And although under Jacqueline Brown's legal supervision we have a great success rate, obtaining asylum is challenging for the reasons discussed in chapter 5.

Representing asylum clients from Central America requires regular research and the updating of country conditions to support asylum applications. Becoming familiar with the root causes of migration is part of being a good asylum lawyer. That research reveals the sordid history of US involvement in those countries.

The United States has played a big role in creating many of the driving forces of migration from Central America. Some of the contributing factors to social, political, and economic instability include CIA involvement in coups and support of right-wing military groups; support for US multinational corporations in Central America; the deportation of gang members from southern California to countries where those individuals formed extensions of the MS-13 and 18th Street gangs; and the fact that the United States plays the biggest role in global climate change, which affects agriculture in Central America. The effect on migration is clear. Those US actions have affected the societal, economic, and political structures in those nations much like racism against Blacks in the United States has been institutionalized.

Thus, the violence fueled by the social, political, and economic conditions in Central America can be directly linked to US complicity. That violence leaves many migrants from Central America with little choice but to flee. Attorneys and the courts try to fit their stories into the framework of US asylum law, but not without difficulties and challenges. However, given what we know about the role that the United States has played in the forced migration, the immigration and asylum systems should be open to claims related to the United States' role in root causes. History professor Aviva Chomsky offers this perspective:

> Isn't it finally time that the officials and citizens of the United States recognized the role migration plays in Central American economies? Where U.S. economic development recipes have failed so disastrously, migration has been the response to these failures and, for many Central Americans, the only available way to survive. . . . At present, migration is a concrete way that Central Americans are trying to solve their all-too-desperate problems. Since the nineteenth century, Indigenous and peasant communities have repeatedly sought self-sufficiency and autonomy, only to be displaced by U.S. plantations in the name of progress. They've tried organizing peasant and labor movements to fight for land reform and workers' rights, only to be crushed by U.S.-trained and sponsored militaries in the name of anticommunism. With other alternatives foreclosed, migration has proven to be a twenty-first-century form of resistance and survival.[2]

This idea of migration as a "form of resistance and survival" is an important way of understanding that many migrants from Central America are forced to leave due to phenomena that are way beyond their control. Yes, they may be reaching US borders without proper immigration documents. But they are left with little choice.

This situation draws strong parallels to the "defense of necessity" in criminal law. Occasionally, a person faces a situation that requires doing something illegal to prevent serious harm. In such a situation, the defense of necessity, which is also called the "lesser of two evils" defense, may come into play. A defendant who raises the necessity defense admits to committing what would normally be considered a criminal act but claims the circumstances justified it. Usually, to establish a necessity defense, a defendant must prove the following:

- there was a specific threat of significant, imminent danger
- there was an immediate necessity to act
- there was no practical alternative to the act
- the person did not cause or contribute to the threat
- the person acted out of necessity
- the harm caused was not greater than the harm prevented

Consider these examples:

A defendant was convicted of driving with a suspended license for traveling to a telephone to call for help for his pregnant wife. He did not have his own phone, and his wife was experiencing back and stomach pains. He first walked to his only neighbor's house to use the phone but found no one home. He then drove a mile and a half to the nearest phone to call his mother-in-law for help. On the drive back home, the police stopped him for a broken taillight and arrested him for driving with a suspended license. Recognizing that circumstances beyond one's control sometimes force a defendant to engage in illegal conduct, an appellate court ruled that the trial court should have allowed the defendant to present a necessity defense.[3]

In *United States v. Contento-Pachon*, a federal court found that duress and necessity could be used as a defense when a man smuggled drugs into the United States based on the threat that if he did not, his wife and child would be murdered.[4]

In *United States v. Haischer*, another court held that the defendant had the right to raise the duress defense in a mortgage fraud case because she had been in an abusive relationship for years and lacked a reasonable opportunity to escape. The threat of harm from her partner would have been immediate if she had refused to sign the loan documents.[5]

For asylum applicants from Central America who have fled their home countries out of duress and necessity, when they have suffered violence or have been threatened by gangs, cartels, or domestic violence, being granted relief is a matter of survival. As such, they should be excused for entering or attempting to enter the United States without proper documentation. Their assertion of duress or necessity should be accepted as a matter of fundamental fairness. Yes, their actions may be an attempt to break the law of entry without documentation. However, their acts are the lesser of two evils—immigration law violations versus facing significant, imminent violence. There is an immediate necessity to act. There is no practical alternative to the act. They have neither caused nor contributed to the threat. Rather, they have acted out of necessity. The harm (entry without documents) is certainly not greater than the harm prevented (being victimized by violence).

BLACK RAGE DEFENSE

Being victimized by US imperialism or an institutionally racist immigration system is relevant to another criminal law-like defense of a different nature.

As early as 1925, famed defense attorney Clarence Darrow introduced the notion of an environmental hardship defense while defending a Black family who shot into a drunken white mob that had encircled their home. Much later, defense attorneys William Kunstler and Ronald Kuby unsuccessfully tried to argue that Colin Ferguson (accused of killing six and wounding nineteen others on the Long Island Railroad) had been driven to temporary insanity by a psychiatric condition they termed "black rage."[6] Kunstler and Kuby argued that Ferguson had been driven insane by racial prejudice and could not be held criminally liable for his actions even though he had committed the killings. The attorneys compared it to the battered-woman defense, post-traumatic stress disorder, and the child-abuse syndrome used in other cases to negate criminal liability. In 1971, another attorney successfully defended a young Black man charged with armed bank robbery, pointing out that "a person's environment can, and does, affect their life and actions, [and] even the most rational person can become criminally deranged, when bludgeoned into hopelessness by exploitation, racism, and relentless poverty."[7]

Forced undocumented migration resulting from US imperialism or a racist immigration system is not a deranged act. Victimization by exploitation, racism, and relentless poverty is evident in many of the clients we see. Explaining that to an immigration judge is an important part of contextualizing the actions of individuals facing removal. And while immigration judges have little authority to simply terminate proceedings out of sympathy in a manner analogous to jury nullification in the criminal courtroom, at the very least, perhaps that contextualization can positively influence the immigration judge's weighing of factors in exercising the discretion that is part of many forms of immigration relief.[8]

While an immigration judge may resist claims of racism as relevant to viable defenses or relief, we should persist in making the record for appeal. And if those appeals bear no fruit, then perhaps an appeal to rulemaking and legislative authorities should follow. At the very least, the evidence of racism must be displayed for all to see the very nature of the system in which we practice.

ACKNOWLEDGMENTS

THERE ARE MANY to thank for my ability to complete this project. Allegra Upton, Marisela Musgrove, Jennifer Ayala, Heather Philson, and Emily Verrill provided me with able research assistance. Lundy Khoy, Zulma Munoz, John Louie, Deborah Lee, Francisco Ugarte, Zach Nightingale, Dan Barton, Raha Jorjani, and Jay Stansell have allowed me to learn from their experiences. Eric Cohen, Sally Kinoshita, and my friends at the Immigrant Legal Resource Center have developed programs whose accomplishments and contributions to immigrant rights have exceeded my wildest dreams. Special thanks to Jacqueline Brown, whose genius, hard work, and unwavering dedication to asylum seekers is a daily inspiration. Of course, there is little I can do without the love and support of my wife, Lenora, while my granddaughters, Madeline and Penelope, provide pure joy.

I also want to acknowledge the important support of my new friends at Beacon Press. Susan Lumenello, Ruthie Block, and Emma Gibbons provided very helpful suggestions at the manuscript stage. In particular, I am most grateful to Gayatri Patnaik, the director of Beacon Press. Her belief in the project was steadfast, and the confidence she demonstrated in me was uplifting.

NOTES

CHAPTER 1: AN INTRODUCTION TO THE RACIAL INJUSTICE OF IMMIGRATION LAW

1. Annika Kim Constantino, "U.S. Border Patrol Will No Longer Use Horses in Del Rio, Texas, After Outrage over Treatment of Haitian Migrants," CNBC, updated Sept. 24, 2021, https://www.cnbc.com/2021/09/23/border -patrol-wont-use-horses-in-del-rio-after-outrage-over-treatment-of-haitians .html, accessed Aug. 11, 2022.

2. Anabel Munoz, "Black Immigrants Rights Groups Denounce Biden Administration's Deportation of Haitian Asylum Seekers," ABC7 Eyewitness News, Sept. 21, 2021, https://abc7.com/haiti-earthquake-haitian-asylum-seekers -deportation-flights/11034012, accessed Aug. 11, 2022.

3. Constantino, "U.S. Border Patrol Will No Longer Use Horses."

4. Aaron Morrison, Astrid Galvan, and Jasen Lo, Associated Press, "Haitians See History of Racist Policies in Migrant Treatment," *NewsHour*, PBS, Sept. 24, 2021, https://www.pbs.org/newshour/nation/haitians-see-history-of -racist-policies-in-migrant-treatment, accessed Aug. 11, 2022; Cindy Carcamo, Andrea Castillo, and Molly Hennessy-Fiske, "Biden Calls Haitian Migrant Crisis 'An Embarrassment.' Advocates Say Racism at Root," *Los Angeles Times*, Sept. 24, 2021, https://www.latimes.com/politics/story/2021-09-24/biden -haitian-migrants-border-critics-claim-racism, accessed Aug. 11, 2022.

5. Dara Lind, "'Abolish ICE,' Explained," *Vox*, June 28, 2018, https://www .vox.com/policy-and-politics/2018/3/19/17116980/ice-abolish-immigration -arrest-deport, accessed Aug. 11, 2022.

6. Lind, "'Abolish ICE,' Explained"; Rachel Levinson-Waldman and Haley Hinkle, "The Abolish ICE Movement Explained," Brennan Center for Justice, July 30, 2018, https://www.brennancenter.org/our-work/analysis-opinion /abolish-ice-movement-explained, accessed Aug. 11, 2022.

7. Julissa Arce, "The Structural Racism of Our Immigration System," *UnidosUS Blog*, July 1, 2021, https://www.unidosus.org/blog/2021/07/01/the -structural-racism-of-our-immigration-system, accessed Aug. 11, 2022.

8. Refugee and Immigrant Center for Education and Legal Services (RAICES), "Black Immigrant Lives Are Under Attack," last modified Aug. 11, 2022, https://www.raicestexas.org/2020/07/22/black-immigrant-lives-are-under -attack.

9. Julian Borger, "US to Send Asylum Seekers Home to Cameroon Despite 'Death Plane' Warnings," *The Guardian*, Nov. 9, 2020, https://www.the guardian.com/us-news/2020/nov/09/us-to-send-asylum-seekers-home-to -cameroon-despite-death-plane-warnings, accessed Aug. 11, 2022.

10. Ali Vitali, Kasie Hunt, and Frank Thorp V, "Trump Referred to Haiti and African Nations as 'Shithole' Countries," NBC News, Jan. 11, 2018, https://www.nbcnews.com/politics/white-house/trump-referred-haiti-african -countries-shithole-nations-n836946, accessed Aug. 11, 2022.

11. Ed Pilkington, "Outcry as More Than 20 Babies and Children Deported by U.S. to Haiti," *The Guardian*, Feb. 8, 2021, https://www.the guardian.com/us-news/2021/feb/08/us-ice-immigration-customs-enforcement -haiti-deportations, accessed Aug. 11, 2022; Jacqueline Charles, "He Wasn't Born in Haiti. But That Didn't Stop ICE From Deporting Him There, Lawyer Says," *Miami Herald*, Feb. 3, 2021, https://www.heraldmailmedia.com/story /news/2021/02/03/he-wasnt-born-in-haiti-but-that-didnt-stop-ice-from -deporting-him-there-lawyer-says/115758308, accessed Aug. 11, 2022; Maria Sacchetti and Arelis R. Hernández, "Black Lawmakers Urge Biden to Stop the Deportation of Black Immigrants," *Washington Post*, Feb. 12, 2021, https:// www.washingtonpost.com/immigration/black-immigrants-deportations-biden /2021/02/12/5f395932-6d54-11eb-ba56-d7e2c8defa31_story.html, accessed Aug. 11, 2022.

12. 42 U.S.C., Section 265.

13. Pilkington, "Outcry as More Than 20 Babies and Children Deported by U.S. to Haiti."

14. Brian Naylor and Tamara Keith, "Kamala Harris Tells Guatemalans Not to Migrate to the United States," National Public Radio, last modified June 7, 2021, https://www.npr.org/2021/06/07/1004074139/harris-tells -guatemalans-not-to-migrate-to-the-united-states.

15. USC 1182: Inadmissible Aliens, Proc. No. 4865: High Seas Interdiction of Illegal Aliens, https://uscode.house.gov/view.xhtml?req=granuleid%3AUSC -prelim-title8-section1182&num=0&edition=prelim, accessed Nov. 30, 2022.

16. Sale v. Haitian Centers Council, Inc., 509 U.S. 155 (1993), https:// supreme.justia.com/cases/federal/us/509/155, accessed Nov. 30, 2022.

17. Bill Ong Hing, *Defining America Through Immigration Policy* (Philadelphia: Temple University Press, 2004).

18. Bill Ong Hing, "African Migration to the United States: Assigned to the Back of the Bus," in *The Immigration and Nationality Act of 1965: Legislating a New America*, ed. Gabriel Chin and Rose Cuison Villazor (New York: Cambridge University Press, 2015).

19. For example, consider Cook County in Illinois. While the vast majority of individuals removed in Cook County are Latinx Americans, Black people are also deported in disproportionate numbers—they compose 7.2 percent of the immigrant population but account for 20 percent of the criminal-based immigration proceedings. Maurizio Guerrero, "Universal Legal Representation Can Make a Lifesaving Difference for Immigrants," *Daily Kos*, Sept. 21, 2021, https://www .dailykos.com/stories/2021/9/21/2053356/-Universal-legal-representation-can -make-a-lifesaving-difference-for-immigrants, accessed Aug. 11, 2022.

20. Alejandro Sanchez-Lopez et al., *The State of Black Immigrants in California*, ed. Opal Tometi, Black Alliance for Just Immigration and USC Center for the Study of Immigrant Integration, Sept. 2018, https://dornsife.usc.edu /csii/black-immigrants-in-california, accessed Sept. 26, 2022.

21. RAICES, "Black Immigrant Lives Are Under Attack."

22. RAICES, "Black Immigrant Lives Are Under Attack."

23. Human Rights First, *"I'm a Prisoner Here"*: *Biden Administration Policies Lock Up Asylum Seekers*, Apr. 21, 2022, https://humanrightsfirst.org /library/im-a-prisoner-here-biden-administration-policies-lock-up-asylum -seekers, accessed Aug. 11, 2022.

24. Southern Poverty Law Center, "Immigrant Advocates Call to End Contracts and Shut Down Two Louisiana ICE Facilities over Racial Discrimination & Abuse," July 28, 2021, https://www.splcenter.org/presscenter/immigration -advocates-call-end-contracts-and-shut-down-two-louisiana-ice-facilities-over, accessed Aug. 11, 2022.

25. Human Rights First, *"I'm a Prisoner Here."*

26. Sanchez-Lopez et al., *The State of Black Immigrants in California*, 22.

27. Sanchez-Lopez et al., *The State of Black Immigrants in California*.

28. Sanchez-Lopez et al., *The State of Black Immigrants in California*.

29. Sanchez-Lopez et al., *The State of Black Immigrants in California*.

30. Sanchez-Lopez et al., *The State of Black Immigrants in California*, 24.

31. Sanchez-Lopez et al., *The State of Black Immigrants in California*.

32. N'dea Yancey-Bragg and Niraj Warikoo, "Patrick Lyoya Escaped Violence in Congo for the 'Safe Haven' of the US. Then Police Killed Him," *USA Today*, Apr. 18, 2022, https://www.usatoday.com/story/news/nation/2022/04 /16/michigan-patrick-lyoya-killing-black-migrants/7318904001, accessed Aug. 11, 2022.

33. Yancey-Bragg and Warikoo, "Patrick Lyoya Escaped Violence in Congo for the 'Safe Haven' of the US."

34. Sanchez-Lopez et al., *The State of Black Immigrants in California*.

35. Borger, "US to Send Asylum Seekers Home to Cameroon Despite 'Death Plane' Warnings."

36. The phrase "paper sons" describes Chinese men who used false papers to claim US citizenship, usually saying that they were sons born in China to US citizen fathers. Others were known to have falsely stated that they were born in San Francisco, but that their birth certificates were destroyed in the 1906 earthquake. Bill Ong Hing, *Making and Remaking Asian America Through Immigration Policy, 1850–1990* (Stanford, CA: Stanford University Press, 1993). I have written about my father's false claim to US citizenship and detention at Angel Island. Bill Ong Hing, "No Place for Angels: A Reaction to Johnson," *University of Illinois Law Review* 559 (2000), accessed Aug. 11, 2022.

37. Bill Ong Hing, "Detention to Deportation—Rethinking the Removal of Cambodian Refugees," *UC Davis Law Review* 38 (2005): 891.

CHAPTER 2: THE INHUMANE TREATMENT OF DETAINED CHILDREN

1. Reno v. Flores, 507 U.S. 292 (1993).

2. Matthew Haag, "Thousands of Immigrant Children Said They Were Sexually Abused in U.S. Detention Centers, Report Says," *New York Times*, Feb. 27, 2019, https://www.nytimes.com/2019/02/27/us/immigrant-children -sexual-abuse.html, accessed Aug. 18, 2022.

3. Emily Stewart, "The Multibillion-Dollar Business of Sheltering Migrant Children, Explained," *Vox*, June 25, 2018, https://www.vox.com/2018/6/23 /17493380/family-separation-shelter-money-children-southwest-key.

4. Jake Offenhartz, "Former Cayuga Center Employee Says She Witnessed 'Psychological Trauma' to Separated Migrant Kids," *Gothamist*, June 29, 2018, https://gothamist.com/news/former-cayuga-center-employee-says-she-witnessed -psychological-trauma-to-separated-migrant-kids, accessed Aug. 18, 2022.

5. Priscilla Alvarez, "Parents of 270 Children Separated at Border Under Trump Have Still Not Been Found, Court Filing Says," CNN.com, Nov. 3, 2021, https://www.cnn.com/2021/11/03/politics/border-separations-trump -administration/index.html, accessed Aug. 18, 2022.

6. Adriana Gomez Licon and Amy Taxin, Associated Press, "'Prison-Like Conditions' at Homestead Migrant Children Facility: Advocates," NBC 6, June 3, 2019, https://www.nbcmiami.com/news/local/prison-like-conditions -at-homestead-migrant-children-facility-advocates/142454, accessed Aug. 18, 2022.

7. Miriam Jordan, "Migrant Children Are Spending Months 'Crammed' in a Temporary Florida Shelter," *New York Times*, June 26, 2019, https://www .nytimes.com/2019/06/26/us/homestead-migrant-children-shelter.html, accessed Aug. 18, 2022.

8. Alexi C. Cardona, "Advocates Denounce Biden Plan to Reopen Homestead Migrant Children's Facility," *Miami New Times*, Feb. 23, 2021, https:// www.miaminewtimes.com/news/biden-to-reopen-homestead-shelter-for -migrant-children-11881926, accessed Aug. 18, 2022.

9. Aaron Blake, "No, Biden Isn't Putting 'Kids in Cages' Like Trump," *Washington Post*, Feb. 23, 2021, https://www.washingtonpost.com/politics /2021/02/23/no-bidens-new-border-move-isnt-like-trumps-kids-cages-not -hardly, accessed Aug. 18, 2022; Associated Press, "DOJ Lawyer: Sanitary Conditions for Detained Migrant Children Doesn't Necessarily Mean Providing 'Toothbrush and Soap,'" KQED, June 19, 2019, https://www.kqed.org /news/11755713/doj-lawyer-sanitary-conditions-for-detained-migrant-children -doesnt-necessarily-mean-providing-toothbrush-and-soap, accessed Aug. 18, 2022.

10. Alistair Graham Robertson et al., *Operation Streamline: Costs and Consequences*, Grassroots Leadership, Sept. 1, 2020, https://grassroots leadership.org/sites/default/files/uploads/GRL_Sept2012_Report-final.pdf, accessed Aug. 18, 2022.

11. Mark Moore, "COVID Cases Reportedly Surging in Illegal Immigrant Detention Centers," *New York Post*, July 7, 2021, https://nypost.com/2021/07 /06/covid-cases-reportedly-surging-in-immigrant-detention-centers, accessed Aug. 18, 2022.

12. In other facilities I have inspected, the team is given permission to walk around. For example, in an ICE detention facility in Dilley, Texas, run

by the private prison company CoreCivic, the guards walked us around. They were very proud to show us classrooms that looked like normal classrooms, a library that looked like a normal suburban branch library, a basketball court, and other outdoor playgrounds. Of course they could not hide the fact that the Dilley detention center was surrounded by barbed wire and armed guards. At Clint, we had to ask the children to describe the conditions.

13. Caitlin Dickerson, "'There Is a Stench': Soiled Clothes and No Baths for Migrant Children at a Texas Center," *New York Times*, June 21, 2019, https://www.nytimes.com/2019/06/21/us/migrant-children-border-soap.html, accessed Aug. 18, 2022; CBS Mornings, "250 Children Living Under Inhumane Conditions at Texas Border Facility, Doctors and Attorneys Say," CBS News, June 21, 2019, https://www.cbsnews.com/news/children-at-border-facility-children-living-inhumane-conditions-texas-border-facility-doctors-attorneys-say, accessed Aug. 18, 2022; Nick Valencia and Catherine E. Shoichet, "Lack of Soap, Filthy Onesies and Too Few Beds Have Created a 'Health Crisis' at Border Detention Facilities, Monitors Warn," CNN, June 21, 2019, https://www.cnn.com/2019/06/20/politics/border-detention-facilities-health, accessed Aug. 18, 2022; Dahlia Lithwick, "Some Did Not Have Socks. Their Hair Was Dirty," *Slate*, July 1, 2019, https://slate.com/news-and-politics/2019/07/kids-at-clint-border-crisis-immigration-lawyer-weighs-in.html, accessed Aug. 18, 2022.

14. Karen Ocamb, "Rep. Judy Chu: Witness to Inhumanity," *Los Angeles Blade*, July 10, 2019, https://www.losangelesblade.com/2019/07/10/rep-judy-chu-witness-to-inhumanity, accessed Aug. 18, 2022.

15. American Immigration Lawyers Association, "Documents Relating to *Flores v. Reno* Settlement Agreement of Minors in Immigration Custody," last modified June 22, 2022, https://www.aila.org/infonet/flores-v-reno-settlement-agreement, accessed Oct. 17, 2022.

16. Based on American Immigration Lawyers Association, "Documents Relating to *Flores v. Reno* Settlement Agreement of Minors in Immigration Custody."

17. Pamela Baez, "The Custody of 'Unaccompanied Children': A Critical Analysis and Recollection of Narratives," master's thesis, University of San Francisco, 2020, https://repository.usfca.edu/thes/1323.

18. Andrea Castillo and Jie Jenny Zou, "ICE Rushed to Release a Sick Woman, Avoiding Responsibility for Her Death. She Isn't Alone," *Los Angeles Times*, May 13, 2022, https://www.latimes.com/world-nation/story/2022-05-13/ice-immigration-detention-deaths-sick-detainees, accessed Aug. 18, 2022.

19. Dana Nickel, "Who Profits from Migrant Detention in the US?" *Globe Post*, Aug. 2, 2019, https://theglobepost.com/2019/08/19/profit-migrant-detention, accessed Aug. 18, 2022.

20. Andrea Castillo, "More Than a Million Could Die Waiting for Green Cards as U.S. Immigration Buckles amid COVID," *Los Angeles Times*, Aug. 4, 2022, https://www.latimes.com/politics/story/2022-08-04/la-na-pol-backlogs-immigration-system, accessed Jan. 19, 2023.

21. It turns out that the crime rates for noncitizens are far lower than those for native-born Americans. In 2018, the undocumented immigrant

criminal conviction rate was 782 per 100,000; 535 per 100,000 legal immigrants; and 1,422 per 100,000 native-born Americans. Alex Nowrasteh, "New
Research on Illegal Immigration and Crime," Cato Institute, Oct. 13, 2020,
https://www.cato.org/sites/cato.org/files/2020-10/working-paper-60.pdf, accessed Aug. 18, 2022.

22. ICE boasts about other aspects of its "alternatives to deportation"
(ATD) approach, which includes the use of cumbersome GPS ankle monitors.
The Biden administration reduced the use of ankle monitors and starting using
a SmartLINK phone app much more. The noncitizens have to download the
app on their own phones. They regularly receive messages to send ICE their
photo, which is confirmed biometrically. A simpler system that the Obama administration used for a time was telephonic monitoring. The noncitizen would
enroll in a telephonic reporting voice verification program and receive an au-
tomated telephone call at periodic intervals, which would require the person
to call the system back within a certain time frame; the computer would recognize the biometric voiceprint and register the "check-in."

23. Although the United States signed the United Nations Convention on
the Rights of the Child (CRC), Congress never ratified it. Arguments can be
made that the United States is still subject to its terms, but that's for courts to
someday determine. For now, the CRC provides some guiding principles from
the Convention on the Rights of the Child, https://www.unicef.org/child-rights
-convention/convention-text:

- Parties shall take all appropriate measures to ensure that the child is
  protected against all forms of discrimination or punishment on the basis
  of the status, activities, expressed opinions, or beliefs of the child's parents, legal guardians, or family members.
- In all actions concerning children, whether undertaken by public or private social welfare institutions, courts of law, administrative authorities or legislative bodies, the best interests of the child shall be a primary
  consideration.
- No child shall be deprived of his or her liberty unlawfully or arbitrarily.
  The arrest, detention or imprisonment of a child shall be in conformity
  with the law and shall be used only as a measure of last resort and for
  the shortest appropriate period of time.

It seems clear that US detention of migrant children violates the CRC because it constitutes punishment, is not in the child's best interest, and has not
been used as a measure of last resort. The United Kingdom has fully ratified
the CRC, and that has made a difference when it comes to detaining migrant
children.

24. "Immigration Detention in the UK," The Migration Observatory, Nov.
2, 2022, https://migrationobservatory.ox.ac.uk/resources/briefings/immigration
-detention-in-the-uk, accessed Jan. 19, 2023.

CHAPTER 3: DEPORTING AGGRAVATED FELONS

1. "Table 41. Aliens Removed by Criminal Status and Region and Country
of Nationality: Fiscal Year 2016," Department of Homeland Security, 2016,

https://www.dhs.gov/immigration-statistics/yearbook/2016/table41, accessed Aug. 31, 2022.

2. Teresa Wiltz, "What Crimes Are Eligible for Deportation?" *Stateline*, Pew Charitable Trusts, Dec. 21, 2016, https://www.pewtrusts.org/en/research -and-analysis/blogs/stateline/2016/12/21/what-crimes-are-eligible-for-deportation, accessed Aug. 31, 2022.

3. Lundy Khoy, email to Bill Ong Hing, May 1, 2022.

4. When lawful permanent resident parents complete the citizenship naturalization process, their children under the age of eighteen automatically become US citizens as well.

5. "Save Lundy—The Story of an American Girl," YouTube video, last modified Aug. 7, 2012, https://www.youtube.com/watch?v=6KT_ZSiucRY.

6. Zadvydas v. Davis, 533 U.S. 678 (2001).

7. Padilla v. Kentucky, 559 U.S. 356 (2010); Chaidez v. United States, 568 U.S. 342 (2013).

8. Agnes Constante, "After Facing Life in Prison and Deportation, Reformed Inmate Receives U.S. Citizenship," NBC News, Jan. 5, 2017, https:// www.nbcnews.com/news/asian-america/after-facing-life-prison-deportation -reformed-inmate-receives-u-s-n703491, accessed Jan. 4, 2023.

9. In fact, the Board of Immigration Appeals has ruled that expungement of crimes and other sentence reduction statutes do not always eliminate the conviction for deportation purposes.

10. Jay Stansell, email to Bill Ong Hing, Apr. 26, 2022.

11. Bill Ong Hing, Jennifer M. Chacon, and Kevin R. Johnson, *Immigration Law and Social Justice* (New York: Wolters Kluwer, 2021).

12. Jay Stansell, assistant federal public defender, Seattle, WA, to Daniel M. Kowalski, attorney, Austin, TX, email, Oct. 18, 2002, 16:02 PST; on file with author.

13. Separate deportation provisions were provided for possession of weapons and prostitution as well. An alien convicted of possession of a sawed-off shotgun or certain automatic weapons any time after entry was subject to deportation. One conviction at any time was sufficient. On the other hand, no conviction was necessary to deport a noncitizen who had engaged in prostitution, as a prostitute, procurer, or recipient of funds from prostitution.

14. As told to author.

15. Ashby v. INS, 961 F.2d 555 (5th Cir. 1992).

16. Varela-Blanco v. INS, 26 F.3d 832 (8th Cir. 1994).

17. Diaz-Resendez v. INS, 960 F.2d 493 (5th Cir. 1992).

18. Jennifer Chacón, "Unsecured Borders: Immigration Restrictions, Crime Control and National Security," *Connecticut Law Review* 39 (Nov. 9, 2007), https://tinyurl.com/2p9xwnj2, accessed Aug. 29, 2022.

19. Chacón, "Unsecured Borders."

20. Yepes-Pardo v. INS, 10 F.3d 1363 (9th Cir. 1993).

21. Valerie Neal, "Slings and Arrows of Outrageous Fortune: The Deportation of 'Aggravated Felons,'" *Vanderbilt Journal of Transnational Law* 36 (2003): 1621.

22. Sor Vann was a thirty-four-year-old construction worker in Houston who was charged with indecent exposure for urinating in public. He was placed on six years' probation. He was caught urinating in public again one month before his six-year probation was completed. Although the offense was only a misdemeanor, violating probation was a felony, and he served four years in prison. That made him a deportable aggravated felon. He had a wife and two young children. Before he entered the United States as a refugee, his parents were murdered by the Khmer Rouge.

23. Nasri v. France: European Court of Human Rights (1995), https://hudoc.echr.coe.int/eng#, accessed Dec. 26, 2022.

24. AR (Pakistan) v. Secretary of State for the Home Department, England and Wales Court of Appeal (Civil Division), July 15, 2010, https://www.casemine.com/judgement/uk/5a8ff70960d03e7f57ea6609.

25. Dana Leigh Marks, "Let Immigration Judges Be Judges," *The Hill*, May 9, 2013, https://tinyurl.com/2p8mjryk, accessed Aug. 29, 2022.

26. Paul Grussendorf, "Immigration Judges Need Discretion," *San Francisco Chronicle Online*, Apr. 12, 2013, http://www.sfchronicle.com/opinion/openforum/article/Immigration-judges-need-discretion-4428406.php, accessed Dec. 26, 2022.

27. Robert Johnson, "Justice System Should Determine Which Immigrants Are Public Safety Risk," *Roll Call*, May 16, 2013.

28. Steven Jansen, "A Prosecutor's Call: Justice for All," *The Hill*, May 21, 2013, http://thehill.com/blogs/congress-blog/judicial/300903-a-prosecutors-call-justice-for-all, accessed Dec. 26, 2022.

29. Jeff Rosen, "Immigration Reform Should End Injustice to Minor Offenders," *San Jose Mercury News Online*, Aug. 9, 2013, http://www.mercurynews.com/opinion/ci_23814309/jeff-rosen-immigration-reform-should-endinjustice-minor, accessed Dec. 26, 2022.

30. Mary Jo White, *Corporate Criminal Liability: What Has Gone Wrong?* (New York: Practising Law Institute, 2005), 815–18.

31. Bill Vlasic and Matt Apuzzo, "Toyota Is Fined $1.2 Billion for Concealing Safety Defects," *New York Times*, Mar. 19, 2014, https://www.nytimes.com/2014/03/20/business/toyota-reaches-1-2-billion-settlement-in-criminal-inquiry.html, accessed Aug. 29, 2022.

32. US Department of Justice, "America Online Charged with Aiding and Abetting Securities Fraud," news release no. 04-790, Dec. 15, 2004, http://www.usdoj.gov/opa/pr/2004/December/04_crm790.html, accessed Aug. 29, 2022.

33. Julia Preston, "The True Costs of Deportation," Marshall Project, June 18, 2020, https://www.themarshallproject.org/2020/06/22/the-true-costs-of-deportation, accessed Aug. 29, 2022.

CHAPTER 4: DEPORTING ANTONIO SANCHEZ
1. I am not using Antonio Sanchez's true name, nor those of his family members, for privacy purposes.

2. 27 I&N Dec. 808 (BIA 2020), https://www.justice.gov/eoir/page/file/1264601/download.

3. Memorandum from John Morton, ICE director, "Exercising Prosecutorial Discretion Consistent with the Civil Immigration Enforcement Priorities of the Agency for the Apprehension, Detention, and Removal of Aliens," US Department of Homeland Security, June 17, 2011, https://www.ice.gov/doclib/secure-communities/pdf/prosecutorial-discretion-memo.pdf, accessed Dec. 28, 2022.

4. Rev. A.M., to Judge Loreto S. Geisse, Feb. 12, 2008, quoting Rev. A.M., executive director, Berkeley (Calif.) Organizing Congregations for Action; on file with author.

5. Quotes here and below are from the union representative, PTA president, friends and neighbors to Judge Loreto S. Geisse, Nov. 1, 2007; on file with author.

6. Quotes in this paragraph are from letters my students collected on behalf of Roberto; on file with author.

7. Quotes here and below are from letters collected by Angie Bean, attorney, filed on behalf of Antonio in immigration court; on file with author.

8. Lorena Cintron to Judge Geisse, 2008; on file with author.

9. Transcript of Oral Decision at 3, In re [Antonio Sanchez], No. A-xx-xxx-xxx (Sept. 12, 2008).

10. Timothy S. Aitken, field officer dir., ICE, DHS, phone interview with author, Sept. 21, 2011.

11. Application for Humanitarian Parole from Bill Ong Hing to USCIS (Nov. 30, 2011).

12. Kathy Lee and John He, "DREAM Deferred," *Harvard Political Review* (Oct. 30, 2010), http://hpronline.org/covers/higher-education/dream-deferred, accessed Dec. 29, 2022.

13. Lee and He, "DREAM Deferred."

14. Lee and He, "DREAM Deferred."

15. Office of Senator Dick Durbin, "Durbin, Reid, 20 Senate Democrats Write Obama on Current Situation of DREAM Act Students," press release, Apr. 13, 2011, http://durbin.senate.gov/public/index.cfm/pressreleases, accessed Dec. 29, 2022.

16. Susan Carroll, "U.S. to Review 300,000 Deportation Cases," *Houston Chronicle*, Aug. 18, 2011, http://www.chron.com/news/houston-texas/article/U-S-to-review-300-000-deportation-cases-2122837.php, accessed Dec. 29, 2022.

17. Office of Senator Dick Durbin, "Durbin, Reid, 20 Senate Democrats Write Obama on Current Situation of DREAM Act Students."

18. Lynn Sweet, "Immigration: Obama Eases Student Deportations with New Policy Applauded by Durbin, Gutierrez," *Chicago Sun-Times*, Aug. 18, 2011.

19. Thomas M. Susman, director, American Bar Association Government Affairs Office, to John Morton, director, ICE, Dec. 15, 2011, http://www.aila.org/content/default.aspx?docid=38021, accessed Dec. 29, 2022.

20. Mickey McCarter, "White House Vows to Drop Low-Priority Cases for Illegal Aliens," *HS Today*, Aug. 19, 2011, http://www.hstoday.us/briefings/today-s-news-analysis/single-article/white-house-vows-to-drop-low-priority-deportation-cases-for-illegal-aliens/22b3625f617e370d2380c4f24b22b889.html, accessed Dec. 29, 2022.

21. Immigration Policy Center, American Immigration Council, *Prosecutorial Discretion: A Statistical Assessment*, June 11, 2012, https://www.american immigrationcouncil.org/research/prosecutorial-discretion-statistical-analysis.

22. American Immigration Lawyers Association and American Immigration Council, "Holding DHS Accountable on Prosecutorial Discretion" (2011), 11, 15, 19, http://www.aila.org, accessed Dec. 29, 2022.

23. American Immigration Lawyers Association and American Immigration Council, "Holding DHS Accountable on Prosecutorial Discretion."

24. "Good Immigration Policy, on Hold," editorial, *New York Times*, Jan. 14, 2012, https://www.nytimes.com/2012/01/15/opinion/sunday/good-immigration-policy-on-hold.html, accessed Dec. 29, 2022.

25. National Immigration and Customs Enforcement Council, "ICE Agent's Union Speaks Out on Director's 'Discretionary Memo' Calls on the Public to Take Action," press release, June 23, 2011.

26. Elise Foley, "Kris Kobach Represents Immigration Agents in Lawsuit Against Obama Administration," *Huffington Post*, Aug. 23, 2012, http://www.huffingtonpost.com/2012/08/23/kris-kobach-immigration-lawsuit-obama_n_1825272.html.

27. Ani Palacios McBride, "Dream Activist Blames Senators Reid and Durbin for Deportations," *La Columna*, Oct. 12, 2011, http://contacto-latino.com/ideas-latinas/la-columna/2003/dream-activist-blames-senators-reid-and-durbin-for-deportations.

28. Posting of Violeta Raquel Chapin, violeta.chapin@colorado.edu, to immprof@listserv.unc.edu and to crimimm@yahoogroups.com, Apr. 9, 2012.

29. Jorge Rivas, "ICE Confirms DREAMer Yanelli Hernandez Deported to Mexico," *Colorlines*, Jan. 31, 2012, https://truthout.org/articles/ice-confirms-dreamer-yanelli-hernandez-deported-to-mexico, accessed Dec. 29, 2022.

30. Hernandez v. Gonzales, 437 F.3d 341 (3d Cir. 2006).

31. 23 I&N Dec. 56 (BIA 2001).

32. Matter of Andazola, 23 I&N Dec. 319 (BIA 2002).

33. Lorena Cintron to Bill Ong Hing, professor of law, University of San Francisco, email, Apr. 17, 2012.

34. Telephone interview with Timothy S. Aitken, field officer director, ICE, DHS, Sept. 21, 2011.

CHAPTER 5: GIVING THE BENEFIT OF THE DOUBT TO ASYLUM SEEKERS

1. US law distinguishes between "refugees," who are granted entry as refugees, and "asylees," who apply for and are granted asylum after presenting themselves at the border, entering without inspection, or arriving with nonimmigrant visas (such as those for students and tourists). The law permits the president to set the annual number of refugees to be admitted from abroad. For example, President Obama established a refugee number of 110,000 in his last year in office. President Biden set the number at 125,000 in his first year in office. In his last year in office, President Trump set the number at 15,000—an all-time low. The vast majority of the numbers are reserved for refugees from Africa, the Near East, and South Asia. Few refugee slots are reserved for individuals from Lain America and the Caribbean. Refugees are admitted only

after being vetted by the United Nations High Commissioner for Refugees, the State Department, and the Department of Homeland Security—a process that can take two years.

2. INS v. Stevic, 467 U.S. 407 (1984).

3. INS v. Cardoza-Fonseca, 480 U.S. 421 (1987).

4. 8 U.S.C. § 1101(a)(42)(A).

5. McMullen v. INS, 658 F.2d 1312 (1981).

6. *INS v. Stevic.*

7. Cardoza-Fonseca v. INS, 767 F.2d 1448 (9th Cir. 1985).

8. Andrea Bianchi, "International Law and US Courts: The Myth of Lohengrin Revisited," *European Journal of International Law* (2004): 10.

9. *INS v. Cardoza-Fonseca.*

10. "Judge-by-Judge Asylum Decisions in Immigration Courts FY 2017–2022," TRAC Immigration, October 26, 2022, https://trac.syr.edu /immigration/reports/judge2022.

11. Matter of Mogharrabi, 19 I&N Dec. 439 (BIA 1987).

12. *Matter of Mogharrabi.*

13. *Well-Founded Fear,* dir. Michael Camerini and Shari Robertson, Epidavros Project, 2000.

14. Matter of A-S-, 21 I&N Dec. 1106 (1998).

15. Matter of A-S- (BIA Chairman Paul W. Schmidt, dissenting).

16. Shrestha v. Holder, 590 F.3d 1034 (9th Cir. 2010).

17. Rodriguez-Ramirez v. Garland, 11 F.4th 1091 (9th Cir. 2021).

18. Cuesta-Rojas v. Garland, 991 F.3d 266 (1st Cir. 2021).

19. Munyuh v. Garland, 11 F.4th 750 (9th Cir. 2021).

20. Mike LaSusa, "3 Tips for Building a Trauma-Informed Immigration Practice," *Law360,* Nov. 8, 2021, https://www.law360.com/articles/1438319/3 -tips-for-building-a-trauma-informed-immigration-practice.

21. Carol M. Suzuki, "Unpacking Pandora's Box: Innovative Techniques for Effectively Counseling Asylum Applicants Suffering from Post-Traumatic Stress Disorder," *Hastings Race and Poverty Law Journal* 4 (2007): 235, https://repository.uchastings.edu/cgi/viewcontent.cgi?article=1039&context =hastings_race_poverty_law_journal.

22. Suzuki, "Unpacking Pandora's Box."

23. Suzuki, "Unpacking Pandora's Box."

24. Affidavit of Annika Sridharan, licensed clinical psychologist, Dec. 20, 2017.

25. Ana Gonzalez-Barrera, "Apprehensions of Mexican Migrants at U.S. Borders Reach Near-Historic Low," Pew Research Center, Apr. 24, 2016, https://www.pewresearch.org/fact-tank/2016/04/14/mexico-us-border -apprehensions.

26. Camilo Montoya-Galvez, "Sessions and Top Aides Pushed for Separating Migrant Families Despite Warnings, Report Finds," CBS News, Jan. 14, 2021, https://www.cbsnews.com/news/jeff-sessions-trump-family-separation -policy.

27. Matter of A-B-, 27 I&N Dec. 316 (2018).

28. These cases are examples of viable political opinion claims based on female subordination: Hernandez-Chacon v. Barr, 948 F.3d 94 (2d Cir. 2020); Rodriguez Tornes v. Garland, 993 F.3d 743 (9th Cir. 2021).

29. Matter of A-R-C-G-, 26 I&N Dec. 388 (BIA 2014).

30. Perdomo v. Holder, 611 F.3d 662 (9th Cir. 2010).

31. Cece v. Holder, 733 F.3d 662 (7th Cir. 2013).

32. Matter of Kasinga, 21 I&N Dec. 357 (1996); Sarhan v. Holder, 658 F.3d 649 (7th Cir. 2011).

33. Ramos v. Holder, 589 F.3d 426 (7th Cir. 2009).

34. Henriquez-Rivas v. Holder, 707 F.3d 1081 (9th Cir. 2013).

35. Villegas Sanchez v. Garland, 990 F.3d 1173 (9th Cir. 2021).

36. Matter of H-L-S-A-, 28 I&N Dec. 228 (2021).

37. Velasquez-Gaspar v. Barr, 976 F.3d 1062 (9th Cir. 2020).

38. Flores-Rios v. Lynch, No. 12–72551 (9th Cir. 2015).

39. Matter of L-E-A- II, 27 I&N Dec. 581 (2019).

40. Matter of A-C-A-A-, 28 I. & N. Dec. 351 (2021).

41. Demiraj v. Holder 631 F.3d 194 (5th Cir. 2011).

42. *Demiraj v. Holder.*

43. *Demiraj v. Holder.*

44. 27 I&N Dec. 303 (2018).

45. However, asylum can still be denied if the government shows that conditions in the country have improved so much that the applicant no longer has a well-founded fear, or if the applicant can reasonably relocate to another part of the country and be safe. 8 C.F.R. § 1208.13(b)(1).

46. Kaur v. Wilkinson, 986 F.3d 1216 (9th Cir. 2021).

47. A dissenting judge would have ruled against Kaur on the grounds that it was not clear that the men who assaulted her did so on behalf of the government.

48. Afriyie v. Holder, 613 F.3d 924 (9th Cir. 2010).

49. "Nicaraguan President Daniel Ortega, from Revolutionary Leader to Opposition Hate Leader," BBC News, July 19, 2018, https://www.bbc.com/news/world-latin-america-15544315.

50. "The 'Reagan Doctrine' Is Announced," History.com, Feb. 4, 2020, https://www.history.com/this-day-in-history/the-reagan-doctrine-is-announced.

51. Anthony Jensen, "Fleeing North: An Examination of U.S. Refugee and Asylum Policy Towards Nicaragua," *Political Science Student Work*, May 2012, https://digitalcommons.csbsju.edu/cgi/viewcontent.cgi?article=1000&context=polsci_students.

52. James Gerstenzang and Juanita Darling, "Clinton Gives Apology for U.S. Role in Guatemala," *Los Angeles Times*, Mar. 11, 1999, https://www.latimes.com/archives/la-xpm-1999-mar-11-mn-16261-story.html.

53. Raymond Bonner, "Guatemalan Army and Leftist Rebels Locked in War," *New York Times*, Dec. 4, 1981, https://www.nytimes.com/1981/12/04/world/guatemalan-army-and-leftist-rebels-locked-in-war.html; James Lemoyne, "Salvador Rebels: Where Do They Get the Arms?," *New York Times*, Nov. 24, 1988, https://www.nytimes.com/1988/11/24/world/salvador-rebels-where-do-they-get-the-arms.html.

54. Jensen, "Fleeing North."

55. Charles Kamasaki, "US Immigration Policy: A Classic, Unappreciated Example of Structural Racism," *Brookings*, Mar. 26, 2021, https://www.brookings.edu/blog/how-we-rise/2021/03/26/us-immigration-policy-a-classic-unappreciated-example-of-structural-racism; Michel Skolnik, "Trump's Racist Immigration Policies Ignore the Real Causes of Migration from Central America," ActionAid, May 30, 2018, https://www.actionaidusa.org/insight/immigration-real-causes-central-america.

56. Sarah Gammage, "El Salvador: Despite End to Civil War, Emigration Continues," Migration Information Source, Migration Policy Institute, July 26, 2007, https://www.migrationpolicy.org/article/el-salvador-despite-end-civil-war-emigration-continues.

57. Orantes-Hernandez v. Smith, 541 F. Supp. 351 (C.D. Cal. 1982); Orantes-Hernandez v. Thornburgh, 919 F.2d 549 (9th Cir. 1990).

58. Michaela Ross and Brandon Lee, "What to Know in Washington: Biden Faces Bipartisan Border Angst," *Bloomberg Government*, Apr. 25, 2022, https://about.bgov.com/news/what-to-know-in-washington-biden-faces-bipartisan-border-angst.

59. Immigrants' Rights Policy Clinic, *The Biden Administration's Dedicated Docket: Inside Los Angeles' Accelerated Court Hearings for Families Seeking Asylum*, UCLA Center for Immigration Law and Policy, May 2022, https://law.ucla.edu/sites/default/files/PDFs/Center_for_Immigration_Law_and_Policy/Dedicated_Docket_in_LA_Report_FINAL_05.22.pdf.

60. *INS v. Cardoza-Fonseca.*

61. Paragraph 203 of the *Handbook on Procedures and Criteria for Determining Refugee Status and Guidelines on International Protection, Under the 1951 Convention and the 1967 Protocol Relating to the Status of Refugees*, reissued (Geneva: UNHCR, Feb. 2019), https://www.unhcr.org/en-us/publications/legal/5ddfcdc47/handbook-procedures-criteria-determining-refugee-status-under-1951-convention.html (emphasis added).

62. *Matter of Mogharrabi.*

63. *INS v. Cardoza-Fonseca.*

CHAPTER 6: DYSFUNCTIONAL IMMIGRATION COURTS

1. Ng Fung Ho v. White, 259 U.S. 276 (1922).

2. Immigrant Law Center of Minnesota, "Death Penalty Cases in Traffic Court Setting," press release, Mar. 31, 2020, https://www.ilcm.org/latest-news/death-penalty-cases-in-traffic-court-setting, accessed Sept. 22, 2022.

3. Priscilla Alvarez, "Immigration Judges Quit in Response to Administration Policies," CNN.com, Dec. 27, 2019, https://www.cnn.com/2019/12/27/politics/immigration-judges-resign/index.html.

4. Immigrant Law Center of Minnesota, "Death Penalty Cases in Traffic Court Setting."

5. Rick Tulsky, "Controversial Cook County Judge Nicholas Ford Retired from the Bench Last Month," *Chicago Sun-Times*, May 13, 2019, https://chicago.suntimes.com/crime/2019/5/16/18628320/cook-county-judge-nicholas

-ford-appointment-immigration-court-controversy-lawyers-group, accessed
Sept. 22, 2022.

6. "Ford Campaign Sign-On Letter," National Lawyers Guild, San Francisco Bay Area Chapter, Nov. 2020, https://nlgsf.ourpowerbase.net/fireford, accessed Oct. 25, 2022.

7. Associated Press, "Immigration Judge, Subject of Complaint by Lawyers, Retires," Apr. 18, 2021, https://apnews.com/article/san-francisco
-immigration-courts-illinois-a42d5d54a798583c7afff8f8e01f1a3f, accessed
Sept. 22, 2022.

8. TRAC Immigration, "Judge V. Stuart Couch: FY 2017–2022, Charlotte
Immigration Court," Oct. 26, 2022, https://trac.syr.edu/immigration/reports
/judgereports/00394CHL/index.html.

9. Nathan Morabito, "Charlotte Immigration Judge Threatened to Sic 'Big
Dog' on Child During Hearing," WCNC, Sept. 11, 2019, https://www.wcnc.com
/article/news/investigations/investigators/charlotte-immigration-judge-threatened
-sic-dog-child-hearing/275-3db2f071-32e0-49ae-a5b8-f455783e0da2, accessed
Sept. 22, 2022.

10. Jerry Markon, "Can a 3-Year Old Represent Herself in Immigration
Court? This Judge Thinks So," *Washington Post*, Mar. 5, 2016, https://www
.washingtonpost.com/world/national-security/can-a-3-year-old-represent
-herself-in-immigration-court-this-judge-thinks-so/2016/03/03/5be59a32
-db25-11e5-925f-1d10062cc82d_story.html, accessed Sept. 22, 2022.

11. These are referred to as Article I courts under the US Constitution.
Article III of the Constitution establishes the Supreme Court and the other federal court below the Supreme Court, the district court (trial courts), and the
federal circuit courts of appeals.

12. 8 U.S.C. § 1153(a)(7) (1972).

13. Members of Congress have the authority to introduce legislation to
grant lawful residence or citizenship to individuals facing deportation. Like
any other legislation, the bill must be passed by both houses of Congress and
signed by the president. The practice has not been used much since the Abscam
scandal (1978–1980), when members of Congress were convicted on bribery
and corruption charges for activities that included introducing private bills on
behalf of noncitizens associated with a casino project in Atlantic City.

14. Bob Egelko, "Ollie Marie-Victoire, SF Judge, Dies," *SFGATE*, Aug. 16,
2012, https://www.sfgate.com/bayarea/article/Ollie-Marie-Victoire-S-F-judge
-dies-3794680.php#:~:text=Marie%2DVictoire%2C%20who%20heard%
20cases,She%20was%2088, accessed Sept. 22, 2022.

15. Lopez-Telles v. INS, 564 F.2d 1302 (1977).

16. 8 C.F.R. § 242.7(a) (1977).

17. Transcript of Hearing Record of [Yelena Gorev], Dec. 4, 2007.

18. Letter from [Yelena Gorev], ICE detainee, to Hon. Anthony Murry, immigration judge, San Francisco Immigration Court, Oct. 29, 2007.

19. Transcript of Hearing Record of [Yelena Gorev], Dec. 4, 2007.

20. Decision of the Immigration Judge in the Matter of Yelena Gorev
(Dec. 4, 2007).

21. The account of Fento's (a pseudonym) case was provided by Holly Cooper, staff attorney at the UC Davis Immigration Clinic; on file with the author.

22. Jeff Adachi et al., "Why We Should Provide Lawyers to Immigrants Facing Deportation," *San Francisco Examiner*, Nov. 29, 2016, https://sfpublic defender.org/news/2016/11/why-we-should-provide-lawyers-to-immigrants -facing-deportation, accessed Jan. 2, 2023.

23. TRAC Immigration, *Representation for Unaccompanied Children in Immigration Court*, Nov. 25, 2014, https://trac.syr.edu/immigration/reports /371, accessed Jan. 2, 2023.

24. Jacinto v. INS, 208 F.3d 725 (9th Cir. 2000).

25. Franco-Gonzales v. Holder, 767 F. Supp. 2d 1034 (2010).

26. Gideon v. Wainwright, 372 US 335 (1963), https://www.oyez.org /cases/1962/155.

27. José Magaña-Salgado, *Detention, Deportation, and Devastation: The Disproportionate Effect of Deportations on the Latino Community*, Mexican American Legal Defense and Education Fund, National Day Laborer Organizing Network, and National Hispanic Leadership Agenda, May 2014, https:// www.maldef.org/wp-content/uploads/2019/01/Deportation_Brief_MALDEF -NHLA-NDLON.pdf, accessed Sept. 22, 2022.

28. Annie Chen, "Universal Representation Advances Racial Equity for Immigrants Facing Deportation," Vera Institute of Justice, Oct. 15, 2020, https://www.vera.org/news/universal-representation-advances-racial-equity -for-immigrants-facing-deportation, accessed Sept. 22, 2022.

29. UK Border Agency, Immigration Group, *Review into Ending the Detention of Children for Immigration Purposes*, Home Office, UK Border Agency, Dec. 2010, https://assets.publishing.service.gov.uk/government /uploads/system/uploads/attachment_data/file/257654/child-detention -conclusions.pdf, last accessed Sept. 22, 2022.

EPILOGUE

1. Operation Gatekeeper was instituted by the Clinton administration to close off the parts of the border that were easiest to traverse. As a result, thousands of migrants have died trying to cross through the desert or another dangerous terrain. See Bill Ong Hing, "The Dark Side of Operation Gatekeeper," *UC Davis Journal of International Law & Policy* 121, no. 7 (2001). In 2022, 748 migrants died at the US southern border because of the dangerous terrain; the figure surpassed the 557 deaths that were recorded for 2021. Priscilla Alvarez, "A Record Number of Migrants Have Died Crossing the US-Mexico Border," CNN, Sept. 7, 2022, https://www.cnn.com/2022/09/07/politics/us -mexico-border-crossing-deaths/index.html.

2. Bill Ong Hing, "Institutional Racism, ICE Raids, and Immigration Reform," *University of San Francisco Law Review* 44 (2009): 307.

3. To access the UFCW report, see Desiree Evans, "Study Finds Workplace Immigration Raids Unlawful," *Facing South*, July 2, 2009, https://www.facing south.org/2009/07/study-finds-workplace-immigration-raids-unlawful.html, accessed Sept. 21, 2022.

4. Jennifer Jung Wuk Lee, "Immigration Disobedience" *California Law Review* (Mar. 24, 2022), forthcoming 2023, Temple University Legal Studies Research Paper No. 2022-09, https://ssrn.com/abstract=4079709; Bill Ong Hing, "Addressing the Intersection of Racial Justice and Immigrant Rights," *Belmont Law Review* 9 (2022): 357; Bill Ong Hing, "Immigration Sanctuary Policies: Constitutional and Representative of Good Policing and Good Public Policy," *UC Irvine Law Review* 247 (2012): 261.

5. Kevin R. Johnson and Bill Ong Hing, "The Immigrant Marches of 2006 and the Prospects for a New Civil Rights Movement," *Harvard Civil Rights & Civil Liberties Law Review* 99 (2007): 42.

6. DREAMers are named for the Development, Relief, and Education for Alien Minors (DREAM) Act, first introduced in Congress in 2001. Over the years, many versions of the DREAM Act have been introduced in Congress. While the various versions of the bill have contained some key differences, they all would provide a pathway to legal status for noncitizens, without proper immigration papers, who came to this country as children. Despite bipartisan support for each iteration of the bill, none have become law.

7. Telephone conversation between Gaby Pacheco and Bill Ong Hing, Dec. 20, 2010.

8. Kate Brumback, "Georgia Immigration Law: 6 Illegal Immigrants Arrested During Protest," *Huffington Post*, June 28, 2011, https://www.huffpost.com/entry/georgia-immigration-law-economy_n_995889.

9. Julie Mason, "On Immigration, Obama Blames GOP," *Politico*, July 25, 2011, https://www.politico.com/story/2011/07/on-immigration-obama-blames-gop-059842, accessed Sept. 26, 2022.

10. Glenn Kessler, "Obama's Royal Flip-Flop on Using Executive Action on Illegal Immigration," *Washington Post*, Nov. 18, 2014, https://www.washingtonpost.com/news/fact-checker/wp/2014/11/18/obamas-flip-flop-on-using-executive-action-on-illegal-immigration.

11. Rebecca Kaplan, "Obama Is 'Deporter-in-Chief,' Says Prominent Latino Group," CBS News, Mar. 4, 2014, https://www.cbsnews.com/news/obama-is-deporter-in-chief-says-prominent-latino-group.

12. National Immigrant Justice Center, "Immigration Detention Bed Quota Timeline," Jan. 2017, https://immigrantjustice.org/sites/default/files/content-type/commentary-item/documents/2017-01/Immigration%20Detention%20Bed%20Quota%20Timeline%202017_01_05.pdf, accessed Jan. 3, 2023.

13. Leighton Akio Woodhouse, "Obama's Deportation Policy Was Even Worse Than We Thought," *The Intercept*, May 15, 2017, https://theintercept.com/2017/05/15/obamas-deportation-policy-was-even-worse-than-we-thought.

14. Amy Goodman, "Plea to End Deportations Heard Nationwide as Activist Interrupts Obama Speech on Immigration," *Democracy Now!*, Nov. 27, 2013, available at https://www.alternet.org/2013/11/plea-end-deportations-heard-nationwide-activist-interrupts-obama-speech-immigration.

15. Ju was one of countless DREAMers with whom I have worked in the Bay Area, speaking at rallies and various events in favor of the DREAM Act and comprehensive immigration reform. A graduate of the University

of California, Berkeley, he was particularly active in a local DREAMer organization: ASPIRE—Asian Students Promoting Immigrant Rights Through Education.

16. Sam Levin, "Airbnb Vows to Be First Company to Defy Trump and Keep Employing Dreamers," *The Guardian*, Sept. 7, 2017, https://www.the guardian.com/us-news/2017/sep/07/silicon-valley-executives-dreamers-daca -trump, accessed Sept. 21, 2022.

17. 8 U.S. Code § 1324a.

18. Dina Bass, "Major Corporations, Including Google and Wells Fargo, Condemn Trump Move to End DACA," *St. Louis Post-Dispatch*, Sept. 5, 2017, http://www.stltoday.com/business/local/major-corporations-including-google -and-wells-fargo-condemn-trump-move/article_eb6bc212-093f-5a42-8908 -e4bf489f2183.html.

19. Thomas J. Donohue, "Clock Is Ticking for DACA Solution," US Chamber of Commerce, Oct. 2, 2017, https://www.uschamber.com/series/your -corner/clock-ticking-daca-solution.

20. Daniel T. Ostas, "Civil Disobedience in a Business Context: Examining the Social Obligation to Obey Inane Laws," *American Business Law Journal* 47 (2010): 291, 299, 312.

21. Ostas, "Civil Disobedience in a Business Context," 291.

22. Cynthia A. Williams, "Corporate Compliance with the Law in the Era of Efficiency," *North Carolina Law Review* 76 (1998): 1265.

23. Bill Ong Hing, "Beyond DACA—Defying Employer Sanctions Through Civil Disobedience," *UC Davis Law Review* 299, no. 52 (2018).

24. Bill Ong Hing, "African Migration to the United States: Assigned to the Back of the Bus," in *The Immigration and Nationality Act of 1965: Legislating a New America*, ed. Gabriel Chin and Rose Cuison Villazor (New York: Cambridge University Press, 2015); Bill Ong Hing, *Making and Remaking Asian America Through Immigration Policy, 1850–1990* (Stanford, CA: Stanford University Press, 1993).

25. Julie Su, "Making the Invisible Visible: The Garment Industry's Dirty Laundry," *Journal of Gender, Race & Justice* 405 (1998): 1.

26. Ironically, years later, Julie Su was appointed California Labor Commissioner by Gov. Jerry Brown, then the California secretary of labor by Gov. Gavin Newsom. Julie was appointed by President Biden to serve as the US deputy secretary of labor and confirmed by the Senate on July 13, 2021. She was a MacArthur "genius award" winner, largely because of her work with the Thai garment workers.

27. ACLU challenged virtually all of the Trump administration's efforts to thwart asylum seekers, including the family separation policy.

28. Peter Schey successfully challenged the attempt by Texas to foreclose K–12 education for undocumented children in Plyler v. Doe, 457 U.S. 202 (1987).

29. Gaby Del Valle, "The Dark, Racist History of Section 1325 of U.S. Immigration Law," *Vice*, June 27, 2019, https://www.vice.com/en/article/a3x8x8 /the-dark-racist-history-of-section-1325-of-us-immigration-law, accessed Sept. 21, 2022.

30. Roque Planas, "Julián Castro Hammers 2020 Candidates over Criminalization of Immigrants," *Huffington Post*, June 26, 2019, https://www.huffpost.com/entry/julian-castro-immigrants-2020-democrats_n_5d143402e4b0d0a2c0ab8e74, accessed Oct. 16, 2022.

31. Jesse Franzblau, "Landmark Decision Finds 'Illegal Reentry' Charges Are Racist In Origin, Discriminatory In Practice," National Immigrant Justice Center, Aug. 26, 2021, https://immigrantjustice.org/staff/blog/landmark-decision-finds-illegal-reentry-charges-are-racist-origin-discriminatory, accessed Sept. 21, 2022.

32. In *Gonzalez-Rivera v. INS*, 22 F.3d 1441 (9th Cir. 1994), the federal Ninth Circuit Court of Appeals suppressed evidence gathered as a result of a stop, based solely on the individual's Latin appearance. Almeida-Amaral v. Gonzales, 461 F.3d 231, 235 (2d Cir. 2006) ("Even where the seizure is not especially severe, it may nevertheless qualify as an egregious violation if the stop was based on race.").

33. Matter of S-M-J-, 21 I&N Dec. 722, 727 (BIA 1997).

34. Alex Chadwick, "Immigrant Aid Workers Face Prison for Smuggling," NPR, Aug. 26, 2005, https://www.npr.org/templates/story/story.php?storyId=4817559.

APPENDIX TO CHAPTER 1

1. My colleague Professor Rhonda Magee writes convincingly: "[S]lavery was, in significant part (though hardly exclusively), an immigration system of a particularly reprehensible sort: a system of state-sponsored forced migration human trafficking, endorsed by Congress, important to the public fisc as a source of tax revenue, and aimed at fulfilling the need for a controllable labor population in the colonies, and then in the states, at an artificially low economic cost.

"Viewing immigration as a function of slavery helps us articulate an important irony: that with respect to immigration, slavery—our racially based forced migration system—laid a foundation for both a racially segmented labor-based immigration system, and a racially diverse (even if racially hierarchical) 'nation of immigrants'—legacies which the Founders may not have set out to leave, but which are among our history's most pernicious and most precious gifts to civilization." Rhonda V. Magee, "Slavery as Immigration?" *University of San Francisco Law Review* 44 (2009): 273, 276–77.

2. Gerald P. López, "Undocumented Mexican Migration: In Search of a Just Immigration Law and Policy," *UCLA Law Review* 28 (1981): 615, 643.

3. López, "Undocumented Mexican Migration."

4. United States v. Martinez-Fuerte, 428 U.S. 543 (1976).

5. INS v. Lopez-Mendoza, 468 US 1032 (1984).

6. Bill Ong Hing, *Making and Remaking Asian America Through Immigration Policy, 1850–1990* (Stanford, CA: Stanford Press, 1993).

7. Hing, *Making and Remaking Asian America Through Immigration Policy*.

8. Peter H. Irons, *Justice at War: The Story of the Japanese American Internment Cases* (Oxford: Oxford University Press, 1983), 105.

9. Bill Ong Hing, *Defining America Through Immigration Policy* (Philadelphia: Temple University Press, 2004), 36.

10. California State Board of Control, *California and the Oriental: Japanese, Chinese, and Hindus*, orig. 1920 (London: Forgotten Books, 2017), 25–30.

APPENDIX TO THE EPILOGUE

1. INS v. Lopez-Mendoza, 468 U.S. 1032 (1984).

2. Aviva Chomsky, "Migration as Resistance," Massachusetts Peace Action, July 21, 2021, https://masspeaceaction.org/migration-as-resistance, accessed Jan. 6, 2023.

3. State v. Cole, 403 S.E.2d 117, 118 (S.C. 1991).

4. United States v. Contento-Pachon, 723 F.2d 691 (9th Cir. 1984).

5. United States v. Haischer, 2012 WL 5416234.

6. Judd F. Sneirson, "Black Rage and the Criminal Law: A Principled Approach to a Polarized Debate," *University of Pennsylvania Law Review* 143 (1995): 2251.

7. Paul Harris, *Black Rage Confronts the Law* (New York: New York University Press, 1997), 202–10.

8. Jury nullification occurs when a trial jury reaches a verdict that is contrary to the letter of the law because the jurors either disagree with the law under which the defendant is prosecuted or believe that the law shouldn't be applied in the case at hand. Because the *not guilty* verdict cannot be overturned, and because the jurors cannot be punished for their verdict, the law is said to be *nullified* in that particular case.

INDEX

Abbott, Greg, 204
ABC (American-born Chinese), 49
Abolish ICE movement, 1–2, 4, 16, 206
Abscam scandal, 239n13
accelerated program, for Haitian migrants, 6–7
ACLU. *See* American Civil Liberties Union (ACLU)
Acosta, A. J., 42–43
administrative closure, of deportation cases, 102
"adversely affected" countries, 217–18
Affordable Care Act (2010), 191
African migrants: forced migration due to enslavement of, 13, 206–7, 243n1; immigration visa requirements for, 7–9
Afriyie, Stanley, 141–42
aggravated felon(s), 52–54; zero-tolerance policy for, 55, 65. *See also* deportation of aggravated felons
aggravated felony(ies), categories of, 35, 52, 54, 57, 233n22
agricultural workers: Chinese, 213; climate change and, 220; Japanese, 214; Mexican, 15, 74, 208, 209; and *Murgia* case, 219
Aguirre, Ramon, 104
AILA (American Immigration Lawyers Association), 102, 198

Airbnb, 194–95
Aitken, Timothy S., 86–89, 102, 103, 110
Albania, asylum seekers from, 135, 137–39
Algeria: asylum seekers from, 122; deportation to, 56
Algerian Embassy, 119
Almeida-Sanchez v. United States (1973), 209–10
Al Otro Lado, 112
alternative to deportation (ATD) approach, 231n22
Alvarez, Juan, 47
American Baptist Churches v. Thornburgh, 144
American Bar Association, 101
American-born Chinese (ABC), 49
American Civil Liberties Union (ACLU): on detention deaths, 32; and family separation policy, 21, 242n27; on legal representation for children, 154; and prosecutorial discretion, 101; and public oversight disruption, 188; on racist immigration laws, 201
American Immigration Lawyers Association (AILA), 102, 198
American Law Institute, 89
America Online (AOL), 62
Anderson, Carrie, 89–90
anger management, 59

release from, 31; sexual abuse at, 19–20, 28, 32; sleep at, 17, 26, 29, 31; standards of care and treatment in, 18–19, 20, 22; supplies at, 30; temperature at, 29, 31; toddlers at, 17, 25, 26
Detention Watch Network, 36
Development, Relief, and Education for Alien Minors (DREAM) Act, 98–105, 191, 205, 241–42n15, 241n6
DHS. See Department of Homeland Security (DHS)
Diallo, Amadou, 11
Diaz-Reynoso, Sontos Maudilia, 133–34
Dilley, Texas, family detention center at, 29–30, 229–30n12
discretion, prosecutorial. See prosecutorial discretion
discretionary authority, of immigration judges, 157–58, 224
discretionary relief, from deportation, 50–51, 55, 57
displaced workers, 13
disruption(s), 186–205; anti-ICE, 186–88; by attorneys, 197–203; concept of, 199; by corporations, 194–97; courtroom strategies for, 219–24; by DREAMers, 191–94; explicit racial strategies for, 201–3; by immigrants, 190–97; of immigration court system, 184–85; legal services program and need for, 195, 198; May Day 2006 march against Sensenbrenner bill as, 190–91; public oversight, 188–90; recommendations on, 203–5
diversion programs, vs. deportation of aggravated felons, 59, 60
diversity visa program, 3, 8, 217–18
document(s): of asylum seekers, 118–19; false, 82, 85. See also undocumented noncitizens
documentary evidence, 118, 124, 178–79

domestic violence, asylum seekers due to, 131–32, 133–34, 136
Dornell, Lisa, 151
DPA (deferred prosecution agreement), 60–63
DREAM (Development, Relief, and Education for Alien Minors) Act, 98–105, 191, 205, 241–42n15, 241n6
DREAMers, 241–42n15, 241n6; disruptions by, 191–94; fundraising for, 73; work permits for, 194, 195
drug convictions, deportation for, 36–44, 48, 49–50, 51
drug rehabilitation program, 50, 59, 60
Du, Miranda, 202
due process, 183
Duncan, Arne, 98
Dundas, Michael, 78
Durbin, Dick, 98, 100–101
duress defense, 222–23
Duvalier, "Baby Doc," 6

earthquake, "conditional entries" due to, 156
East Bay Asian Youth Center, 82
"economic migrants," 144
Educators for Fair Consideration, 73
18th Street gang, 220
El Paso Border Patrol sector, 30
El Salvador: asylum seekers from, 131, 135–36, 139–40, 143, 144, 184, 220; unaccompanied minors from, 22, 198
employer sanctions, 3, 195–97, 211
employment visas, 8
Enforcement and Removal Operations, 103
enforcement raids, 3, 186, 189–90, 204
English Learner Advisory Committee, 79
environmental hardship defense, 223–24

EOIR (Executive Office for Immigration Review), 82, 151
equal protection clause, 202, 219
Ethiopian refugees, 165–67
European Convention on Human Rights, 56–57
European Court of Human Rights, 56
exclusionary rule, 219–20
Executive Office for Immigration Review (EOIR), 82, 151
executive order, 7, 192, 194

Facebook, 196
fairness: and Dedicated Dockets, 150; and Fourth Amendment violations, 220; and immigration court reform, 155, 157, 171; and necessity defense, 223; and proportionality, 58; and providing legal counsel, 173, 183; and public oversight, 188; vs. speed, 145
false documents, and deportation of undocumented noncitizens, 82, 85
family-based asylum seekers, 136–39
Family Case Management Program (FCMP), 33
family detention centers, 17, 25, 29–30, 32, 131
family members, persecution of, 136–39
family reunification: as basis for immigration, 8, 9, 13–14; detention facilities for children and, 18, 19, 20–21, 23, 24; and immigration court system, 159–64, 171–74
family separation: and Board of Immigration Appeals, 106; due to deportation, 158, 185; and Flores settlement agreement, 31; and hardship requirement, 111; after ICE raid, 190; under Obama, 193; and prosecutorial

discretion, 97; racist origins of, 201–2, 204; under Trump, 1, 19, 20, 21, 22, 24–25, 33, 201, 242n27. See also detention facilities for children
family ties, and deportation of undocumented noncitizens, 77–78, 82–83
farmworkers. See agricultural workers
FCMP (Family Case Management Program), 33
Federation for American Immigration Reform, 99
Feinstein, Dianne, 87, 88, 187
female genital mutilation, 135
Ferguson, Colin, 223
filibuster, 100, 191
Filipino immigrants, 214–16
Fitz, Marshall, 99
fixed checkpoints, 210
Flores, Jenny Lisette, 22
Flores, Martha, 87, 88
Flores, Yvette, 91
Flores inspections, 28, 29, 188
Flores settlement agreement, 18–19; additions to, 30–32; and Office of Refugee Resettlement detention, 20; and unaccompanied minors held as bait, 144; violations in Clint, Texas facilities of, 22
Floyd, George, 3, 5, 203
flu, at detention facilities for children, 27–28
Fong, Ivan, 87
food, at detention facilities for children, 26–27, 31
forced immigration system, of chattel slavery, 13, 206–7, 243n1
Ford, Nicholas, 152–53, 184
foreign students, as nonimmigrants, 7–8
Fourth Amendment, 209–11, 219–20
France, proportionality in, 56
freedom fighters, 143

Freedom of Information Act request, 96–97, 166
funding, for immigration services, 182

Gámez, Francisco, 77
Gandhi, Mahatma, 196
gang-related crimes, 45, 48
gang violence, asylum seekers due to, 131–32, 135–36, 220
Garland, Merrick, 132, 137
garment workers, trafficking of, 200–201
Geisse, Loreto S., 81, 82, 84
Gelernt, Lee, 201
gender, asylum seekers due to, 134–35
General Motors, 196
Gentlemen's Agreement, 214
Geo Group, 10
Ghana, asylum seekers from, 141–42
Gideon v. Wainwright (1963), 183–84
Gingrich, Newt, 68
Gleason, Paul, 87, 88
globalization, 14, 207
Golden Gate University, 197
Gomez, Laura (pseudonym), 74, 75
Google, 196
Gorev, Ricky (pseudonym), 160–61, 172
Gorev, Yelena (pseudonym), 158–65, 171–74, 187
GPS ankle monitors, 231n22
Great Britain. *See* United Kingdom (UK)
group living arrangements, *vs.* deportation of aggravated felons, 60
group therapy, 59
Grussendorf, Paul, 57
guardian ad litem, 166
Guatemala: asylum seekers from, 143, 144, 176–81, 184, 220; indigenous women from, 133–35, 136; unaccompanied minors from, 131, 198

Guatemala Human Rights Commission, 135
Guatemalan migrants, 5–6
guerrillas, 144
Gulf War veterans, 128–29
Gutiérrez, Luis, 98, 100, 101
Gyamfi, Nana, 1

Habitat for Humanity, 36
Haiti, asylum seekers from, 142–43
Haitian migrants: accelerated program for, 6–7; bonds for, 10; detention of, 9–10; interdiction on high seas of, 7; racial injustice for, 1, 4, 5–7
"Haitian program," 6–7
Haitian Refugee Center v. Gracey (1985), 7
halfway house, 49
Hansen, Joe, 189
hardship, due to deportation, 51, 53, 55, 58, 97, 151, 167
hardship requirement: appeal of decision based on, 69, 79, 80, 82–85, 89–93, 106–7; qualification for, 66, 111
Harris, Kamala, 5–6, 204
Hatch, Orin, 53, 98, 99
Hawaii, Japanese immigrants to, 213–14
Haynes, Jim Tom, 44, 64
Health Insurance Portability and Accountability Act (HIPAA), 166
health law provision, 5, 143, 145
Hernández, Kelly Lytle, 202
Hernandez, Yanelli, 104–5
HIPAA (Health Insurance Portability and Accountability Act), 166
Holder, Eric, 153
Holquin, Carlos, 22–23, 24, 30
Homestead, Fla., children's detention center at, 21–22
Honduras: asylum seekers from, 131, 143, 184, 220; unaccompanied minors from, 21, 23–24, 198

Khoy, Lundy, 36–44; aggravated felony by, 162, 168; background of, 36–37; crime committed by, 37; deportation order after prison term for, 38–40, 54, 55; legal representation for, 43–44, 64, 199; and need for reform, 32–33, 59, 65, 187; overturning deportation order for, 43–44; pardon request for, 40–42
Kidane, Nunu, 12–13
Kiernan, Mia-Lia, 39
Kim Ho Ma, 44–47; aggravated felony by, 34–37, 64, 162, 168; background of, 44–45; deportation after prison term for, 40, 45–47, 54, 55; legal representation for, 43, 45–47; and need for reform, 32–33, 64, 65, 187
King, Martin Luther, Jr., 196
Kino Border Initiative, 112
Kobach, Kris, 104
Korean immigrants, 214, 215
Kosovan refugees, 128
Kuby, Ronald, 223
Kunstler, William, 223

labor recruitment: of Chinese immigrants, 211–13; of Filipino immigrants, 214–16; of Japanese immigrants, 213–14; of Mexican immigrants, 207–8, 209
Latin America: asylum seekers from, 142–43; deportation of aggravated felons from, 35
Latinx residents: deportation of, 68; and DREAM Act, 100, 193; racial profiling of, 9, 227n19; role models for, 80
Latinx voters, 193
lawful permanent resident status: demographics of, 8; and deportation of aggravated felons, 35, 36–37, 40, 47, 50, 52, 53, 55, 62, 64; and deportation of undocumented noncitizens, 70, 71, 83–84, 94, 96, 98, 111; and

DREAM Act, 98; and family reunification, 8, 14
law school immigration clinics, 164, 165–66, 167, 169–70, 173, 192, 197, 220
least restrictive setting, 18–19, 20, 22
Lee, Deborah, 186–88
LeFevre, Ronald, 84, 85
legal representation: for asylum seekers, 132, 145, 146; for children, 154, 175, 183, 198–99; for clients with mental illness, 164–71; for deportation hearings, 164–71, 172–73, 174–84, 185; effectiveness of, 174–75; functions of, 175; and ICE detention, 169–70, 172–73, 174–75, 182; and misunderstandings, 176–81; pro bono, 43, 113, 146, 170, 171, 173, 181–82, 183, 184; for unaccompanied minors, 198–99
Legal Services for Children, 72, 76
legal services program: for asylum seekers, 146; and deportation of aggravated felons, 48, 55, 94; and need for disruption, 195, 198; and need for reform of immigration court system, 173, 181–82, 183, 184
Lennon, John, 96–97
"lesser of two evils" defense, 221–23
literacy test, 7
Lloyd, Jesse, 72, 86
Lofgren, Zoe, 154–55, 158, 184
Lopez, Francisco Javier, 179–81
López, Gerald, 207–8
Lopez-Mendoza, Adan, 210–11
Lopez-Telles, Juana Zoraida, 155–58, 187
Los Angeles Immigration Court, 145–46
Lugar, Richard, 98
Lydon, Susan, 116, 120, 147
Lyoya, Patrick, 12

treatment program, *vs.* deportation, 50, 59, 60
Treaty of Guadalupe Hidalgo, 3, 207
Trillin, Abigail, 72, 76, 78
Trump, Donald: ACLU challenges to, 242n27; armed ICE workplace raids under, 190; and asylum seekers, 131–32, 137, 143, 145, 235n1; and DACA program, 192–93, 195–96; and deportation of aggravated felons, 42–43; and disruptions, 186–87, 190; and DREAM Act, 104, 105; family separation policy of, 1, 19, 20, 21, 22, 24–25, 33, 201, 242n27; immigration court system under, 151, 152–53, 182; on Mexican migrants as criminals, 53; targeting of Black immigrants by, 4–5
"T" visas, 201
Tydings-McDuffie Act (1934), 216

UC (University of California) Davis immigration clinic, 164, 165–66, 167, 169–70, 173, 197
UFCW (United Food and Commercial Workers Union), 189–90
UK. *See* United Kingdom (UK)
Ukrainian migrants, 5
UN. *See* United Nations (UN)
unaccompanied minors: alternatives to detention for, 25, 34; arrest and detention of, 25; attorneys for, 174–75, 182, 198; classification of, 25; cost of detaining, 21; detention policy for, 18, 19, 25; Flores settlement agreement for, 18–19, 20, 22; held as bait, 22, 144; least restrictive setting for, 18–19, 20, 22; legal representation for, 198–99; media attention to, 5, 130; number of, 20, 25; problems with current policy for,

130–31, 144–45; surge in, 22; in UK, 33–34, 231n23
unauthorized workers, law against hiring, 3, 195–97, 211
"underrepresented" countries, 218
undocumented noncitizens: criminal provisions for, 14; detention of, 193; employment of, 195–97; pathway to citizenship for, 98; proposed bill making felony of being, 191; providing aid to, 203–4; trafficking of, 200–201. *See also* deportation of undocumented noncitizens
Ungar, Don, 113, 116
Ungerman, Leslie, 78, 88
United Farm Workers, 219
United Food and Commercial Workers Union (UFCW), 189–90
United Kingdom (UK): detention of migrant children in, 33–34, 231n23; immigration court system in, 184; proportionality in, 56–57
United Nations (UN): on asylum seekers, 117; Convention on the Rights of the Child, 33, 231n23; High Commissioner on Refugees, 147
United States v. Brignoni-Ponce (1975), 210
United States v. Contento-Pachon, 222
United States v. Haischer, 222
United States v. Martinez-Fuerte (1976), 210
universal representation for noncitizens facing removal, 184
University of California (UC) Davis immigration clinic, 164, 165–66, 167, 169–70, 173, 197
University of San Francisco immigration clinic, 182, 197, 220
urinating in public, 54, 233n22
US Chamber of Commerce, 196